Advance Praise for *What Happens Now?*

"In today's egalitarian and pluralistic management environment, business leaders cannot only be good at their business. They need a broader view of the human enterprise and the skills to lead extremely complex and sophisticated organizations. John Hillen and Mark Nevins, experienced and thoughtful leadership scholars I came to know at the Aspen Institute, have written a practical and enriching guide for leaders seeking to be effective at the highest levels of performance."

> —**Walter Isaacson**, former President and CEO of The Aspen Institute
> Best-selling author of *Steve Jobs, Leonardo da Vinci, Einstein*, and
> *Benjamin Franklin* and *Time Magazine* honoree of their annual list,
> 100 Most Influential People in the World

"Over the course of my career leading companies, government agencies, and NGOs, I have seen leaders struggle with having the strategic and interpersonal skills they need to go to the next level. It is not always obvious about the new mindsets and behaviors leaders need to adopt to be effective as their organization changes and grows. It is hard to find a fresh way to think through this age-old problem, but *What Happens Now?* is one of the most effective books I've seen to show leaders how to stay ahead of their enterprises."

> —**Henrietta Holsman Fore**, former Director of the US Mint and
> Administrator of the US Agency for International Development

"Over the many years I have watched and commented on the best performing companies, I've observed the best leaders reinvent themselves and their role as fast as they've grown their firm. This book helps leaders see challenges in advance and charts a way for them to stay out in front of their enterprise as they take it to new heights. A practical and insightful guide to executive development in growing companies."

> —**Larry Kudlow**, CNBC's Senior Contributor

"John Hillen and Mark Nevins have written a must-read primer for any leader seeking to successfully navigate in today's dynamic social, financial, and technical environments. In my time running several companies and in leading at all levels during 30 years in the Navy, I've seen leaders confront these issues time and again. Read this book; its solution orientation is both timely and refreshing."

—**Admiral William "Bud" Flanagan**
Former Commander-in-Chief of The US Atlantic Fleet

"Success can breed bad habits in executives. John Hillen and Mark Nevins add to that research by showing the changing circumstances that accompany growth and change can exacerbate these habits and cause leadership stalls. Their framework for seeing and working through them will help leaders at all levels grow and develop as fast as their businesses in order to stay ahead of these challenges."

—**Marshall Goldsmith**
Author of one of Amazon.com's top 100 leadership books of all time,
What Got You Here Won't Get You There
Voted by Thinkers50 as one of The World's 50
Most Influential Leadership Thinkers

"Hillen and Nevins recognize the need for leaders to have a range and depth of expertise extending far beyond operational and technical skills. Without having those mistakenly named 'soft' skills, leaders cannot effectively lead change or contend with important issues relating to organizational culture and ethics. The authors' sophisticated and multidimensional approach to leadership is both philosophically sound and eminently practical. Think of this as 'a leadership coach in a book'!"

—**James O'Toole**
Author of *Leading Change* and *The Executive's Compass*

"The practice of management badly needs disruption. The practice of management doesn't need improvement—it needs changing. This book gives us a great start in this important journey as human development now occurs primarily in the workplace—leadership and purpose matters more than ever."

—**Jim Clifton**
Chairman of CEO of Gallup, author of *The Coming Jobs War*

"John Hillen and Mark Nevins astutely focus on how leaders must behave in order to become adaptable in today's increasingly dynamic world. *What Happens Now?* is a necessary read for leaders combatting the reality that what worked in the past will no longer be good enough in the near future."

—General Stanley McChrystal
Author of *New York Times* best-seller *Team of Teams: New Rules of Engagement for a Complex World* and former commander of the US Joint Special Operations Command

"Hillen and Nevins have hit the mark in describing what it takes to lead at the highest levels of dynamic organizations. Based on my own experiences as a CEO, their key insight rings true: as organizations change and grow, their leaders must adopt new mindsets and behaviors rather than relying solely on those that have made them successful in the past. Adaptability and agility, they rightly argue, will be distinguishing characteristics of those leaders who succeed and a notable gap for those who fail. This is an important book for leaders taking on new challenges and asking what they must do to rise to the occasion."

—David McCormick
Co-CEO of Bridgewater Associates

"We live in a world where nobody has all the answers, yet I have observed that truly great leaders are masters of sophistication. They engage and listen to those who don't think like themselves. They connect thoughts and patterns from within complexity and find simplicity on the other side—always grounded in a moral compass. John and Mark, great sophisticated leaders themselves, have unpacked the evolution of a leader and what it takes today in a very fresh—but recognizable—way. Only the two of them could have created such a guide that will help so many people who are looking to making a huge difference in the world."

—Beth Brooke-Marciniak
EY Global Vice Chair - Public Policy

"Over the course of my 50-year career in consulting, I've watched a few consulting companies grow and prosper, while most crash and burn because the technical skills that got their leaders to the top were not suited for growing their businesses, and the leaders could not adapt. In *What Happens Now?* John Hillen and Mark Nevins walk the reader through seven common stalls that can block the leader's ability to lead. They provide guideposts for how the leader can adapt by not focusing on 'technical management' and solving complexity, but instead building the personal and interpersonal skills required to define and strengthen purpose and values, build stronger teams, develop other leaders, and engage and influence stakeholders. I had the good fortune to have the help of one of the authors, Mark Nevins, in adapting my own leadership style when I was working to transition my firm from a small specialized company with an uncertain future to a large, prosperous, and growing company built for the long run. I am very happy that the learnings that benefitted me are being made available to others."

—James C. Burrows
Vice Chairman, Charles River Associates

What Happens Now?

What Happens Now?

Reinvent Yourself as a Leader
Before Your Business Outruns You

JOHN HILLEN AND MARK NEVINS

Keep Re-Inventing!

SelectBooks, Inc.
New York

This edition published by SelectBooks, Inc.
For information address SelectBooks, Inc., New York, New York.

First Edition

ISBN 978-1-59079-453-1

Library of Congress Cataloging-in-Publication Data

Names: Hillen, John, author. | Nevins, Mark D., author.
Title: What happens now? : reinvent yourself as a leader before your business
  outruns you / John Hillen and Mark Nevins.
Description: First edition. | New York : SelectBooks, [2018] | Includes
  bibliographical references and index.
Identifiers: LCCN 2017057099 | ISBN 9781590794531 (hardcover book : alk.
  paper)
Subjects: LCSH: Leadership. | Management.
Classification: LCC HD57.7 .H555 2018 | DDC 658.4/092--dc23 LC record
available at https://lccn.loc.gov/2017057099

Jacket and book design by Janice Benight

Manufactured in the United States of America
10 9 8 7 6 5 4 3 2 1

We dedicate this book to our fathers,
John F. Hillen Jr. and Albert E. Nevins Jr.,
our first and best teachers for what it means to be a leader.

We both lost our fathers in 2009, too early, but their influence
lives on in us, in our work, and in our children.

Contents

Foreword

by Norman Augustine

Thousands of books have been written about leadership, a few of them even worth reading. This book is most assuredly one of the latter. While most authors provide guidance on how to *become* a leader, this book also tells how to *remain* a leader. The importance of this distinction is that leadership demands new attributes when one takes on greater responsibilities as one's career progresses. There are, of course, certain fundamental qualities of leadership that are foundational and perpetual, such as integrity, caring, and determination—but new demands arise as one's scope of engagement expands. Individuals who cannot grow their own personal qualities accordingly are at risk—past accomplishments notwithstanding.

I was educated to be an aerospace engineer—a "rocket scientist," if you will—but in the final years of my career found myself working almost exclusively with lawyers, bankers, and politicians! There was nothing I learned in engineering school that equipped me for that change in environment.

While serving on boards of several Fortune 100 companies I have a few times been given the unfortunate assignment of informing CEOs that their services were no longer needed. These were honorable people who had succeeded at every level of the dozen or so stages that separate a new employee from the position of the topmost executive in a major firm. With that sort of background, how could they possibly have failed in the end? That is a question that the Hillen and Nevins answer in the pages that follow—and, more importantly, tell what can be done to avoid such outcomes.

Between them, the two authors offer the perspective of a sound educational foundation—Duke, Oxford, Cornell, Holy Cross, Harvard. They also offer the perspective of a life in the trenches advising some of America's best known firms, both large and small, and serving in that ultimate crucible of leadership: a battlefield as a military leader.

My own favorite definition of leadership is actually to be found in the British Officers' Cemetery in Normandy, where it is engraved on a tombstone. It reads, "Leadership is Wisdom, Courage, and Carelessness of Self." I would offer just one addition to that monument so that it would read, "Leadership is Wisdom, Courage, Character, and Carelessness of Self." Great leaders focus on their mission and the followers for whom they bear a fiduciary responsibility—never upon themselves.

Many years ago I made a list of 30 people whom I had the privilege of knowing personally and considered to be great leaders. I have been very fortunate in this regard: my list begins with such individuals as General Omar Bradly, General Jimmy Doolittle, and Admiral Arleigh Burke, and ends with Sandra Day O'Connor, Elizabeth Dole, and Warren Buffett. After each name I put on my list, I wrote down the reason why I included him or her. Clear patterns emerged as to fundamental qualities of leadership embodied by these individuals, even though their personalities and styles varied widely. I only recently discovered that the authors of this book recommend that individuals assuming leadership responsibilities undertake this same exercise.

In observing individuals with whom I worked over my four careers in industry, government, academia, and charitable organizations, I have tried to understand why some of the most capable and effective people seemed to hit ceilings as they advanced through their careers. I concluded that there were actually three phases to a career, each with its own set of hazards. Early in one's career, failures are usually attributable to a lack of knowledge in the individual's own purported field, such as a lawyer who doesn't understand the First Amendment, an accountant who doesn't understand Generally Accepted Accounting

Principles, or an engineer who doesn't understand the Second Law of Thermodynamics.

Ironically, the most outstanding individuals who successfully graduate from this initial phase are often the most vulnerable to failure in the second phase. These are people who failed to discover that they could no longer rely solely upon their own talents, but had to rely on the talents of others as well. This is of course called leadership—and it includes evaluating people, trusting people, and, importantly, delegating to people. Failures in this phase of a career are often exacerbated by the would-be leader, propelled by earlier successes to focus on the next job he or she *wants* and not on the job he or she now *has*.

Those who succeed in reconfiguring their leadership skills and succeed in these two phases will likely find themselves at a level of management that can be a lonely place where decisions must be made under uncertainty, where intangibles weigh heavily, where risks and consequences are substantial, and where every meeting includes people who know more about each topic that arises than they do. This phase is when career failures are usually attributable to an inability to deal with people. One of the greatest assets one can possess in this phase is a selfless colleague who will occasionally close the door to your office and say, "You are really messing this up!" Warren Buffett once told me that the most important lesson a person in a position of responsibility can learn is always to have someone around to tell the emperor he has no clothes. The next most important lesson is, presumably, for the emperor to listen to that person.

Of course, not everyone can—or even wishes to—make the transition from the early stages of leadership to the more advanced stages. But one owes it to one's self as well as to one's colleagues to recognize when this is the case and to act accordingly. Among the most interesting examples familiar to me relates to a startup company founded by three engineer friends of mine who were astoundingly successful from the very outset. But as the firm grew, these leaders began to realize that they enjoyed technical challenges far more than management challenges. Recognizing this, they hired an experienced leader to serve as the firm's CEO—while each of the founders, who continued to own most of the firm, took positions as vice presidents for specific technological areas. They actually made this work very well, and the firm continued to be prosperous. Leadership demands adapting to changing circumstances—always while maintaining one's core values.

In my own career, and as a person largely aware of his own strengths and weaknesses, I have lived through IPOs, mergers, acquisitions, divestitures, market collapses, restructurings, attempted hostile takeovers, and more. Each demanded its own skill set as a leader. Simply stated, one must grow as the nature of one's responsibilities grow. Doing so is not always easy, but it is always essential.

As I think about it, my life would have been easier had I read this book at the beginning of my career rather than near the end!

NORMAN R. AUGUSTINE
Retired Chairman and CEO, Lockheed Martin
Former Under Secretary, US Army

Preface

"There is a tide in the affairs of men, which, taken at the flood, leads on to fortune; omitted, all the voyage of their life is bound in shallows and in miseries. On such a full sea we are now afloat; And we must take the current when it serves, or lose our ventures."

—WILLIAM SHAKESPEARE, *Julius Caesar*

Why do so many leaders have trouble with a second act? They win applause from their followers and bosses in one run of their career but hear only nervous throat-clearing in the next. When they have to play at the next level, they go from stars to has-beens. How could that be when they have so much talent and such a record of success?

We wrote this book to answer those questions. Over the decades, we've seen leaders at all levels struggle in organizations of all sizes and types, from small private companies to big public conglomerates to nonprofit organizations. They struggle no matter what their leadership style, personality, or role. And we've even struggled with second acts ourselves.

If you're a leader, the most common explanation for slumps in your leadership performance is that you mistakenly assume that if you were a star at the last level, you'll succeed when you take the next step by behaving the same way and tapping the same skills. The past was prologue, and you expect a long, steady ride as your career advances.

That kind of thinking often turns out to be exactly wrong. You face what feels like more difficult challenges or problems at the next level. You're not sure how to master them. The needs of the organization seem to have outrun your capabilities as a leader. And then, in the words of this book, you *stall*.

Our aim is to help leaders at all stages to see, understand, and overcome such stalls. Too few leaders devise and put in place clear and pragmatic plans to grow themselves with the same deliberate processes and energy they use to grow or change their organizations. They pay attention to the needs of the institution but not to their own needs. We would like to help leaders change that habit, and we have some experience-based knowledge to help them do so.

In our decades as managers, C-level executives, consultants, teachers, and members of boards, we have rarely come across leaders who are not seeking growth and change for their organizations. The byproduct is that they encounter greater levels of complexity as the job becomes bigger, faster, and more demanding. They also run into unfamiliar levels of sophistication, and the job seems very different and more disorienting.

In our view, it is not so much the new complexity but the new sophistication that triggers stalls. That's because new levels of complexity call on you to practice the abilities you have become familiar with and succeeded with in the past: the skills of managing an organization. On the other hand, the new levels of sophistication call on you to tap into capabilities you may not be as familiar with, a set of capabilities, behaviors, and mindsets critical for leading a human enterprise, often in a time of great change. This is not a matter of just managing more activity or people.

As a rising leader, you thus face a dual challenge. When we get calls from leaders for help, those calls almost *never* come from leaders who want us to help them in mastering greater complexity. They mostly come from leaders who need help with mastering new capabilities of *sophistication*—capabilities these leaders may not be aware of or have historically undervalued. Mastering the sophisticated leadership capabilities now demanded can be especially difficult because doing so calls on you to make a personal change and reinvent *yourself* as an entirely different kind of leader—one with a new mindset, new capabilities, and new behavior.

The leadership bookcase is a crowded one, but in writing this book we offer a new layer of insight from our in-the-trenches work with leaders of all kinds. In our journeys as executives, board members, consultants, coaches, teachers, and friends, we have been repeatedly told by our clients and colleagues that our approach to solving vexing problems is unique . . . and uniquely helpful. And we've also been encouraged that our perspectives on how to view leadership problems and address them are distinctive and insightful. This book, then, is a testament to our shared experiences and many conversations—as well as a way to leave a legacy of our work and friendship.

As coauthors, we approach the challenges of leadership with an atypical inside/outside mix of experience and perspectives. John, formerly CEO of Sotera Defense Solutions, which he took public in one of the few successful US IPOs in 2009, speaks with an executive insider's view. In his experience as COO or CEO of four different companies, and as a board chairman, director, consultant, and business school professor, he has seen scores of what we call "leadership stalls" and encountered a few himself. Mark, earlier in his career the top executive in global people development and human resources at both Booz Allen Hamilton and Korn/Ferry, speaks with an outside advisor's view framed in his two-decade career as consultant and executive coach. His insights are grounded in work with hundreds of leaders and executives who have encountered stall points, and who in turn have found powerful ways to reinvent themselves.

Rooted in different backgrounds and experiences, our insights cut across history, disciplines, and fields of endeavor. John's career includes service as a former US Army officer and combat veteran, a US assistant secretary of state, and a director of twelve companies. He has worked with leaders in the military, government, business, and charities in their most heated moments. Mark, a Harvard PhD and former literature professor, takes a view informed as much by universal themes of the human condition as by the pragmatics of how to engage, develop, and lead people at organizations large and small, in both the public and private sector, spanning many industries and in dozens of countries.

Our commitment is to share what we've learned with you and provide you with practical and useful new ways to think and to develop yourself—and soar to new levels of success. A leadership stall can be a scary experience. And they can happen to any and every leader regardless of intelligence, experience, or capability. In fact, paradoxically, often stalls are a consequence of success in growing or changing your organization when you realize, after having led significant change, that the world has changed around you, and you may begin to feel less effective or no longer up to the task. Why am I not getting the results I used to? We explain why this happens—and we do so with the stories of a diverse group of leaders who also show and tell how to address these stalls and how to pull through them, with the support of proven tools to get you back on the track to leadership success.

One caveat: The leaders and executives who generously allowed us to present them as examples in this book illustrate the concepts of complex and sophisticated leadership. However, the passage of time changes everything. All executives retire someday. Some fall from grace, others may be forced out by palace intrigue in the boardroom. Even leaders who have attained a high degree of sophisticated leadership are not immune to time or fortune. Nothing lasts forever. Yet readers should not allow changes since this book's publication to rob them of the insights we have gathered here. The lessons and insights transcend the individuals who embody them.

Our hope is that when you finish this book you'll have an immediate action plan to take yourself up a level and catch up to the aspirations you have for your organization. When you wonder, "What happens now?" you'll have this book to help you respond.

Acknowledgments

We owe a great debt to the many people who have helped us write this book.

First, we'd like to thank the many leaders and executives who over the years have shared their stories with us. Those hard-won experiences and insights helped us perceive and formulate the arguments we are making in this book. Some of these wise people are clients and some are colleagues, and we count all of them as friends. Without them, we couldn't have seen just how frequently leaders are threatened by stalls—and in turn how the best leaders summon the courage to reinvent themselves to be successful.

We would especially like to thank a number of people who spent significant amounts of time sharing with us their personal experiences and challenges in great detail: Michael Barnett, Hector Batista, Trevor Boyce, Jonathan Bush, Jim Burrows, Sid Fuchs, Dawn Halfaker, John Hassoun, Chris Howard, Dev Ittycheria, Ron Jones, David Kriegman, Frank Lavin, Dominique Malard, Ali Manouchehri, Taryn Owen, Kim Pendergast, Jean-François Poupeau, John Rogers, Jeff Rubenstein, Hervé Sedky, David Singer, Gary White, and Bob Zoellick. Each of these leaders detailed his or her experiences, often with a humbling degree of vulnerability, and many of them appear as illustrations or "case studies" in this book.

We'd also like to thank the hundreds of clients, colleagues, employees, students, peers, and friends who have contributed in so many ways to our thinking on leadership and on life. In particular, we wish to express our appreciation to the many leaders we have dialogued with in the Aspen Institute executive seminars we have co-moderated over the years. Aspen's intensive and original approach to values-based and sophisticated leadership has had an enormous impact on us. The lessons we've learned from those seminars and in our work together are woven throughout the book.

We have been blessed to be influenced at close quarters by some of the best minds of our time on the subject of leadership. We have learned from these bold and energetic thinkers to understand leadership as its own competency—not just as a facet of something else. They led us to study and teach leadership in addition to our work of applying it. What Sir Isaac Newton said about standing on the shoulders of giants seems an apt description for our experience of building on their discoveries.

There are too many of these great leaders and thinkers to call out by name here, but John was especially touched in his leadership life by the late Phil Merrill, and Mark would especially like to express his appreciation to Jim O'Toole for decades of mentorship and friendship. For each of us, these great men have been our most profound teachers of leadership.

We would also like to thank our content, editorial, publishing, and marketing team: our researcher, editor, and guide, Bill Birchard; our agent Carol Mann; our publishers Kenzi, Kenichi, and Nancy Sugihara at SelectBooks; our copyeditor Lucy Zepeda; our photographer Mike Cohen; and our publicity team at Cave Henricks Communications, especially Nina Nocciolino, Kimberly Petty, Jessica Krakoski, and Barbara Henricks. Without the help of all of these amazing professionals, this book could not exist. Mark would like to offer special thanks to his colleague and thought partner of many years, Kristina DiStasio, whose ideas and creativity have informed more than a few examples in this book. Jay Marshall and Steve Gladis, two leadership gurus whom we intensely admire, were kind enough to read early drafts of the book and provide helpful guidance.

Friends, clients, and companies with whom we are affiliated, especially Laurence Belfer, SOS International, Big Brothers Big Sisters of NYC, and IAP Inc., lent us conference rooms in various cities in which to work and where much of the writing of this book was done. And we must also thank Buddy Dive Shop in Dominica, which provided the conference room and the terrace where we came to one of our main epiphanies.

Finally, we would like to thank our families, from whom we stole too many evening and weekend hours to complete this book. Thank you for your support, patience, and love, Maria, Ndingara, Jack, Chris, Katie, Olivia, and Declan.

JOHN HILLEN
MARK NEVINS
March 2018

Introduction

THE DAY EVERYTHING CHANGES

"The important thing is this: to be able at any moment to sacrifice what we are for what we would become."
— CHARLES DU BOS, *Approximations*

"It's no use going back to yesterday, because I was a different person then."—LEWIS CARROLL, *Alice's Adventures in Wonderland*

When we work with executive teams on improving leadership effectiveness, we sometimes start with an old but revealing icebreaker. "Think of the best leaders you've ever worked with," we say. "What specifically did they *do* that made them so effective? What behaviors made you admire them and want to follow them?"

We then ask the executives, working in teams, to draw a picture of their "Best Leader Ever" based on the leadership qualities and characteristics each of them articulated. The purpose of the exercise is to reveal what seasoned leaders value in other leaders. What capabilities and traits define the best ones? (Only occasionally is anyone much of an artist, so the exercise also reveals people's sense of humor in exposing their rudimentary drawing skills.)

The groups are routinely surprised by what emerges. Rarely do the drawings show gutsy "type-A" leaders with sleeves rolled up working on the front lines. Or leaders with their chins into the wind like commanders on a battlefield. Or leaders with their brains bulging like Einstein's as they rattle off all the answers to the business's problems.

Instead we see depictions of figures with warm smiles and prominent symbolic features: Oversized hearts for encouragement. Large ears for listening. Big eyes for vision. Raised thumbs to show supportiveness. Light-bulb brains for sparking creativity. Broad shoulders for

1

supporting others. Down on one knee to reveal a willingness to serve others and a greater cause. Offering a hand to develop their followers and pull them to the next level.

When we ask the participants to explain their pictures and lists of characteristics, we get into a deeper conversation. We end up talking about leadership behaviors and competencies that have little to do with so-called "hard" business skills such as technical or functional knowledge or management expertise. The actions and capabilities most commonly identified include coaching and developing others; effectively managing stakeholders; initiating important conversations; listening with empathy and perception; broadcasting a vision with clarity and purpose; shaping strategy to lead change; and providing feedback, support, and opportunities to grow.

We call these *sophisticated* leadership capabilities.

We use the word "sophisticated" deliberately because our experience shows that the capabilities required of leaders as their organizations grow are divided into two groups. The first includes those skills and abilities to deal with complexity in a traditional management-centered way, such as knowing how to design and implement processes and systems, and having the required technical and functional knowledge. The second group relates to sophisticated abilities and, often, mindsets to address growth challenges at the human and more fundamental transformational level. Rapidly growing and changing organizations require both kinds of capabilities from their leaders, and yet most leaders focus on the former set (complexity responses) at the expense of the latter set (sophisticated responses), and doing so can lead to suboptimal outcomes or even failure.

In our experience in over fifty collective years as executives, consultants, board members, teachers, and students of leadership, we have consistently found that one insight is pivotal: Understanding the mindset, capabilities, and behaviors for dealing with challenges of greater *sophistication* is the secret to becoming a "Best Leader Ever."

When thinking about how people can become better leaders, we start with a simple assumption: What will separate great leaders from average ones will not only be the ability to rack up quarterly accomplishments. It will be the sophistication to lead others in doing so.

When we say that leaders must get more sophisticated, we mean that they have to respond to and solve challenges presented by their organizations and stakeholders by applying new capabilities related to political, personal, strategic, and interpersonal skills. These challenges are different from those where one applies conventional structures and systems of management, often "best practices" used across many organizations.

Distinguishing sophistication from complexity is powerful. It allows leaders to know where to focus their efforts to ensure success as well as the best outcomes for their followers. If complexity calls on you to change the mechanics or structure of your organization, sophistication calls for you to change yourself and others. If complexity calls for changing your skills, sophistication calls for changing behaviors. If complexity calls for management initiatives, sophistication calls for leadership mindsets.

The devil of it all is that tackling a sophistication challenge with complex skills usually won't work. You're not going to take a dysfunctional team to the next level of sophisticated performance with spreadsheets or a restructuring of systems. On the other hand, tackling a challenge of complexity with sophistication skills will not work either. You can't solve a problem related to, say, incompatible legacy IT platforms via coaching. You need the right approach for each kind of challenge.

The Seven Stalls of Leadership

All of this brings us to the core problem our book addresses: What happens when you have trouble rising to meet the more ambiguous challenges of sophistication? When you're called on to be astute instead of analytic? Or strategic instead of performance-driven? Or hands-off instead of hands-on? Or indirect instead of direct? Or persuasive instead of precise? Or empathetic instead of energetic? What happens then?

The answer is that you'll often have a hard time. In fact, you may experience a stall. If this occurs, the odds are good that you'll lose some credibility or clout. You may lose the capacity to lead, or even your job. You may kick yourself, because you probably had a growth plan for your organization, but you overlooked the critical need to create a parallel growth plan for yourself. You stall because of self-neglect—falling behind in growing yourself as a leader.

We see this misstep so often that we've identified seven specific stall points that bewilder just about every leader, regardless of role, style, or personality. These stalls happen at junctures of organizational change or growth. They are times when your performance seems to grind to a stop. You're left on the side of the highway, and as much as you crank the ignition key, you can't get your leadership engine to turn over and start up.

To choose the right way to develop yourself as a sophisticated leader, you'll need to understand these seven dangerous stalls. You're likely to face at least one or two at some point in your career:

1. When you can't create an organizational story that delivers meaning and purpose.

2. When you can't align your team to deliver high performance as one.

3. When you can't amplify your influence among important stakeholders.

4. When you struggle in your ability to explain and lead change.

5. When your authority slips in the eyes of followers.

6. When you fail to focus your time and energy to have the most impact.

7. When you can't develop your own leaders or prevent them from failing.

If you've ever tried to lead an organization through growth and change, you'll know what we mean by encountering one of these trouble spots—and know all too well the unnerving sensation of not delivering the leadership or performance you expect of yourself. Over a career, you are almost sure to hit stalls. It doesn't matter if you're a leader in a big organization or a small one, or in a corporation, nonprofit, or government agency. Stalls happen to everyone.

In almost every case, you will stall at an inflection point that demands that you take a more sophisticated approach to leadership. You're challenged to take your organization to the next level, but doing so demands that you take *yourself* to the next level of leadership to keep up. You're struggling with what it takes to guide people through successive tiers of sustainable growth to ensure that the company will thrive. And if you delay too long, you may have trouble restarting.

We hear all the time from leaders who have excelled in taking their organizations to a new level of performance but then can't figure out how to keep the momentum going. Although they just celebrated a triumph of growth, they feel they don't have the leadership capabilities required for the next, more difficult problem they face. Sometimes these leaders tell us, "We need to find someone who has solved this type of problem before!"

Of course, many times your organization *does* need a fresh perspective and the capabilities of someone with experience you don't have. Maybe you're completely out of your depth. You're expanding regionally for the first time. Or courting stockholders as a new public company. Or devising a turnaround to transform the way you operate. You feel you just must go outside to hire.

But the reflex to hire externally often signals a shortcoming: You think you need somebody else's help—even though you're capable of the job—*only because you haven't recognized the nature of the challenge and how you need to reinvent your mindset, capabilities, and behaviors to overcome it.*

This reality explains why, as a good deal of research shows, bringing in a "white knight" from the outside only works in some circumstances.

It's easy to misread the problem as a shortage of experience rather than a shortage of your own personal growth. You assume the solution to the challenge lies with changing the leadership makeup of the institution, not the makeup of your own abilities. But our experience argues that if you're an aspiring leader, you can—and should—plan to lead your organization to the next level of performance yourself. You don't always need a savior.

When you're a leader beset by a host of new challenges, the learning and practice of more sophisticated leadership may elude you. But if you can figure out how to embrace new learning, you can plan to grow and change personally as fast as you grow or change your organization. Our conviction is that the solution is to master sophisticated leadership capabilities that are too often seen as "nice to have" rather than fundamental for success.

Feeling outrun by the growth and change of your organization is perfectly normal. It's even sometimes inevitable. But don't fall for thinking you can simply outwork the problem and use brute force to get through it. Some leaders double down on the skills that made them successful at the previous level. Although they don't hire someone new, they put in more hours, seek out new tools and systems, request more data for decision-making, call in consultants to map and analyze processes, and restructure the organization. They are tapping *only* into their skills to manage complexity.

Whether you're a high-potential young manager or in a top position in a high-performance organization, identifying, getting ahead of, and reinventing yourself to power through leadership stalls is critical. Mastering sophistication, rather than merely complexity, demands self-development, and over time, radical change of yourself. You need to adopt mindsets and behaviors you haven't been fully aware of before. And you need to become a student of a new process for doing so.

Overcoming the Stalls

Our objective in this book is to equip you with that process, which gives you the insights and actions to speed up your leadership engine when it threatens to stall—and restart your engine when the stall does come. That's why, unlike business books that address the tools leaders need for complex management, this one highlights the tools for developing the less tangible capabilities of sophisticated leadership.

When you master these abilities, you become a leader whom other leaders want to follow, learn from, and perform for. You become your best leader ever—not best performer, not best manager, but best *leader*. And you will skillfully overcome the stalls that may hold others back.

We start our book by devoting chapter 1 to the insight that underpins every following chapter: that the root cause of stalls is mistaking new challenges of sophistication for ones of complexity. We offer different ways to think about these most-often-overlooked challenges. Overcoming them doesn't demand years of experience. But it does require a commitment to improving your leadership awareness and acumen, especially related to issues of judgment and character, strategic thought and system-wide thinking, and personal style and presence.

We devote the rest of the book to rolling the camera on leaders struggling with each of the seven stalls. In a rich set of real-life examples, we detail the experiences of leaders like you—and in turn try to highlight what you need to watch out for and grapple with. Our intent is to answer the burning question: "What do I do now?" What do you do when you're trying to grow but things aren't clicking? When you're losing your bearings? When your vision or engagement or teamwork or performance is suffering and you're not sure why?

In short, how can you succeed as leader when the job gets bigger than you are? How can you jumpstart your success?

In chapters 2 through 8, after we describe the nature of each stall, we share ways you can assess whether you're at risk for lapsing into one.

We then provide a handful of simple but powerful tools you can use to avoid each stall or recover from it. These are the field-tested tools our clients have found most helpful. At the end of each chapter, we summarize in a breakout summary how to improve your awareness, troubleshoot your stall, and recover to achieve greater success.

Our intent is to help you to convert your passage through the inflection points that trigger each stall from a time of struggle to a time of personal growth. From a career-stopping calamity to a career-advancing opportunity. Instead of stalling out, you will be able to surge forward skillfully, executing one gratifying breakthrough after another in your lifelong journey as a leader.

In chapter 2, we explain how to escape what we call the *purpose stall* by assessing whether you are inspiring people with a meaningful story about the organization's mission. We show how you can and must craft a story that carries your people forward on an inspirational, shared, purpose-based quest—a story that can guide their actions when you are not there to give specific direction at every new turn.

In chapter 3, we show how to overcome the *teamwork stall* by assessing your effectiveness in aligning your team's priorities as well your own critical role in creating a high-performing team. In turn, we reveal time-tested tools to straighten out misalignment and bind people together into a true "A-team."

In chapter 4, we uncover how to eliminate the *stakeholder stall* by assessing who holds power in your universe of internal and external constituencies and how you can engage them to achieve your desired outcomes. In turn, we offer tools for "lifting and shifting" your influence to stakeholders you don't control but who will pave the way for your future success.

In chapter 5, we detail the way to avoid the *leading change stall* by assessing how readily employees and stakeholders receive and embrace your messages about change, and offer new behaviors and practices for engaging people so they grasp, welcome, and act on your initiatives.

In chapter 6, we look at how to handle the ***authority stall*** by assessing your own sources of leadership authority and planning for self-development. We then propose actions that will inspire people to follow you based on trustworthiness, empathy, breadth, balance, and gravitas.

In chapter 7, we explore how to anticipate the *focus stall* by assessing how you allocate your time and energy, and in turn suggest techniques for dividing your focus among "do," "manage," and "lead" tasks—mastering the perennial secret to high-powered leadership.

Finally, in chapter 8, we focus on how to overcome the ***leadership development stall***, the most crucial of all, by assessing your leadership talent and committing to coaching and developing new leaders as your main job. You will become a leader of leaders, multiplying your own leadership success through the success of others.

The Wisdom of It All

What can you expect in reconsidering your development as a leader in terms of understanding inflection points to vanquish stalls? The leaders we have worked with have shifted the ways in which they look at the world, their organizations, their followers, and themselves. In some cases, they have learned to avoid dangerous stalls altogether. Sometimes the shifts to overcome a stall seem subtle, but that's the nature of mastering the challenges of sophistication. The subtle changes—which over time you may come to realize are not so subtle at all—make all the difference.

The magnitude of that difference is reflected in the word "sophistication." The etymology of "sophistication" is rooted in the idea of *wisdom*. The word comes from the Greek, *sophistēs* "wise man," and ultimately from *sophia*, "wisdom." Thus "sophistication" contrasts with the nature of leadership challenges related to complexity. "Complexity" derives from a more straightforward etymology, "composed of or weaving together many parts"—*com + plectare*.

As you tap into the sophisticated leadership capabilities you may have underappreciated or underdeployed, you'll see fresh wisdom in the way you deal with people. You'll move from giving them the answer to pointing them to where they can find the answer. From talking and telling to listening and asking. From convincing others with your technical knowledge to engaging them via bigger-picture non-transactional conversations. From leaning in to standing back. From dictating "what" to coaching "how." From asking people to solve issues through processes and reports to solving them through their own more sophisticated approach to people and personalities.

You'll also see wisdom as you shift the way you deal with work in your organization. For instance, from making decisions on every issue to making them on only a critical few. From drilling into present problems to envisioning the future. From fine-tuning the status quo to innovating anew. From focusing on concerns only within the organization to focusing outside. From solving the right problems to asking the right questions. From managing performance to managing risk. From decision making to decision prepping.

The list could go on. Subtle but not so subtle. And when you evolve yourself as a leader in this way, you'll discover that when you see a stall coming, you can act preemptively to work through it. And when you get used to acting early often enough, you will avoid stalls because you will have built a leadership foundation to sustain both your own growth and that of your organization.

You may have wondered at some point why sustaining personal growth as a leader is so difficult. Why are so many leaders a master of the universe at one level but then struggle mightily at the next? Is it just because the job and organization get bigger and more complicated? Not quite. There's a further element to this story. One of the added reasons for stalls is that an increasing need for more sophisticated leadership responses appears, and reappears, in new forms and contexts. Each stall looks different, even to seasoned leaders. And yet there are many similarities as well, and after struggling with the stall, it ends up feeling like déjà vu.

The truth is that your growing organization's demands *will* outrun your capabilities at some point if you're leading a thriving business. It's inevitable. And the higher you go in an organization, the faster these demands could outrun you. Have no fear: The occasional crisis of confidence that comes with a stall can, if you look at the upside, be helpful and instructive. The sooner you recognize a crisis in the making, the sooner you can act on the need to think differently. A stall may be the signal for reinventing yourself as a leader.

If you're a new leader, we have some specific advice: Don't just focus on adopting new skills or capabilities. You will also need to abandon—or downplay—old ones. Almost everyone is tempted to stay loyal to their initial trade. You think of yourself as an engineer, or a factory manager, or a financial whiz, or an operations guru, or a marketer, or a scientist. But as you move up, you must reshape your sense of who you are and what you project to others. As we say in the pages ahead, overcoming stalls is a matter of backing away and elevating your perspective on the challenges confronting you, and learning to do so repeatedly during your career.

When you take a step back from a crisis in the making, you rethink the capabilities you need as a leader and how to move them to the foreground. You reconsider which tasks you should do versus which you'll let others do. When you elevate your view, you in turn elevate your responsibilities as befits a higher-level player on your team—and in turn a higher level in your organization, in your sector, and in society.

When you repeat this kind of growth again and again during your career, you position yourself to evade the pain and consequences of being caught in future stalls. When you ask yourself, "What happens now?" you'll be ready to answer: "I will look inside, see myself as others see me and as they want and need me to be, and act to remake myself." You won't blame your troubles on your organization or people, or ask,

"How do I change the institution to overcome these challenges?" You'll see yourself as the source of the slowdown. And then you'll be ready to become your own "Best Leader Ever."

CHAPTER 1

Why Leaders Stall

Confusing Challenges of Complexity with Those of Sophistication

"Just because we don't understand doesn't mean that the explanation doesn't exist."—Madeleine L'Engle, *A Wrinkle in Time*

"Any intelligent fool can make things bigger, more complex, and more violent. It takes a touch of genius—and a lot of courage—to move in the opposite direction."—E.F. Schumacher, *Small Is Beautiful*

Trevor Boyce has been a CEO for thirty-five years. A surfer who once made annual pilgrimages to a secret spot in Puerto Rico, he has observed firsthand how, as in surfing, at many junctures in the life of a leader the waves get bigger in ways you don't expect. The same skills, the same knowledge, and the same behaviors from the past don't deliver the results needed *now*. That's when you might get anxious. Or alarmed. You may realize the job—the wave!—has swollen beyond your capabilities.

And that's when, as a leader, whatever your level in your organization, you can lose your footing. Or slip off the board. Or wipe out in the surf.

Boyce has observed this danger in his role as the head of Microbac Laboratories. Microbac, the largest independent testing lab in the US, posts $100 million in yearly sales and has grown over 10 percent a year. Operating in twelve states, it serves customers with every possible testing need—from bicycle manufacturers gauging the flex of carbon-fiber frames to chemical giants sampling hazardous waste.[1]

Boyce started with the company in 1982, working for the founder, his father. In 1991, when Microbac reached $10 million in sales, he bought his father out. Since then, he has acquired more than eighty testing companies, steadily expanding Microbac's capabilities, services, and footprint. Over the decades he has observed patterns in leadership that many managers don't get the chance to see, and his story heralds the message of this book.

Boyce pinpoints the moments in his industry when the challenges of growth tend to get the better of most leaders. These moments of truth, which we observe across organizations, are the inflection points when leaders discover they don't know what they need to know—or to do— to keep their companies growing. We call them stall points.

If you've ever led a team or organization, you'll know what we mean by a stall—and the unnerving sensation triggered by not delivering the kind of leadership your people need. Over a career, everyone is almost sure to hit at least a few stalls. Sometimes you'll feel like you're failing, and sometimes you'll pull out of the stall on your own. But you can't avoid the threat of stalls any more than a surfer can avoid gnarly waves.

In our experience as executives, consultants, board members, coaches, and leadership instructors, we see stalls time and again. We're convinced too few leaders know how to see them in advance or handle them when they happen. Stalls usually don't stem from your making a mistake. Nor are they caused by having a debilitating personality trait or bad habit. Rather, they come about when your organization hits one of those inflection points—usually as it grows and changes, or the industry or world changes around it—where you need to deploy entirely different skills and behaviors as a leader. The changing organization needs something new from you, not just your trusted talents of the past.

Stalls are often a consequence of your success, making them hard to fathom. They are the points when you're challenged to build on your acclaimed record to deliver bigger or different results, often depending on skills you undervalue or didn't think you needed. Aglow from past achievements, you get confused, frustrated, maybe panicked—beset by flagging momentum with possibly lifelong impact.

Take heart. Stalls are predictable, and if you recognize the warning signs that show they're happening to you, you'll have a good chance of surfing right past them. Boyce is a great example. Based on three decades in the commercial testing industry, he has concluded that leaders of startup laboratories face their first stall at $3.5 million in sales. That's when scientist owners "trained in school to have their hands on the entire experiment" end up stunting growth. Why? Because they persist with micromanagement and their need to be involved in all aspects of the business.

The second stall comes at around $10 million. That's when two scientists, as partners, do the same. They micromanage their way to a partnership crossroads. The third is at $25 million. That's when the business demands more computer technology, science PhDs, global standard (ISO) quality controls, formal sales forces, and savvy CFOs to deal with big customers like Monsanto and DuPont.

"For a lot of the companies we bought, these were permanent stalls," Boyce says. "And that's why they went up for sale, because the owners could not get beyond those points."

Not getting beyond those points. Just what is it that can stymie you such that you have trouble leading a next phase of growth or transformation in your team or organization? What are you missing? In what circumstances might you hit a stall that stops you from sustaining your personal and professional leadership trajectory? What could turn a career advance into a career-stopping derailment?

Boyce has some answers. His latest fight to avoid a stall came four years ago, when Microbac reached $75 million in sales. "One day I looked at where we were and just asked a very simple question," he says. "We were doubling in size every seven years . . . so the question was, were the systems and the management team in place to get through that next doubling? Would we survive it?"

"And in my mind, the answer was 'no,'" he admits. "We wouldn't have done it well. And I was not at all sure we would have survived it." He was worried that a bigger company could have gobbled up Microbac. "That was a huge wake-up call for us," he says. "Our culture of semiautonomous labs was not going to stand the test of time." He realized that to pull out of this stall he needed to do something different as a leader. The growth waves were getting bigger and rougher.

That's when Boyce restructured the business, remaking a company led by people in autonomous labs into one with an integrated corporate structure. The restructuring was a traditional management response to the increasing complexity of the business. But the harder part was the required change of culture and the demand for a new philosophy of leadership. Every lab boss was, overnight, becoming responsible and accountable to a leadership team at headquarters. As Boyce raised his sights as a leader, he had to ask his people for different mindsets and capabilities. "And that was without a doubt the most painful thing I've ever been through in business," he says. "It nearly took us under."

Pain and Doubt

Why was this inflection point so painful? For the same reason it is for all leaders: because, while leadership involves many kinds of challenges, the ones that usually stymie you at inflection points are those that require what we call increased *sophistication*. Facing challenges of fresh sophistication requires not just that you change your team or organization, but that you change yourself and others. This means not just changing structure and systems. It means changing thinking and behaviors. And it means that you must not only apply conventional tools of management, but that you must develop subtle shifts in and enhancements to your judgment, style, gravitas, and *savoir faire* as a leader.

You're not alone if the challenges we're describing strike you as somewhat abstract. Matters of leadership sophistication don't get the same attention as what we call the challenges of *complexity*: namely the responsibilities for managing the systems and processes in your organization. If you're like most leaders, you find it easier to embrace complex challenges: You can document them, measure them, and subject them to analysis and data crunching. You can document and capture them in spreadsheets and on organization charts.

But you may find it more difficult to discover solutions for problems not easily measured or explained by the "hard" data. That's only natural. Faced with a new territory to explore, who wouldn't plan their next journey across the landscape that they can see most clearly? You wouldn't set your path across lands hidden from view. We refer to this as the "dark side of the moon" problem. As a leader, you're drawn to territory that shows up in highlight, the sunlit part of the moon, the side facing Earth. You reflexively hesitate to deal with what you can't see. This dark side—or "far" side as astronomers say—is more mysterious and harder to study with conventional tools, so it doesn't get as much attention.

And yet both sides of the moon, and both sides of leadership, matter. You can't lead as a full, holistic leader without seeing and responding to the challenges presented by both sides. If you focus on the near side, the complexity, you're in league with most leaders. Why not roll up your sleeves and bridge craters in the moonscape you are used to? That's what most leaders are taught to do: attack obvious gaps and structural problems armed with tools they know best, relying on reams of data and analysis, support from consultants, and whiteboards full of plans.

But the terrain on the far side requires a different approach—that's where the bigger risks and greater challenges are. These challenges are often less urgent and less straightforward. They are also more painful to handle, because they oblige you to develop less familiar people skills. Skills to manage your time and energy toward different ends. To orchestrate the alignment and motivation of your people in new ways.

To modify how you act in tackling a host of new personal, interpersonal, strategic, and political issues.

No matter what your leadership role is, you might get so flummoxed at times by the challenges of sophistication that you will be at a loss to accelerate growth or confront change. It doesn't matter what level you are or if your organization is big or small, corporate or nonprofit, fast-moving or slow, civilian, military, or political. It doesn't even matter what kind of leadership style or set of experiences you have. The ground has shifted under your feet, often as a result of your own efforts. The setting has changed and you face new challenges to your leadership that were not necessarily present at your earlier level of responsibility. You are inevitably going to face stalls. In this book we describe in detail the seven most common stalls and how you can pull through them.

You're a rare leader if you have never encountered a stall. And when you first hit one, you'll probably react as most people do—by redoubling your efforts to engineer a revival by reorganizing, bringing in outside experts, hiring new, talented executives who have "been there before," building organizational infrastructure, re-crunching the data, running tests, and changing business processes. In other words, you'll do the same things that have worked in the past. You'll tackle the well-illuminated stuff with your standard portfolio of skills.

But that's where the danger lies—in following that reflex. You think, "If the tried-and-true building blocks worked before, they'll work again, won't they?" And then you end up succumbing to a flaw afflicting most leaders: maintaining sight of one half of the challenge, the illuminated side, but losing sight of the other half. The first half requires handling increased complexity—increased but not unfamiliar. The second half requires handling increased sophistication—a new, unfamiliar, and (just as on the far side of the moon) rougher landscape.

Most of the tools, techniques, and training available to you as a leader will help you to master increased complexity. If you have more customers, more locations, more products, and more employees, then you rework reporting lines, information sources, logistics systems, manufacturing processes, risk-management procedures, budgeting approaches, and so on. If you can't, you hire consultants who can and acquire technology that helps. You make the most of the management innovations of the past twenty years—lean management, Six Sigma, total quality management, business process reengineering, big data analytics, and so on.

But the most effective strategies and capabilities to bring increased sophistication to your work as a leader are not available off-the-shelf or through hiring others. They depend on your taking initiative largely on your own and leading and doing things in a different way than you did before. If you don't, you can find yourself crippled by new challenges. Your efforts to spur teamwork result in strife. Plans you polish up to communicate change are met with yawns. New stakeholders control your future and push an agenda confounding yours. Accomplished executives you recruit can't or won't work well together. Your sources of authority as a leader no longer command respect.

Based on our work with hundreds of leaders, this error of addressing the challenges requiring increased sophistication with solutions more fit for increased complexity is the consistent—often maddeningly so—source of most leadership stalls. We hear the same story again and again. Leaders become baffled as to why they can't drive higher performance, and the reason is that they are caught up in using tools for solving complexity issues when they need to develop the capabilities to lead in a more sophisticated way. If there is any common thread that binds together the stories of leaders who stall, this is it.

The Insidious Trigger

Imagine you're a CFO who has developed a robust set of processes for overseeing payroll, vendor payments, customer billing, treasury, forecasting, and accounting. All of a sudden, your boss, the CEO, asks you to help raise money from new, outside funders, namely bankers or share-holders or private-equity investors. The new task requires an almost completely different set of skills than the ones that helped you succeed so far. If you're like many financial leaders, you'll feel out of your depth—and will probably stall.[2]

Or imagine you're a technology leader, highly regarded for your aptitude in overseeing product development. You have long kept the organization clicking as it expanded to multiple regions. All of a sudden, your boss asks you to ramp up innovation by partnering with other organizations via joint ventures. Your mastery and mindset for overseeing the team underneath you do not translate to managing people in enterprises who do not report to you. If you're like many leaders, you'll fear that you've been thrust into a dynamic of new relationship-building challenges you don't know how to navigate, and will probably stall.

Perhaps you've been in a situation similar to those of these finance and technology leaders. You stalled when you found yourself out of your depth in terms of the strategic, political, and interpersonal skills you needed—lacking the sophisticated leadership capabilities to respond. You belatedly recognized the insidious thing about stalls. When they happen, you're usually, in some vague way, aware of them, but can't figure out how to respond. You're unable, on the fly, to grasp the nature of your trouble or turn things around to regain your footing and drive results.

If you want to overcome—or avoid—the tragedy of a stall, you have to start by asking a basic question: How aware am I of how my organization's operating environment is changing, and what that will require from me? Do I see that new challenges require something more than or different from the tools and solutions I have historically brought to bear? Can I recognize the need for developing my own leadership sophistication as I'm taking the organization into different waters, in unfamiliar weather, with different people watching and counting on me?

To come at this in another way, when you face challenges of complexity, do you see that, in most circumstances, you're being asked to do *more of the same job*? More finance processes that work in similar ways. More technology innovation of the same kind. And when you face challenges of sophistication do you see that you're being asked to do *more of different jobs*—or do the job *in a different way*?

In a growing and changing organization, you do have to master complexity as a leader. That's a given. And we're not saying it's easy. But it's not sufficient. If you don't recognize the challenges of sophistication as well, you are destined to go wobbly in the chop and scale of bigger waves. You risk wiping out, forced to haul yourself out on the beach, banged up and disoriented.

Of course, most leaders we work with are not oblivious to sophistication. Neither are they unaware of the broader capabilities that the changing organization requires. Nor do they undervalue these leadership abilities. But caught riding the crest of past success, they don't take stock of just how much their next success depends on navigating the unforeseen trough ahead. As it turns out, the new job almost always requires that you drop your old self—all the skills that made you a good leader in the first place—and reinvent yourself for a new future.

And that's daunting. We can't tell you how many times we've heard from seasoned leaders we've worked with, "As a company, we don't have the technical knowledge to play at the next level." Or "I need to go out and find someone who has done it before." Or "I don't think I can run the show anymore." We hear this even from seasoned C-suite executives. Sometimes an element of alarm electrifies these moments. Maybe you've felt it firsthand: All eyes are on you. People are looking at you dance in the spotlight to see your next steps—and those steps better be snappy.

But the solution isn't to take faster steps of the same kind of dance. You must take sophisticated new steps. This should include role-modeling new behaviors, understanding divergent value systems, managing more and different stakeholders, making weighty ethical decisions, projecting greater presence, communicating matters that will change the course of your organization, and shaping leaders to lead other leaders. You have to develop a new and deeper leadership repertoire—deep enough to inspire people to embrace a mission, nurture relationships, energize teams, groom successors, and more.

Some leaders simply leave the dance floor—or are asked to step away. They tap an outsider to take their place, or a boss or board member taps somebody for them. But from long experience, we can testify that you *can* learn to lead at a new level, maybe even at the top level. You don't have to let your organization outrun your capabilities. You can commit to developing yourself as a sophisticated leader, learning to act and behave differently. So when you ask yourself, "What happens now?" you know the answer: Take steps to evolve with more depth, breadth, and sophistication. In a world where no organization stands still, you have no choice.

The Two-Sided Challenge

Seeing, avoiding, and handling stalls starts with confronting a hard reality: Where are you today? Do you really know? Are the challenges in front of you what you think they are? In the military, the challenge you face is called "situational awareness."

An enterprise can get more complex in many ways. The most common is one we introduced earlier: multiplicity. More of everything. More employees, more offices, more products, more offerings, more customers, more systems, more meetings, more decisions—just *more*. More usually stems from growth, which is an indicator of success. And if you're like most leaders, even of privately held or nonprofit companies, you make regular plans to spur your organization's growth.

In understanding complexity, take your cue from a huge body of research. The way in which organizations grow in complexity has a consistent pattern. So much so that, in the 1970s, Larry Greiner, an emeritus professor at University of Southern California's business school, documented the stages in a typical business. His work has been copied and extended ever since. Even with successive booms in technology and hyper-growth startups, Greiner's pattern holds as follows.[3]

In the first phase of growth, everyone is a doer and nobody is a leader. The founding boss hits a crisis, and the crisis persists until the boss recruits professional managers. The pros in turn install a hierarchical structure, accounting systems, budgeting processes, work standards, and so on. The new managers are able to tame the chaos of growth.

The pros then hit a crisis themselves because the structure, which allayed chaos, becomes a straightjacket. Workers chafe under the weight of too many directives, and managers lose track of what's happening on the front lines. The boss and other leaders are forced to ease up on centralization. They add a new structure to decentralize and give responsibility for profits and management to people near the front lines. This is an era of delegation, in which leaders manage by exception.

With more growth, the ever-more-elite managers lose control again, because they delegated *too* much. They re-impose controls—planning procedures, review programs, capital-spending processes, centralized data processing. Alas, although they quell the new crisis, it leads in turn, with more growth, to yet another, when the organization is beset by rigidity and red tape. At that point, top managers often form a matrix organization. They build cross-functional teams and introduce formal incentives to motivate people to serve the whole organization rather than parochial groups.

The evolution Greiner describes comes in lots of varieties, but you get the picture. Although the model helps illuminate the challenges of complexity, its focus exclusively on structure suggests that all leaders are interchangeable. All they have to master are the standard systems and processes to manage growth. Greiner was astute in explaining how leaders have to relentlessly attack complexity during growth—and become master mechanics of organizational management.[4]

Trevor Boyce had to be that kind of mechanic. When Microbac was small and all the lab heads ruled, he imposed little structure beyond centralizing accounting. At $25 million in sales, he added new building blocks: a formal sales force and a high-performing IT department. He also adopted scientific and quality standards to meet lab accreditation requirements to serve big corporate customers. At $75 million in sales, he instituted an integrated structure, and that's when entrepreneurial lab heads had to relinquish their autonomy and join the corporate fold.

In other words, to grow to $100 million in sales, Boyce began operating with a set of new structural elements. He hired a range of experts, from finance to logistics to quality. He redesigned the organization to stress one central hierarchy. He revamped supply chain management to gain efficiencies via consolidated buying. He reworked data management to provide customers new analyses, reports, and tools.

But he then had to take into account increasing sophistication, or the other, rockier, side of the moon. This was the half that mattered most in getting beyond the $75 million stall. And this required more than Lego-like reassembly of organizational structure and processes. "What I wanted to do was to be *different*," he says, "not just a different Microbac, but I wanted to be different from every other laboratory company I knew of, as a matter of business differentiation."

But he hadn't yet figured out how to iron out all the wrinkles in the subtle, often-intangible capabilities related to how he would lead in a more sophisticated way. How would he get his people to better handle personal relationships and manage conflict? Or to solidify values to create a corporate culture that prized cross-organizational teamwork? "A stumbling block early on in our cultural shift was getting these guys to realize that $1 + 1 = 6$," he says. "And if you're not working together $1 + 1 = 0$, not 2." As a result, he recalls, "We went through three or four years of cultural change in our company that was sheer pain and torture."

In effect, Boyce had to reinvent himself as a new kind of leader. He was no longer in the business of laboratory testing. He was now in the business of creating more leaders. For years he had spent 50 percent of his time in the field helping lab managers, 25 percent on selling, and 25 percent on acquisition development. He reallocated his time away from operations, and now he now spends 50 percent of his hours working with his team so everyone can get better at coordinating, motivating, and developing their own teams across the company.

That work includes coaxing people to cross-sell services in a national organization to national accounts. Microbac's once-specialized lab leaders—experts in food, pharmaceutical, or environmental testing—had to learn how to work together to sell packages of services nationwide, with uniform data services and national pricing. They also had to learn how to expand by following customers who are growing instead of the customers following Microbac. To make these transformational changes, Boyce oversaw a new effort in which the company put labs on wheels to serve customers wherever they needed testing services. If people couldn't or wouldn't come to the lab, Microbac would bring the lab to them. "That was a major transition," he says.

When we talk about improving your awareness of the challenges of increased complexity and sophistication as a leader, we admit to distinguishing between two fuzzy concepts. Don't they overlap? Yes, the challenges of the two are always married, but learning to distinguish them has a way of explaining an otherwise mystifying fact: No matter the size or kind of organization, if you're like most leaders, you have a good chance of stalling just as you're hitting your peak of success. And our experience is that leaders easily misidentify their biggest challenges, and in turn misapply their responses for tackling them.

Complexity challenges, which often come with growth in scale, can make your job bigger in ways you can anticipate. Sophistication challenges, which usually come with change in kind, make the job broader in ways you don't anticipate. If you're like most leaders, you'll display more comfort with complexity and decidedly less comfort with sophistication. See Table 1.1 for a sampling of what we mean. Note how distinct the challenges are—and how different the corresponding solutions have to be.[5]

TABLE 1.1 TWO DISTINCT LEADERSHIP CHALLENGES

Complexity Challenges	Sophistication Challenges
Unfulfilled mission	Uncompelling mission
Poor communications	Poor inspiration
Inadequate reports and processes	Inadequate collaborative capability
More products, locations, vendors	Different products, locations, vendors
Undersized administrative structure	Obsolete business model
Poor team performance	Poor team commitment
More insider constituencies	More outside stakeholders
More direct competition	New indirect competition
Slow growth in current markets	No growth in undeveloped markets
Falling customer sales	Failing customer relationships
Weak organizational culture	Outdated organizational culture
Noncompliance with rules	Noncompliance with values or ethics
Weak training programs	Weak leadership development, coaching, and succession planning

Leadership challenges have a dual nature. Sometimes they call for something more, and sometimes for something new or different. "More" and "different" don't fully capture the distinctions between these two sets of challenges. But if you feel you can deal with a challenge through a "best practices" approach at an operational level, you're likely talking complexity. In that case, plug in a solution you've used in the past or a new best practice—"more"—and play for future growth in the same way as in the past. For example, hire a new technical person (or hire more) for capacity problems you've seen in the past, and you get more factory throughput.

On the other hand, if you feel you can't plug in a solution—or more likely you've tried one and the square peg hasn't fit into the round hole—you're talking "different," which probably means sophistication. That challenge will require change at the personal level for you, the leader. The simplest example of something different is when your organization grows into serving new or changing customers. You might have to oversee new sales approaches and different types of sales people. You'll also have to understand customers who behave differently and have different expectations. You will have to get your people to understand a new and changing strategy, and you may even need to find ways to *stop* them from doing what they've always done.

At that point, you can't succeed only by hiring more people and expanding the same systems to multiple states. You'll need a lot that is new. A new story that communicates purpose in a different way. A new approach to managing your team and stakeholders. A new allocation of time and energy. A new emphasis on developing the next generation of leaders. And a new answer to your followers' question: "Why should we follow *you* in this new and different world?"

Not Just Business

The challenges of increasing sophistication cut across all sectors of the working world. If you wonder what it might look like in nonprofits, take the case of Hector Batista, CEO of Big Brothers Big Sisters of New York. Batista accepted the top job in that agency in 2010, a time when new organizations were challenging BBBS's century-old status as the gold standard for mentoring urban youth. Big Brothers Big Sisters was facing competition in upstarts such as iMentor, which was seeking to disrupt the business using technology and nontraditional approaches. "We thought our name and reputation would carry us forward," Batista says. "But the reality is your name only carries you so far. We had to deliver differently and better, and change with the times."

Batista did respond with the tools for handling increased challenges of complexity. He updated human-resources systems and processes for salaries and performance appraisals. He funded tools and technologies to better connect and support mentored youth, their families, the mentors, and the agency. He reduced the number of senior administrators and increased the ranks of field people. He replaced obsolete finance and data systems. In restructuring and implementing new standards, he also persuaded board members to bring more structure to their own meetings. And he pushed through a strategic plan to raise funding 24 percent and serve 30 percent more children.

But Batista didn't aim merely to spur growth in the number of boys and girls the agency served with "bigs"—the "big brother" and "big sister" mentors. He worked with his new senior team to think differently about the purpose of the organization and in turn create innovative new mentoring services. What did kids—the "littles"—and their families and communities need in a changing world? How could BBBS respond as it served immigrant populations from unfamiliar cultures? Or respond to littles living in transient housing or suffering homelessness? The question for Batista was the same as for so many organizations: How could the agency serve its constituents better even if it meant doing different things in a different way?

Similarly, if you wonder about what this kind of change looks like in government, take the case of John Hillen, this book's coauthor. In the mid-2000s, as US assistant secretary of state for political-military affairs, he was called on to help fight counterinsurgencies in Iraq, Afghanistan, the Southern Philippines, and elsewhere. Up until then, ambassadors and their staffs in the US State Department worked almost exclusively from comfortable offices in national capitals or major cities. They recorded and analyzed information, negotiated with other diplomats, and wrote cables to dispense measured, dispassionate advice to decision makers elsewhere. Their work followed rules, and it unfolded in a controlled environment where people talked embassy-to-embassy, one formal channel to another.

But turmoil in Iraq and Afghanistan convinced General David Petraeus, in charge of framing a counterinsurgency doctrine and strategy for the US military, that the nature of his challenge was not all military.

It was 80 percent political. Petraeus had authority only over professionals in uniform, so for the effort to succeed he needed participation from other US government missions around the globe. And he didn't just need "more" people from the State Department or other civilian agencies, as if numbers alone mattered. He needed US government civilians from outside the Pentagon to perform in ways they never had before.

The counterinsurgency effort demanded that US diplomats and civilians get on the ground alongside the US military. The diplomatic and civilian forces had to go face-to-face with warlords and head-to-head with provincial leaders. For the US to have an effective government-wide counterinsurgency capability, military, diplomatic, and foreign-aid officers would have to work together. They would have to put themselves in unfamiliar situations, doing everything from cutting ribbons at community centers in the Southern Philippines to cutting deals with warlords in Kandahar. Needless to say, agency leaders, including Hillen in the State Department, didn't see the challenge merely as one of complexity. It was not a matter of opening more consulates or embassies, even in difficult places.

Hillen and other leaders of Condoleezza Rice's State Department couldn't respond to the challenge just by hiring someone and saying "fix" or "install" a new process. Even though Hillen was in charge of political-military affairs at the State Department, he had neither the legal authority nor the budget to put civilians from multiple agencies to work in the "red zones" of conflicts. The complexity of moving more people into such roles—outside the familiarity and safety of "green zones"—was huge. But the more notable challenge was one of sophistication. Beyond changing deployments and restructuring units, the change demanded that Hillen launch a government-wide campaign to develop a shared sense of purpose, to persuade skeptical stakeholders, and to build teams in new forums to cooperate around a new mission.[6]

As with Batista, so with Hillen, and probably with you: The challenges of sophistication have a way of stretching leaders like never before. To overcome those challenges, you first have to heighten your awareness of what you're facing. That's why, for example, we have advised leaders to adopt a rule during rapid growth of not taking on two significant "new" challenges at the same time. By all means, we say, stretch to seek work with new customers. Or stretch to provide an existing customer a new offering. But be wary of trying to do both at the same time. Your coauthors have both tried to do that and learned the hard way it doesn't work. The rule: No two "news" at once.

We don't mean to diminish the challenges of mastering complexity. But responding to increased levels of sophistication demands that you do something much harder. You must fundamentally rethink how you spend time, where you focus energy, how you communicate, with whom you develop relationships, and how you look at the big picture to understand when, where, and how to act. And to do so you have to rely on developing your own capabilities. You have to create a new you, starting with an awareness of how the challenges around you are changing.

Becoming Sophisticated

As you take up the task of developing yourself as a more sophisticated leader, you have to take stock of your own capabilities: Are you aware of the shrinking efficacy of your technical skills? Of the growing power of new interpersonal and strategic abilities, mindsets, and behaviors? Take a look at Figure 1.1. Where do you fall on the graph? Where should you fall? How will you change to get there?

This figure raises an obvious question: What *are* the new capabilities on which your leadership success will depend? But it also raises a less obvious one: Which skills that you value today should you deemphasize—or resist exercising at all? As you rise as a leader, you'll be obliged to master relationship management, raising outside funding, grooming new leaders, redefining purpose in times of wrenching change,

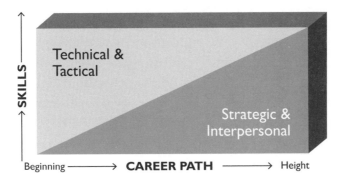

Figure 1.1 Your Mix of Capabilities as a Leader

handling reputational risk or ethical challenges, and much more. You need to figure out the right way to evolve your leadership from the left side of the graph to the right as you take on more responsibility and more sophisticated challenges.

As an example, take the challenge of moving your organization into a new market, especially a foreign one. Although "going global" increases complexity, it often increases the sophistication of your operating environment even more. To begin with, new cultures demand you communicate in new ways. How do you handle the challenge of introducing just this "one new facet," even if it's simply selling an existing product?

Our friend Frank Lavin, former undersecretary for international trade at the US Commerce Department, advises companies on doing just that in China. CEO of Export Now, the advisory firm he founded in 2010, Lavin poses the question: What if the Hershey Company wanted to market its chocolate in China? What are the challenges of selling a respected good from the West to Chinese consumers? What new skills, mindsets, and behaviors would you need? What are the show-stopping challenges you would have to overcome?

In the US, expanding sales of products like chocolate is mostly a matter of distribution: Most growth strategies are nothing more than distribution strategies. Most leaders assume the same is true going into China, says Lavin. They of course grasp the extra complexity: They need to learn to figure out foreign-exchange systems, capital remittance, business licenses, labeling, testing, customs clearance, and so on. But they often forget a critical element of sophistication, the art of courting the consumer. "Products have a very different place in the consciousness of people in China," Lavin says. "It's not just the utility of the product that matters."[7]

What executives often miss, he says, is that "nobody in China knows, likes, or understands your value proposition." He adds: "You think you know what the Chinese like because you inhabit one universe. But there's a parallel universe abroad. What does Hershey's chocolate mean to those consumers?"

"In China," he explains, "this product will only be bought as a gift. It's a boutique product, an exotic item, worthy of premium price, and it's bought as sign of respect for someone else. You have to endow it with premium attributes so it's an appropriate gift to an officemate during a promotion. The product in China is part of the consumer's identity."

To adapt to that sophisticated new way of thinking, he says, leaders of a US business like Hershey would need to learn to be more self-aware, self-diagnostic, and innovative. "The answer is not improving US models, but adding consumer experience with the product." Doing so requires that the consumer have what he calls a "conversation" with the product. People want to know which movie stars use the product. They want to know about the history of the brand and its health benefits. "In China, you're not making a transaction, you're joining a club," he says.

In other words, there's a world of difference between a strategy for increasing distribution and one for joining the Chinese club. Of course, the China experience is a special situation, but you can see how much bigger the job becomes when you're facing growing sophistication and not just complexity. If we are to generalize, we can say that as you advance as a leader, the technical and tactical skills you need—distribution expertise, for example—pale in comparison to the strategic and interpersonal.

When you see this distinction, you'll understand that you have to employ different faculties. Daniel Goleman, known for his work in social and emotional intelligence, has done more than anyone else to promote this kind of thinking. He argues convincingly that traditional leadership competencies, such as cognitive ability, technical knowledge, and subject matter expertise are necessary but not sufficient for success. The most effective leaders rely heavily on emotional intelligence to engage followers, work through conflict, lead change, and get commitment to results. Emotional intelligence includes self-awareness, self-management, motivation, empathy, and social skill—exactly those elements needed at the right side of our graph on page 31.

Goleman's research, together with that of others across hundreds of companies and thousands of managers, provides strong evidence that sophisticated capabilities like emotional intelligence can be much greater differentiators for leaders than cognitive or technical ability, especially at higher levels of management. For example, Goleman concludes that for senior leaders, assuming a baseline level of IQ and specialized ability (such as legal, financial, or technical acumen), up to 90 percent of the difference between average and star leaders can be attributed to emotional intelligence.[8]

That's why so many leaders and business writers today stress a mastery of the so-called "soft stuff" as paramount for top leaders. We strongly agree that intellectual and technical capability are not enough for leaders to overcome the stalls they may suffer as their organizations grow or change rapidly. Leadership sophistication depends on many more intangible competencies, among them the ability to apply emotional intelligence during your mastery of new strategic and interpersonal capabilities.[9]

The bigger message of what it takes to become a sophisticated leader, however, is that it is a matter of changing *how* you go about what you do.

How you pull back and understand the bigger realities of the job. *How* you approach doing the job having done so. *How* you think and behave so your people eagerly receive your leadership. Getting the *how* right is the challenge when it comes to mastering sophistication.[10] That's what we see in the stories of Trevor Boyce, Hector Batista, and many other leaders—and perhaps your own as well.

Another friend of ours, Sid Fuchs, president and CEO of MacAulay-Brown, Inc. a Dayton, Ohio-based engineering and cybersecurity firm, tells a story about his own past. Fuchs, a Louisiana State University engineering grad, has held top positions at Northrop Grumman and served as CEO of two mid-size tech firms. He is also a veteran of the CIA. He recalls that, as a new CIA officer, he was trained, motivated, and rewarded to be assertive and aggressive. And he was a self-admitted "bull in a china shop."[11]

And when Fuchs got into industry, he discovered that style didn't play well. "It took me a little while to figure it out," he says. "People would tell me, 'Sid, you're really smart, but the cost of doing business with you is high.' I'm wired with a fast motor, a fast tempo. So that was a blind spot for me that people brought to my attention. My aggressiveness was holding me back."

Fuchs hired an executive coach and collected more feedback about adapting his behavior to get the interaction he wanted and needed from others. He came to see he had been making decisions autonomously. Sometimes he had interacted with people in ways that stifled empowerment or caused them not to feel heard or involved. Now he catches himself and "opens up a space for people to explore, be creative, and take risks."

He says, "To some people, feedback is like poison. 'How dare you tell me that—that hurts me!'" Fuchs says. "For people who are open to constructive criticism, it's like building muscle. Muscle only gets stronger when you break it down. You look at weak spots and rebuild where you need to."

Many leaders faced with new sophistication challenges will reach into their timeworn tool bag to apply what they're familiar with. Such an approach clearly wouldn't work for leaders like Boyce, Batista, Lavin, Fuchs, and many others we feature in the pages ahead. As leadership gurus Warren Bennis and James O'Toole wrote, "Most of us wear the concrete shoes of our earlier successes"—and we pay the price.[12] We need to put on our gym shoes and rebuild muscles instead.[13]

The Missing "S"

Developing yourself as a more sophisticated leader demands inner work, and that's neither simple nor easy. We sometimes run into leaders who, perhaps without realizing it, work diligently to *avoid* changing themselves. A classic case is when a leader hires a chief of staff to manage workflow, generate reports, and even communicate with the senior team. The new staff chief often comes in after a rash of recruiting, firing, reorganizations, changes in meeting formats—you name it. But this new chief gets poor traction because the problems can't be solved by establishing a new box on the org chart. It turns out that the boss is the problem, not the team.

Back in the early 1980s, McKinsey & Company consultants Bob Waterman and Tom Peters developed a now-well-known way for leaders to frame elements of organizational effectiveness. Dubbed "The Seven S Model," it depicts seven factors that must be aligned and reinforce each other for an organization to perform well: strategy, structure, systems, staff, skills, style, and shared values. The model proved wildly popular for leaders attempting to diagnose problems in their organizations.

But that framework left something out—something critical. What about the factor that trumps all other factors when sophistication challenges increase: *yourself*? In our increasingly complex and sophisticated world, the model seems to demand an eighth S: "self." Your work on yourself as a leader is often the S that gets most neglected when it actually demands the most attention. No matter how strong the other parts of the system, if you're not regularly challenging yourself as a leader—questioning what you're doing and how you're doing it—you risk a stall that you can't afford.

We are sometimes surprised when we have to point out this reality. A promising team leader in her twenties stopped us recently in a break-room to ask how to address a problem with her team of three software developers. "How can I explain where we're going with our work and why it matters?" A certified project manager and developer, she could easily spell out the work that needed to get done to get to the next proj-ect milestone. But she was struggling to help her people understand how that work fulfilled the purpose of the company. We suggested she needed to crystallize why *she* came to work every day. She had to exam-ine herself—and only then could she give her team a visceral sense of what mattered.

As with a front-line leader, so with leaders at all levels: Your first task is to discover the pieces of yourself that you must reinvent to master sophisticated challenges. When he arrived at Big Brothers Big Sisters of New York City, Hector Batista had a storied record of leadership at the New York City Housing Department and the American Cancer Society. At the housing department, he had 9,000 employees. And in his growth and evolution as a leader, he had come to realize that he had often made decisions that did not reflect the input of everyone on his team.

"I learned that hard lesson when I was at the Housing Commis-sion," he says. "I went in and started making changes, but I didn't get buy-in from the field, and I didn't understand the field's challenges." The worst part of it was that he was then "beat up" by the unions pub-licly, in the newspaper, as they took him to task for those decisions. [14]

Today, he says, "I seek to build my team with people who tell me what I *need* to hear and not what I want to hear. I purposely hire peo-ple who will challenge me. I want and need to have people around me who have different points of view. I can't surround myself with 'yes' people." Now he relishes getting feedback even when it contradicts his intuitions. And both he and the agency are better for it.

Dealing with openness to feedback requires a commitment to changing your behavior and mindset. Batista, for his part, now holds two meetings each month with his team members. The first, with each individual one-on-one, is "their" meeting, he says, and the direct report can raise any issue at all. The second, with the whole team, is "my" meeting, he adds. Even then, Batista doesn't run the meeting. He delegates that job to someone else. "Everyone has a voice," he says. "Even though it's my meeting, I don't lead the meeting, and that allows dialogue to take place."

And that's what sophistication is all about. A leader takes a new approach, a new *how,* by combining new objectives-based meetings with new ways to foster conversations that produce novel decisions. It is in this way that any leader rises to the stiffer challenges of organizational growth. As a sophisticated leader, you go from personally leading the problem-solving to asking the questions of the problem-solvers. You go from addressing issues through processes and reports to approaching them through people and personalities. You go from leaning in to standing back, from using business skills to using political skill, and from dictating how to accomplish a goal to coaching others how to do so. You are practicing two distinct leadership jobs. See Table 1.2.

The Inevitable Stall

If you don't work to reinvent yourself the way we're describing in this chapter, it's likely only a matter of time until you stall. Look at the scientist-founders who sold laboratories to Trevor Boyce. They got to the point where they couldn't master the new challenges of sophistication. They couldn't delegate responsibility for lab experiments. They couldn't manage the flow of work and data as their companies got bigger. They couldn't create relationships with big corporate customers. And they couldn't craft a compelling vision of the future of their companies.

TABLE 1.2 TWO DISTINCT LEADERSHIP JOBS

To Tackle Complex Challenges	To Tackle Sophisticated Challenges
Grow or shrink an organization	Create a new business model
Change your reporting structure	Change your mindset and behaviors
Take on more responsibility	Give away more responsibility
Manage more insider constituencies	Manage more outside stakeholders
Generate more data and reports	Adapt your style
Build more technical skills	Develop self-awareness and range
Grow sales with customers	Create relationships with customers
Work inside organizational boundaries	Work outside organizational boundaries
Make legal decisions	Make ethical and risk-based decisions
Establish controls	Empower leaders
Supervise new leaders	Coach new leaders
Advocate a near-term direction	Clarify an exciting future vision
Expand organizational systems	Evolve a new culture
Issue new communications	Inspire new followers

Stalls plague all leaders—they are inevitable even if sometimes avoidable—and the consequences of a stall for senior leaders are huge. A now-classic example is that of Lululemon, the maker of high-end, hip yoga clothing. Although Lululemon is studied in business schools as a case on how leaders manage organizational change, we view it as a useful illustration of how leaders can't or won't change themselves as their businesses outrun their capabilities.

Chip Wilson, the founder and CEO of Lululemon, was a Vancouver entrepreneur. He had built the company by going town-to-town cultivating communities of yoga activists. Only after his team had ignited the passions of a local community of yoga advocates did the company open a nearby retail store. He called sales people "educators" and customers "guests." The guests, primed by his community building, snapped up Lululemon's products. In a nearly cult-like way, they fell in love with Wilson's original—if slow—method of retailing.[15]

Lululemon's growth exploded along with a growing mainstream interest in yoga. Lululemon then took the next step: advancing into the US market with capital raised from professional investors. But expanding at the rate demanded by investors took the company into uncharted waters. Lululemon was to become as much a real estate-acquisition and management business as a business of community building. Struggling, seeing his limits, and perhaps having less personal excitement for this kind of executive role, Wilson stepped down to make way for Bob Meers, a CEO who had expertise in US retail store expansion.

As the CEO job got bigger, Lululemon now faced two challenges. The first was scaling up a complex retail store expansion. The second was maturing the company's unique, sophisticated marketing approach to branding and selling active lifestyle and yoga wear. The new CEO's job, in our terminology, now included a tall complexity challenge as well as a broad and deep sophistication one.

For people watching Lululemon, Meers was a virtuoso in matters of complexity. Opening US properties at a rapid pace, he could pop out new stores with the managerial equivalent of an efficient formula, straightforward even if multifaceted. But in matters of sophistication, his performance raised questions. Lululemon was no longer making time to inspire each community's love for yoga. It was failing to propagate the sense of community and intimacy that had made the brand so popular and its consumers so passionate. Nor did it nurture the "Lululemon vibe," a reflection of British Columbia's active, outdoorsy culture.

The leadership capabilities required to transition Lululemon's carefully developed and peculiar marketing strengths to rapid expansion in a new country seemed to escape this CEO. And so the second CEO of Lululemon gave way to a third, Christine Day, and the real reason for the turnover was not because the job had gotten bigger and more complex, but because it had gotten bigger and more sophisticated. Meers had the ability to hire people for replicating stores and building the infrastructure of a big real estate machine. He was a talented manager of organizational engineers. But he may not have fully grasped or prioritized the need for a more sophisticated approach to expand the brand affinity for a rising Canadian clothing star.

Building for the Future

The Lululemon story and other stories in this chapter should have you reconsidering how you look at your own capability as a leader. Ask yourself: When I'm leading an effort and it gets more complex, can I engineer the new technical, functional, and organizational machine to handle it? We bet the answer is usually "yes." In fact, when you need to implement *more* hardware to build the machine and work harder to run it, you probably do yourself proud. But when you need to implement *new* machine software and engage in development of *new* behaviors and mindsets, you may find yourself struggling.

That's when it should dawn on you: You may not be focusing on the proper side of the moon. Are you keeping aware of the rocky half? Are you failing to focus on *how* you're leading—and how you could be leading in a more sophisticated way?

Getting caught unaware by a stall—or unprepared—happens to even the most capable leaders. Stalls test your awareness as a leader because, unlike in an airplane, no alarm bells go off as you start to stall. Often a stall happens at a peak in growth or change. You "inexplicably" lose lift. You may have no idea what to do about it. What happens now? Can you use the tried-and-true nuts and bolts of management to get yourself through? Or do you need to rethink your mindset and behaviors as a master of sophisticated leadership?

Sometimes you'll ask the fateful question: Do I need to build new skills, buy them by hiring others, or sideline myself as unfit for further growth? We call this the build-buy-bail decision. We argue that if you are thinking about buying or bailing, you may have misunderstood the challenge posed by your stall—or you are backing away from it. Put another way, you may be shrinking from overcoming a perennially reemerging flaw among leaders: the inability to realize you need to become more sophisticated.

Steady yourself: If you're reading this book, you have to be interested in *building*, not buying or bailing. What happens now? Our answer is that you commit to reinventing and building a new leadership self.

You *can* face the common and predictable stalls that every leader will eventually run into. You *can* restart your engine to propel your way through each of them. You *can* recreate yourself to become a new leader fit for the future. That's what Trevor Boyce and Hector Batista and the many leaders in the pages ahead have done. And that's what you will do, too—become a new leader, whether next week, next month, or next year.

CHAPTER 2

LEADER WITHOUT A STORY

Stalling When You've Failed to Provide Purpose

"See first that the design is wise and just; that ascertained, pursue it resolutely."
—AESOP, as recounted in *The Fables of Aesop* by George Fowler Townsend

"Where there is no vision the people perish."—PROVERBS 29:18

W hen Michael Barnett started a business out of his Northern Virginia home in 2011 he didn't set out to change the world. After all, he had the simplest of ideas. He wanted to produce software that would give people at events and trade shows a way to meet each other and capture the information on each other's business cards using their smartphones. He did not aspire, as that legendary Silicon Valley genius Steve Jobs had years earlier, to "put a dent in the universe."[16]

But in fact, Barnett *was* looking beyond the technology. A Texas-born philosophy major at Virginia Tech, Barnett's core idea was to empower and enrich human relationships. His product would do so by connecting people in real life and, once connected, help them electronically capture the information on each other's business cards. In other words, he would remove impediments to people meeting and greeting and staying in touch—and thus facilitate the building of communities.[17]

At the startup phase of what he called InGo, this bigger story didn't matter that much. Although his cool new technology pleased people registering for events and trade shows, none of the customers he sought—the trade-show operators—wanted to pay for it. Barnett had to spend three years developing a product that fit the market, a product the big operators would be willing to buy.

That's when the bigger story mattered so much that it would determine his future. He realized, as his company grew to twenty-five people, that he had to explain his business in a new way. How he thought about, constructed, and narrated the deeper story was elemental to motivating both his customers and his employees to see and marvel at the enrichment of human interaction he was promising in his product.

The irony is that earlier in his career Barnett had taught leadership development, and in helping his students understand how to inspire both employees and customers he had preached that appealing to *why* something mattered was one of the strongest ways to create human bonds. "But with my own company, I hadn't done that," he says. "It's embarrassing on some levels."

Barnett's software today is a social media tool that helps event attendees find and connect with friends and colleagues they either know or should know. If you were planning to attend a trade-show and signed on to register, InGo's software would make it easy for you to see which of your friends were going and, with the click of a mouse, to invite others.

For trade-show operators Barnett was offering a new way to fulfill a coveted marketing objective: Spur word-of-mouth recommendations. InGo harnesses each registrant's excitement to inspire him or her to issue invitations and endorsements to friends and colleagues through websites, emails, and mobile apps. For marketers, this word-of-mouth connection ability is massively helpful, as any company's most promising future customers circulate in the company's existing customer networks. InGo provides an instant way to reach them.

The challenge for Barnett was that as he started staffing up his company for growth, neither the people inside nor outside the company entirely grasped the community-building angle. The truth of this situation was galvanizing for Barnett: "A year and a half ago, I recognized that when I told my grandmother about my business, she couldn't tell anyone else what we do."

"People couldn't repeat the story," he explains. "They couldn't repeat it to customers, employees, or other people." On the one hand, they could repeat the "small" story of InGo's unique marketing approach, but they couldn't repeat the "big" story of InGo as a force for building human relationships. The problem Barnett was wrestling with—and we see this often even in mature businesses—is that he could talk about the "what" and the "how" of his business, but not the "why," or the *why it matters.*

As Barnett entered the market with his product in 2014, he was delivering great results for his customers in the trade-show business. He expanded the number of trade-show registrants served by InGo from 80,000 to 2 million in three years. But then he hit a wall. Sales started to flatline. And he suspected the reason was that he couldn't invest InGo's story with the meaning and purpose needed to engage and motivate people both inside and outside. He hadn't explained well enough why InGo's work mattered at a deeper level.

One challenge was that the product couldn't easily be described by referring to something people had already heard of—for example by saying, "It's like Facebook, but for connecting and inspiring businesspeople." Even some employees assumed that the strategy was just another gambit to capture personal data to serve up ads—another Google imitator. And understandably so, because this was in an era when everyone thought that what counted on the web was grabbing eyeballs and data to create the next advertising cash machine.

But InGo's core purpose was not to collect clicks and click-throughs. It was to help people fulfill a basic human need: the desire to build personal communities and get recognition and gratification for doing so. InGo inspires people to build meaningful relationships online, inspires them to engage others in their enthusiasm, and inspires them to bring their community to events and trade shows—which of course boosts his clients' community size and revenues.

"Nobody got this part," Barnett says. Not employees. Not customers. Not even his grandmother. "I was beating my head against the wall to tell the story," he says. "This is revolutionary. Why isn't anybody understanding it?"

People understood pieces of the story. But without his being able to show how the pieces about product, strategy, and marketing created a more compelling human story, Barnett was experiencing a stall sickeningly familiar to many leaders. In times of growth, or during rapid market change, you can hit a showstopping juncture—when different people in the organization see different realities. They see different visions, different missions, different strategies. People across the organization "own" different stories. And hitched to conflicting storylines, they pull the organization in different directions, with different motives and rationales.

Leaders facing this stall do not have just a newly complex communications problem, although they do need to communicate well to be effective. The real problem, subtler and less visible, is failing to define and articulate purpose in a way that unifies direction, values, and strategy. This is different from having to explain more things to more people because the organization has grown or changed. That is a challenge of complexity, which you can tackle with more communications tools, people, and strategies. Having to articulate purpose in creative, compelling, meaningful, and powerfully simple ways to multiple constituents is a challenge of sophistication.

Tackling a sophisticated challenge like this is not a matter of breaking the task into discrete and manageable steps. It's not just a matter, in other words, of making a singular effort to write a vision, or mission, or values, or strategy. It requires developing sophisticated capabilities to clarify, weave together, and coordinate a single, elaborate, and yet understandable narrative. The narrative itself is delivered and received in scores of ways and manifestations—some silent! But this is a narrative which, if you succeed, will resonate with people, and in turn help them resonate together in a high-performance organization.

When you create a winning story it will reflect not an off-the-shelf value proposition, but the invention or reaffirmation of a purpose that energizes you *and* your people. With your purpose clarified you can set an example of behaving in concert with it. You will serve as both the chief story author and chief storyteller. And you will be able to engage those people thirsting for a deeper sense of meaning to work as one in a larger human enterprise they consider their own.

Unfortunately, no matter your level in an organization, you as a leader are often the last to know if you've failed to come up with a winning narrative. At first, you will probably fault your people for misunderstanding the strategy or vision: They're not taking the time to listen, you think. But at some point, hopefully not too late, you realize *you* are the one to blame. You are a leader without a compelling narrative. You are the one who can't show your people how and why they will break free of present organizational limitations and constraints and achieve great results they care deeply about.

When you get to this point, you could be at a risk of stalling. In Barnett's case a mentor pointed it out. He recalls: "It was clear we were not all marching off the same sheet of music. Each time people heard the story, they would take away something, but not necessarily the *right* thing."

Each person on Barnett's senior team had ideas for accelerating business growth in different ways. Some felt InGo should spur revenues by adding another product, some urged opening another market, and others pushed for expansion into another country. One relentlessly urged adding more features. Each of these executives—experienced, skilled, and well-intentioned—wanted to try new things instead of pulling together to grow the business in line with its core purpose.

What was Barnett missing? It was not the ability to communicate—a subject we cover in chapter 5. He's smart, articulate, inspiring, and knew the business intimately. It was, more deeply, his difficulty in crystallizing explicitly how everyone would find meaning in their own lives by working in their jobs at InGo. Creating purpose, a purpose threaded artfully through a narrative of mission, vision, and strategy, is one of the most basic tasks of a leader, and especially in a growing or changing organization.

Management gurus since Peter Drucker have reminded leaders about the motivating and defining power of purpose.[18] Yet in our work as executives, board members, advisors, consultants, and coaches, we see leaders repeatedly stall when it comes to recognizing and carrying out this most fundamental duty. Even the most senior leaders sometimes react indignantly when we suggest they may lack a story to inspire followership. The common refrain? "Well, of course we have a purpose! We're experienced executives, and we know this space!"

But however apparent these leaders think their company's purpose is, many important stakeholders—employees, customers, industry analysts—may simply not get it. The rickety narrative vehicle being offered doesn't rumble with meaning. That's because the leaders believe the more important vehicle—the vehicle that matters—has nothing to do with narrative. They think the vehicle that needs to run smoothly is an organizational control system. So they issue new policies, publish new handbooks, require new report formats, rework reporting lines, or craft goals to cut costs, raise sales, adjust debt, or juice the stock price. And if those don't work, they hire management consultants. They try to control the organization by applying more management machinery or setting new financial goals.

If you respond in this way, with just more complex systems to master more complex operations, you will be glossing over the more sophisticated work required to provide clarity and direction, set priorities, and bind stakeholders to a common purpose. You will have neglected the power of *meaning* to drive commitment and productivity. You may have detailed the managerial steps to get people to work efficiently or achieve next quarter's financial goal, but your efforts to gain control of people's activities will come at a cost: You will fail to elicit bold action by people inspired by a larger purpose.

In contrast, if you wield more sophisticated narrative capabilities, you'll have a narrative of sufficient clarity to guide your people when they face situations not covered in the employee handbook, the policy manual, the quarterly earnings call, or your directives. Creating a narrative rooted in a *raison d'être* can take time and long reflection by any leader. But then you will have people who will make decisions on the fly, on their own, and based on long-term corporate intent, the mission of the enterprise, and organizational values, culture, and tradition. If you can't or don't create this fully loaded narrative vehicle, a vehicle to which people can hitch their hopes and dreams of the future, you will be left by the side of the road as people build their own.

Beware: Stories in Tatters

One of your first jobs as a leader is to watch for the signs that you don't have that holistic, purpose-driven narrative. You are the chief, and the tribe looks to you for more than supervision. Have you, personally, originated a story that kindles excitement about traveling to a land of new opportunity? Or are you seeing warnings that you've let that job slide—and all you've offered is a textbookish, ho-hum description of direction?

The surest sign of stalling is when the decisions you see people making conflict with the direction or priorities you thought everyone understood. People may be making up their own stories, because, by default, people have to make decisions based on some criteria. That's when they take direction from their favored biases, often related to circumstances, their own analysis, outside advice, orders from a boss, pending goals, personal experience, personality, style, you name it. If you don't anchor people in a story tied to purpose, other motivators will guide them. In the worst of cases, people can be tempted into ethical wrongdoing, as when engineers at Volkswagen rigged software to fudge emissions test results.

We sometimes hear from executives running public companies that their purpose is to raise the stock price or "create shareholder value." That's a sure sign that the CEO and other leaders have crafted a story of the organization's future in which any sense of purpose was left out. Although public-company executives need to be responsible as fiduciaries, they also have to paint a picture of the future that shows people how and why to climb from the valley of the status quo to the mountain of success. The trail upward is always hard for people to find. You need to give people a focal point to inform and motivate their day-to-day decisions for the march uphill.

The most embarrassing sign that you've stalled in your task of establishing purpose is when other leaders in your organization go blank when you put them on the spot to repeat it. Do they really understand the vision, mission, values, culture, and strategy? Do they know how these pieces all work together in a way that will engage and motivate the workforce? Or do they just see pieces of the landscape but not how they go together, and how the whole offers a greater future than the sum of its parts? When you ask for a snapshot, what do people at any level of your organization say? Do they eagerly describe an action they just took that aligns with your purpose?

Barnett woke up to the incompleteness of his work when he walked the floor of a trade show with a customer who absolutely loved InGo's product. If anyone could explain InGo's story, he figured, this woman could. She had been singing the praises of InGo all year. And yet, when she stopped to introduce him to another industry heavyweight, she fumbled when she tried to tell the story. "It was a mess," Barnett admits. "We had had two years to educate her, and she had heard fifteen different versions from people in marketing, delivery, and sales. But when she was left to introduce me, her referral—which could have been extraordinarily powerful—was a bit meaningless for lack of clarity. The other person went, 'Huh?'"

She was able to pull some of the puzzle pieces from her pocket. But where was the full picture? "I went back to my team and said, 'This has to end.'"

The power of the product was just too great to allow an inarticulate testimony at such a crucial moment. InGo's community-building potential was also growing in new ways, which required that the core story be that much clearer. Today, InGo serves more than trade show operators. If you're an operator of a fan club, for example, InGo can help connect fans with each other. If a fan is watching a football video, he or she will be guided by InGo's software to suggest which of his or her friends would love to see the same video—and then allow them to send an invitation instantly.

Fragmented stories that don't champion a cause célèbre can create harm as well as embarrassment. When Hector Batista was named the CEO of Big Brothers Big Sisters of New York City in 2010, he sought to revitalize a venerable nonprofit that had lost its edge. "There was not enough investment in the organization, the physical plant, technology, how we looked internally and externally, in our marketing materials, in the services to the community we were responsible for," he says. The organization had a national brand with an amazing reputation, he adds, "but because of that it functioned as if we were the biggest and baddest."[19]

But the truth was different. The organization was not providing the state-of-the-art services to the city that Batista felt it could. The number of children served had scarcely risen for years. Batista was a manager seasoned in the ways of business, nonprofits, and government—a rare trifecta of leadership experience. But his challenge was new: He had inherited from his predecessors an organization whose purpose had blurred.

Founded in 1904, BBBS showcased an enduring mission: "Providing and supporting committed volunteers who have one-to-one relationships with children and youth." But that mission, and the purpose that underpinned it, had loosened its hold on everyone's mind. "The reality," Batista says, "is that BBBS had lost its place in the field. We were the premier mentor organization in the country, but we were losing our place to other organizations like iMentor that were newer and fresher, even though they were not as impactful as we were."

All the signs were flashing that a crisis was at hand. Nobody was evaluating the effectiveness of the agency's programs, and if they did, they sometimes reported incorrect numbers. Some senior managers led via hierarchy and secrecy to protect their fiefdoms. Even the services BBBS offered had not kept up with the changing needs of the people BBBS served. This meant the "littles," the affectionate name for little brothers and sisters, weren't getting help with their performance in school, the help they needed to gain an advantage in a more sophisticated and competitive world. And the "bigs," the volunteers that sign up as mentors, weren't getting the tools they needed to assist them. How was BBBS going to help youngsters in need succeed academically?

The story for how BBBS would guide itself into the future still had some missing pages. Says Batista: "People would say, 'We've been doing this for one hundred years!' And I would say, 'Okay, we've been doing this for one hundred years, but by the same token, we're not getting the kind of results we need, so let's see how we can improve by doing things differently.'"

Times had changed but the story had not. People in the organization simply weren't benefitting from a leadership legacy in which a grander narrative spurred them to doing even greater good in a changing world. "What people painted and what was reality were two different things," Batista says.

Batista inherited this stall, but all too often even experienced leaders unintentionally set the stage for one. Take, for example, the story told by Gary White, formerly the CEO of Gymboree, the children's clothing store. White was tapped to lead Gymboree after a career at Dayton-Hudson, now Target. At Dayton-Hudson, the story of retail operations was clear: run clean stores, stock plenty of product, keep salespeople smiling, and provide solid customer service.

At Gymboree, a specialty store with 1,900 square feet, he moved right from the start to take that same approach.[20] What happened? "Sales dropped 20 percent!" he says. White was the boss, and yet he realized he had gotten the fundamental narrative wrong. "Humble pie!" he exclaims. As it turned out, his stall was not merely about a misfire in how to conduct operations. It was about failing to tap into purpose—the focal point of his narrative painting was washed out, and he had to put new brush strokes on his canvas quickly.

White's head of store operations was diplomatic: "At Gymboree," she said, "moms come in with newborns and toddlers. They expect us to do things like blow up balloons and entertain kids in the stores so they can shop. This is specialty retail—big-box-style efficiency and customer service aren't what set us apart." She reminded White that Gymboree's mission is living—and bettering—a day in the life of mothers. The company's purpose was not rooted in operational efficiency as it is at big retailers. Rather, it was rooted in being close to customers and providing them with a distinctive experience.

"That was the first big learning for me," White says. "Park the ego, take the tie off, and get in the role . . . I listened. I learned. And then I took what I thought was the best of all I heard to meet our mission to grow and be bigger." And with a fresh and purpose-driven story, he turned the organization's results right away. Even he could then get in the role and become, as chief storyteller, a reflection of what the company stood for. When he made store visits as the CEO, he says, "Kids would be running out of the store into the mall. I had to chase down toddlers while mom was trying to shop. That was our world!"

Think of all the decisions you and your team make each week: Add this feature now, or later? Price it here . . . or there? Go exclusive for a time . . . or not? Reward people for this . . . or that? What is going to guide all those decisions? Is everyone understanding the purpose of the broader enterprise and the impact it should make? Or do splits between leaders result in clashing initiatives, signaling that the story doesn't provide a uniform way to align priorities, decisions, and the factors motivating everyone? It's a bad sign if, instead of running alongside each other down the road of change, your people are wrestling on the sidewalks.

Peter Drucker once said that the failure to ask what is right for the enterprise virtually guarantees a bad decision.[21] But how can anyone know what's right if they don't have a visceral sense of what the enterprise is about? If your people can't speak for the enterprise as if they're speaking from their own inner sense of what matters, you may have stalled. You, the leader, have not constructed and personally manifested a story people can absorb so thoroughly that it becomes part of their identity.

WARNING: YOU'VE HIT A PURPOSE STALL

You lead an organization where people cannot express the vision and mission—let alone feel motivated or inspired by it. Even your closest colleagues seem like soldiers fighting a tired battle. You start to wonder: Why are decisions so conflicted, actions so inconsistent, and people so dour? There is no compelling and consistent story that captures the reason your organization exists, what it hopes to accomplish, and the traits it should be known by.

Assess: Is Your Story Dull and Disconnected?

How can you better assess whether you've hit a stall in failing to establish purpose? How do you know if your narrative doesn't grip people and rouse them to focus on the right things? Start by honestly answering the question: Have I crafted a strong, explicit narrative that is memorable and repeatable? Does it engage people? Or does the story fail to seize and energize people to the point that they can shout it out to their own people? Is the response to my story, "Okay—so what?"

Think back to the lessons of your high school English class. If you were to tell the story of your organization, could you instantly identify the theme and plot? Could you detail elements of character and motivation that define and govern the characters'—your stakeholders'—actions? If someone asked you whether you had crafted a riveting story imbued with purpose—a story your workforce couldn't put down—what would you say?

Human beings are narrative creatures. When you appeal to narrative, and get a meaningful story wired firmly in place, people can and will do amazing things. Great things happen when people see themselves as protagonists in their own personal stories. Their stories have to be embedded in a compelling and larger organizational one that you create. People stay fired up when they can say, here's the challenge we're taking on, here's my role in it, and here's why the outcomes are worth striving for.[22]

You may object to this literary analogy as too "fluffy" and tangential to leading a high-performing organization. But if we overstate the analogy with literature, we do it to make a point: The leaders with the best stories, all else being equal, will win. Win at motivating workers. Win at strategic execution. Win at imbuing values. Win against competitors. And if you don't have such a story, if you don't have the capability to tell it in the ways we will describe in chapter 5, you *will* stall. So if you are finding yourself frustrated by conflict among your people, poor decision-making, odd behaviors, or ineffective prioritization, check your narrative. Maybe it's time to hone your storytelling skills. See Table 2.1.

TABLE 2.1
THE STORYTELLING COMPONENTS YOU ALWAYS KNEW

Classic Components of Literary Story	Classic Components of Organizational Story
Conflict/complication	Challenge/problem/opportunity (current reality)
Plot/journey	Mission and strategy
Theme	Purpose
Character	Capabilities, values, and culture
Resolution (satisfying closure)	Vision (inspirational future state)

The Kitchen Table Test

If you feel you may have stalled in your job as the leader who provides clarity and purpose, see if you can tell the story out loud. If you need an audience, who better than your grandmother? Or if she isn't handy, try a cousin, neighbor, or friend. Or colleagues from other organizations. Sit down at the kitchen table and evaluate your story as you tell it to a person unaffiliated with your work.

Michael Barnett tested his story this way, and he found it and his ability to tell it wanting. And it's not because he was not perceptive. It's because sculpting the lines of a story requires a lot of chipping and polishing—and that's after the extensive brainstorming and soul searching.

Who, what, when, where, why, and how—they all go into the story, but especially "why," which clarifies for people that your organization is a place they belong, a place that matters, a place where they will help accomplish memorable things. A good story should raise the pulse of your people. No bump in the pulse, no bump in performance.

When you talk to your grandmother, does she tilt her head and lean closer? Or does she look away and peer into her tea? As a leader, you are a student of human nature. Your story doesn't necessarily have to entertain, but it does need to create an emotional draw that pulls people through the workday and motivates them to make your enterprise their own.

When you try to tell the story simply, do you get tangled in a spaghetti of plotlines and drowned in a bland sauce of themes? As Oliver Wendell Holmes is often credited with saying: "I would not give a fig for the simplicity this side of complexity, but I would give my life for the simplicity on the other side of complexity." A great story gets to the other side of complexity. It connects vision, mission, values, culture, and strategy into a single driving narrative.

Developing and sharing this narrative is an act of the highest leadership sophistication. It animates your vision, mission, and strategy, which can otherwise come across as lifeless and sterile. Imbued with the right meaning, it allows people to join in personally meaningful ambitions, linked to a moving tale of success. If done well, you make the story so clear and compelling that people can (and will!) repeat it eagerly and make it their own. Does the kitchen table test tell you you've accomplished that objective?

Above all, have you established, at a gut level in your stakeholders, the purpose of your organization, the impact it is seeking to have on the world, and the character and identity by which it should be known? If your people understand your story on an intellectual level you will have piqued their curiosity. But if they embrace it viscerally you will have invoked their passion. The story, as the expression goes, is "a boss when the boss isn't around"—able to help drive coherent action across the organization.

Walk Back the Cat

Even if you think you've woven a narrative of this quality, check to see if decisions in your organization demonstrate that people understand it. People in the intelligence services sometimes talk about "walking back the cat." One intelligence service agent plants a story to elicit a trail of responses by others. Once tracks emerge at the end of the trail created by the plant, they "'walk back the cat" to identify connections or culprits they couldn't see before.

Do the same in your organization. Look at the decisions by your people after you plant your story. Walk the decisions back step by step to see if everyone, at each step, followed the narrative.

Barnett in effect walked back the cat in early 2017 when he worked with Wilbert Hiejmans of InfoSalons, an InGo partner in the Middle East. InGo does 25 percent of its business in the Middle East. His partner had assembled a pitch to customers, and Barnett reviewed it with him. One of the first slides showed data on trade-show registrants— how many registrants inspired their colleagues via InGo's software to also sign up. What really stood out, however, were the half dozen pages that followed in which his partner featured the names of the most prominent people motivated to use InGo. Among them: high-level government leaders and CEOs of Fortune 500 companies.

"This was a shocking moment," Barnett says. A host of the most impressive movers and shakers had chosen to wield their influence through his software. All of them had attended the Abu Dhabi International Petroleum Exhibition and Conference. Even the top brass in government and industry were helping, via word of mouth, to sell more registrations for the trade-show operator. "I mean, what would you pay to have those people do more word-of-mouth marketing for you?" he asks.

The names showed that Barnett could walk back the presentation plans to the story he had shaped himself. The purpose of InGo was getting through. Not only could InGo's partner recite the story, he could illustrate it with the names of powerful people making the referrals InGo promised. "We were able to move the needle dramatically for our marketing customer," Barnett says, "inspiring top leaders in the petroleum industry to do word-of-mouth marketing for the event."

If you don't get this kind of response from people you work with, how do you react? Do you blame and criticize your employees and partners for fumbling their execution of the mission? Or do you look in the mirror and rethink your own actions and efforts? Walking back the cat doesn't have to take much time. Look at a single piece of business you won. What was it about the win that made your people go after it? How did they price it? If your story is about an organization that targets premium customers and premium pricing and your people pitched a cut-rate deal, you know people are not getting the narrative.

Survey the Crowd

To understand the scope of your purpose stall, be sure to inquire far and wide, inside and outside the organization. Survey people in a variety of situations, locations, and positions. People need time to internalize a story and express it in a way that's authentic to them. One CEO we worked with was known to give pop-quizzes at employee town halls or when walking the halls: "What's our company's vision?" He also included in his balanced scorecard a measure of how well people could tell the story about the company's mission, vision, and values.

At BBBS, Hector Batista starts all senior meetings with a "mission moment," when he calls on people to report on good things the organization has done that illustrate and connect back to the organization's reinvigorated purpose and strategy. What's important is that you hear a high-fidelity echo of the narrative you've been reciting.

"People need to feel the mission," Batista says. "Each member of our senior staff has to bring a story about a match between a child and a big brother or sister or another feel-good thing, something incredible." He cites one mission moment when a staffer talked about a "little" who just landed a spot as a freshman at Columbia University, due in no small part to the mentoring received through BBBS. "That kind of thing reminds us what we're here doing. It's not about me or you—it's about the kids we're serving."

Such moments are a chance to survey how well everyone is understanding, translating, and embracing the story. Are people feeling drawn to the purpose—and do they feel driven to contribute in a purposeful way? "Hey, what are you up to lately?" you can ask people. "Really? Sounds fantastic! How do you think that's serving the strategic imperatives or values we talked through in the all-hands meeting?" When you bump into customers and partners, query them similarly. Are they seeing the story in action? Better yet, are they caught up in it themselves?

Or play the old game of "Why?" Ask people, "Why did you do that task? Why did your boss ask you to do it? Why does that matter for the organization?" If you don't get answers in which you hear people repeating the deeper themes of your organization's purpose—translated into each person's own words—you're in an unfortunate situation where people don't get or care about the purpose. And you've stalled.

Watch the Audience

Take the next step and ask people directly what behaviors they see every day that demonstrate that their colleagues or employees have internalized the story. What are the telltale behavioral signs that reveal people's interior understanding? What does the head of finance, for example, consider the litmus test of someone on his team truly getting the story? Do people show they understand and own both the small and big stories? As chief storyteller, you'll get a quick reading as to whether your narrative has seized people's attention.

At BBBS, Batista wasn't sure that the new story was penetrating. He had been hired as a change agent but sometimes he couldn't tell if people were hearing the part of the story about a need for change, innovation, and improved efficiency. He says, "People would say, 'You're running this place like a business.'"And he would respond, "That's true, but that's because we're a not-for-profit business, and we have people we're responsible for, our donors, our benefactors, and lots of other people."

That more business-like story didn't sit well with some of his veteran employees, and it showed he still had work to do. "There were some people who were like, 'No!' They just didn't want to accept that we had to promise our donors the same efficiency and effectiveness of a business," he says. "This wasn't something they were comfortable with or wanted to do."

As for Barnett, once he worked through the incompleteness of his story, he got a reading that he had gotten beyond his stall. Even as he felt he was still refining the narrative, he asked for a volunteer to script a video to explain the company's vision and mission. A junior person jumped right up. Recalls Barnett, "And I was like, well, this will be cute . . . I'll give this over to him, and we'll see what he comes back with."

"And he came back with something mind-blowing," says the chagrined CEO. "It was a clearer distillation of the InGo story than I could have created. I was like, whoa, that's *my* job; I am the person who should do that. I don't know if I'm comfortable because all of a sudden some-body has done the job I thought only I could do. Which is great, right?"

Recover: Get Your Story Mojo Back

The depth of a stall in conveying your purpose and story can be far greater than you think. We hear from leaders regularly who call us to help them troubleshoot teamwork problems. But before we get far into the conversation, an uncomfortable truth emerges: Teamwork is not the problem—or at least not the most serious one. The real issue is that the team doesn't grasp the organization's story and purpose. They lack what's most important for getting aligned.

When we ask about team members, we hear that the company's engineers are fantastic, the products amazing, and the sales team is all over the ramp-up. Sensing that the problem is more basic, we probe, "Where are you planning to be in three years?" Or "What's the world going to look like in three years, and how will that affect your busi-ness?" The leaders often don't have a good answer. Some of them tell us about their terrific three-month goals, but then they admit, "We don't have a story about where we're going. Or how we'll get there. Or why anyone should care."

At one company we worked with, the CEO was meeting with his top team, and after we asked the "how will we get there?" question, nei-ther the CEO nor anyone else seemed to grasp what we were getting at. The chief strategy officer, thinking he had caught our drift, pushed us away from the whiteboard. He turned the entire session into an effort to distill five tactical goals for the next six months.

And he was a seasoned leader, not a newbie—but one caught in a stall he was not even beginning to see. At such times, or under extreme pressure or slipping performance, you may make the same error: You decide a new business plan is what you need for a motivating story. But whether short- or long-term, your plans lay out just mile markers in the story. They don't ensure clarity of the longer journey or why you're asking people to brave the long road to a distant destination in the future.

That's a point that business writers Jim Collins and Jerry Porras famously addressed in their studies of management: Even as business strategies and practices change with the times, an organization needs core values and a core purpose for the long haul. The values and purpose should remain constant: The enduring character or identity of the organization transcends products or market life cycles, technological breakthroughs, and individual leaders or administrations.[23]

When we work with executives, we often see a compulsion to substitute a list of near-term objectives for a larger story. The danger of letting this happen plays out over time. Followers know what to do in the next quarter, but not why they should feel gratified to work in the organization. Why (they will want to know, even if they don't ask) does this organization exist? If they can't understand and be moved by the company's purpose, values, and identity, you'll have detached, obedient employees at best.

People can't get excited just by perpetuating an institution. Once they are part of the institution, they want to know if they are on the road to doing something that counts. A story that effectively serves that purpose is often "heroic." Characters in heroic stories learn they can't stay where they are, that they need to develop themselves to advance, and that with enough effort and new insight they will arrive at a better place and make a mark on the world. In other words, when the curtain comes down, they want to feel pride in what they have done both individually and collectively.

The heroic story cannot be captured in a company memo or newsletter. You need to find it in your gut and be able to tell it from the heart to your team—and have the words to repeat it in the hallways, on the phone, and in meetings with customers. The story has to be crafted so people can internalize it and tell it themselves. Constantly interrogate yourself: Is my story a match for our current challenges and objectives? Or should I evolve some elements of the story, as did Hector Batista at Big Brothers Big Sisters of New York?

Collins and Porras argued that in a few organizations the vision and identity can last for a century. But they were writing more than two decades ago. Times and pace are different today, and you'll need to refresh your narrative and story to capture purpose more often. But at the end of the day you should be reaching as much for values and identity as for business plan goals or short-term strategic objectives.

Fashioning a narrative of purpose and meaning usually requires a change in your mindset. You have to develop new behaviors to check constantly that everyone understands and evolves with the story as you do. And also check that they can adapt the story to changing circumstances. As Barnett observes, "Really brilliant people become ossified in their thinking about the mission, vision, and product. When the market changes, what used to accelerate company growth is now its own threat." Can you learn new narrative capabilities so you're not your own threat?

Creating story and purpose is a task you cannot delegate, even though you should enlist others as coauthors. You have to "own" this job. If you are to recover from this stall, change the way you think of your role: You are not to think just as a strategist or communicator. You are the chief of the tribe, a torchbearer for the organization. How can you make the themes of your narrative burn hot with purpose, and in turn, fire the passions of your people?

Conduct a Story Session

That brings us to some actions we suggest for developing a narrative that gets people to sign up for the long, hard journey you have embraced yourself. Since humans are apparently hard-wired to think in terms of story, why not piggyback on that element of human nature? In any progression, people want to know, "And then what happens?" The story of people moving to fulfill an organization's higher aspirations, which shows how your people will advance as heroes in their own right, makes the story come alive.

Since in many cases you shouldn't be the sole author of the story, ask other people to help you with elements that they may grasp better. Barnett admits that, although he was the creator of the first few drafts of the InGo story, that was only the start. "Stories are created several times," he observes. "First, a story is created in the mind of the leader. Then he has to get it created in the mind of the team." And then the odds grow that it will come to life in the mind of everyone in the organization, and in the marketplace as well.

When you sit down with your team to craft the narrative, think of your team as your teacher. If you're getting it wrong, you'll know. For example, imagine a meeting where you are proposing a course of action, and everyone looks at you quizzically. You can read in their eyes what they're thinking, "Hey boss, do you not get what we are about?" Especially if you're a leader who has recently joined the organization, you then know you need to refine. That's the process of, first, evolving your thinking and, second, crafting a story.

To answer "what we're about," we suggest you break down the story into the elements in Table 2.1. While you need to create each piece alone, you also need to assemble them into a single structure. When you address each piece, don't limit the people whom you recruit for help to those who work directly for you. Ask rising stars from all over the organization to contribute. Everyone brings new insight to the six story elements:

» Vision: Depict the future state you're striving for and what the world you touch will look like if you are successful.

» Mission: Explain why you exist and what you hope to achieve.

» Purpose: Clarify why those accomplishments will fulfill the vision and make a difference.

» Strategy: Map the path to accomplish your mission, goals, and "how we will get there."[24]

» Values: Cite the norms of motives and behavior you'll hold everyone accountable to.

» Capabilities and culture: Describe what you need to do and how you'll work together—detailing "the way we do things around here."

Remember, when you're recovering from a storytelling stall you're not just looking for "the answer." That is, you're not merely on task to come up with a deliverable. You're building your story-thinking and story-construction abilities. The headwork, the heart work, the surfacing of meaning, the unifying narrative—these are not tasks to be delegated. Don't make the mistake of abdicating your role and ceding the torch bearing of the organization's flame to the marketing group.

Reestablish Baseline Values

There's no right way to craft a story that captures why your organization exists, what your community of people hopes to get done, and much else besides. The order depends on what your organization demands now. Sometimes the place to start is with values. That was a target for Dev Ittycheria, CEO of MongoDB, a New York City database startup. Ittycheria was recruited in 2014 as a change agent CEO. A veteran of two other startups, he came to a 250-person organization enjoying meteoric growth but an array of confusing values.[25]

As he settled into his leadership role, Ittycheria launched an effort to clarify a narrative that everyone could get behind. That was complicated by Mongo's highly technical product—a new type of software to run and manage the biggest databases, long the domain of Oracle. "I didn't expect people to sing Kumbaya," he says, "but I wanted to be clear on what values we'll tolerate and what behaviors we won't. That was important to galvanize the organization around how we would operate."

In tandem with people across all levels of the organization, Mongo came up with six core values: existing traits people could "double down on" to advance the company and drive results. "There were some people who had some really big ideas, and we wanted to reinforce those," says Ittycheria. So Mongo adopted a value called "Think Big, Go Far." On the other hand, he says, "Sometimes the organization was not great at figuring out where it should spend its time to have the biggest impact. And sometimes it would confuse activities with accomplishments." So they created a value called "Make It Matter."

Ittycheria also favored being intellectually honest. "We want to be constructive but at the same time give practical feedback on what's going well and what's not, and how we can we be better. This is not a license to be a jerk or be super-aggressive. But I think people deserve candid feedback on how they're doing, because people will say, 'If something is wrong, I'd much rather know sooner than later.'" That honesty, a reflection of Ittycheria's own style, spurred a transformation of the sales organization and establishment of better recruiting processes.

Ittycheria's aim was, in part, to create an environment for making better decisions. "If you have two organizations, the organization with better decision-making is going to outperform its competitors," he says. "You never have perfect decisions, but you can have *good* decisions day in and day out." That focus improved communication and collaboration and gave everyone a stronger sense of pulling in the same direction.

Ittycheria wanted his people to take risks, but smart risks; to be honest with each other; to voice feedback and explain why; to be accountable. He knows he's making progress when he hears people say, "It's so much easier to make a decision now." In earlier days, he notes, "one decision could be countermanded by another, it was not clear who was in charge, we had a lot of matrix management, a lot of people were into things but not accountable for things."

In a variation of Chicago Mayor Rahm Emmanuel's dictum "Never let a crisis go to waste," Ittycheria made the most of the disorder in a feverishly growing company. Like him, sophisticated leaders find in every major discontinuity an opportunity to affirm or reaffirm the narrative by which they guide the organization. Clarify for yourself, clarify for everyone else, and role model how people should act in light of the disruption. If ever there was a time to reinforce "What are we about?" an inflection point in the nature of your organization is one.[26]

Be a Culture Warrior

You will want to take a similar approach with organizational culture, another means that you can use to recover from a stall in projecting a powerful, purpose-driven narrative. What can you do to affirm or reaffirm the organization's culture? And how can you articulate it and model it to reinforce the purpose everyone is working to fulfill?

Ittycheria wanted to change the culture along with its values. "When I came to the organization, it was balkanized," he says. "Sales, engineering, finance, international—they all had different cultures. Everyone had their own microcultures." For starters, he says, "Our success depended on marrying great product with great distribution. So I told people that just as the product created a competitive advantage, I wanted the sales and marketing organizations to create a competitive advantage."

That philosophy was one that Ittycheria brought with him from experience working in other high-tech startups. He believed it was critical that the organization have a sales approach as robust and sophisticated as its engineering approach. The very idea of such a culture change energized his sales team, since the company to that point was dominated by engineers who had taken a bit of an only-engineers-can-understand approach to selling their product. "The change in culture really drove the organization," Ittycheria says.

A leader with a similar commitment to culture is Ali Reza Manouchehri, CEO of two companies, MetroStar Systems, a high-tech government contractor with over 220 employees, and analytics startup Zoomph. "If people are our number one asset," says the Reston, Virginia-based CEO, "how do we nurture culture, how do we unlock knowledge, and how do we embrace the whole collective mind?"

Manouchehri emphasizes how he shapes the environment in which people work. "Innovation happens when you put smart people together to solve a problem and each has a different way of looking at it, because one came from the humanities, one from engineering, one from computer science," he says. "And they all brought a different way of solving that problem to the table, and together they came up with something beautiful."

"I always want a huge investment in culture," says Manouchehri. He doesn't cut office costs, for example, by dispersing his people to home offices. He insists on a culture that stresses face-to-face, elbow-to-elbow teamwork. He scoffs at companies that cut overhead in hopes of getting people to be more creative in their pajamas, operating "efficiently" but isolated from each other in their own bedrooms.

To be sure he stays on his chosen cultural course; Manouchehri keeps an ear to the rail of employees' chatter. He relies on continuous engagement throughout the year and checks various channels, physical and digital, where people talk about MetroStar. He also pays close attention to how MetroStar ranks in "best places to work" surveys. Attending to these things provides him with a sort of dashboard to continuously monitor people's sentiments in real time. "I want to know people's hopes and fears," he says. "You can't make decisions off Excel spreadsheets and think the organization is going to respond the way you want it to."

As an added tool in stewarding the culture at MetroStar, Manouchehri keeps a "culture balance sheet" that tracks how people fit with the cultural traits he desires. If an employee is new, he wants to know if they are being rejected like a bad organ transplant. He sits side-by-side with his human capital chief to look at this nonfinancial balance sheet every Tuesday. Along with keeping track of people's skill sets, he knows attrition rates, diversity, educational achievement, and workforce distribution.

"To break through to the next level, the entire organization has to have that mindset and has to be aligned," he says. "It doesn't work if the CEO wants growth, but then managers of managers only think about operations. So everything has to be aligned down and up, and up and down, the organization."

As a leader, you are a cultural warrior. Anoint other cultural warriors in the organization, and when people go awry, act as judge and jury to fix common objections. If you hit a stall when people show they have a divergent belief system, you have to stress and model different patterns of behavior. Like Manouchehri, you also have to monitor constantly. That's what's required to use culture to keep the organizational narrative on track.[27]

Check for Fit

A final way to recover from the purpose stall is to address how all the pieces of your narrative fit together: vision, mission, values, culture, and strategy. Are they all in sync? Do they dovetail and interlock? Or do they butt up against each other and sometimes knock each other askew? Up to now, you have probably largely addressed these independently. But of course they interact, and your constant practice in making them congruent is a powerful way to recover from a stall. Can you tune the entire system?

As you rise as a leader, you exert less and less control by pulling hierarchical strings (and rank). Given the ready availability today of data analytics, leaders have a smorgasbord of management information tools at their disposal to try to keep control of purpose, decisions, and behavior as enterprises get more complex and grow.

But as a leader your real capabilities will not show up in a spreadsheet or analytics report. Your most important capability for propagating purpose and values as the organization grows is making the fit between people, processes, values, and structure. All need to be interconnected and reinforce each other, and bringing that about is more art than science. Challenges of sophistication will require that you increasingly rely on establishing congruence between strategy, vision, mission, values, and culture.

While this may seem abstract, coordinating the narrative vehicle in action is easy to describe by example. Take the case of Ikea, founded and run for over fifty years by Ingvar Kamprad, who invented a narrative for a new kind of retailing that was revolutionary and inspirational in its social impact of providing quality furniture at the lowest possible prices.

Kamprad detested complex rule-driven solutions to managing growth, so much so that he would hold "anti-bureaucracy" weeks. He conquered first European and then North American furniture-retailing markets by hammering away at his mission, vision, values, culture, and strategy. Leaders on Kamprad's front lines could make decisions on the spot without complicated chain-of-command procedures. One manager said that the only guidelines needed for an entrepreneur to set up a new Ikea store was "Ingvar's thesis and a general objective."

Kamprad lived his story—and it was so vibrant and infectious that so did his leaders. He turned to structural or systemic fixes to further his aims when needed. For example, Ikea trained "ambassadors" to police the company's culture. But he lived the Ikea narrative himself, staying in cheap hotels when visiting stores, showing up at 5:00 a.m., taking a dozen pages of notes at store inspections, and approving new initiatives without testing.

These behaviors reinforced the cultural attributes of Ikea management: They were hard-working, frugal, highly attentive to detail, and willing to experiment with new ideas. "Ingvar's thesis" became a powerful narrative. This was not a structured command-and-control system. It was an unstructured one, which he operated by constantly shaping and aligning the pieces of the organization narrative.

Ikea today has changed, and more conventional command-and-control systems now guide store managers. But the finely honed and coordinated components of a purpose-driven narrative became the leadership foundation for building a global retailing colossus. Kamprad's story is an illustration of how you can tap into sophisticated tools and behaviors as a leader. These are not tools you delegate, like management information systems, because they start with your living the narrative as much as Kamprad did.

Kamprad is no easy act to follow. And yet his example highlighted another aspect of mastering the purpose stall. When you're the one "in charge," you always want to be able to "take charge," or maintain control of the organization. That challenge grows—and the stall grows in its potential impact—as you rise in the organization. You can install structure, of course, according to the pattern documented by Larry Greiner in the last chapter. But to personally live a story you may need to rethink your role, change your hands-off mindset, and immerse yourself in the narrative and why it matters to all your stakeholders.

As the chief storyteller, you have a highly sophisticated responsibility to fulfill and re-fulfill. In devising a vision, you have to act partly as futurist. With a mission, partly evangelist. With values, partly ethicist. With strategy, partly intellectual. With purpose, partly philosopher. This slate of roles—sophisticated ones—are challenging to play even before you add the day-to-day and month-to-month operational demands of your organization. But they are the key roles of a sophisticated leader.

If you've been a star performer, as most leaders have been, you may find it hard to play all the needed roles and to reconceive how you approach leadership when it comes to purpose and story. You are probably used to driving yourself hard to meet goals. But your job as a more sophisticated leader is to make sure others meet their goals, and you need a way to engage and excite them to do so. If you are not to be outrun as a leader, answering one question in all its dimensions is necessary: "What kind of company are we?"

Neither your business plan nor your annual budget answer that question. They articulate no higher purpose, stem from no self-reflection, demand no real mindset or behavioral change, prescribe no values for you to role model. What happens now as you seek to reinvent yourself is clear: You must probe for and develop an incisive, straightforward, heroic tale that changes you, and then your people.

See the following breakout summary as a guide. Everyone wants to know: "Why are we here?" Can you tell them?

~Reinventing Your Leadership~

A Purpose Stall?

Create and Champion a Compelling Story.

BEWARE THE DANGER

- People's decisions are at odds with your vision, mission, strategy, values, or culture.
- You see conflict in how your leaders resolve issues or handle crises.
- Your team or employees act contrary to your values or culture.
- You are facing ethical misbehavior because people have been tempted into questionable actions.
- You hired someone who now seems to clash with everyone he/she meets.
- After a bad quarter, people suggest fixes that go against the organization's mission or purpose.

ASSESS & TROUBLESHOOT

- Try the kitchen table test: Do your vision, mission, values, culture, and strategy hold together when you tell a friend or relative?
- Using the "walk back the cat" exercise, see if you can trace the trail of decisions your people are making back to the story you've been telling.
- Informally survey your people to see if their work contributes to the mission and purpose of the organization.
- Do people know the story in action when they see it? Ask them to cite examples of behavior exemplifying your story.
- Ask team members to list their priorities—are they in line with the story?

Recover & Reinvent

- Hold a story-creation session with people from all levels of the organization. Make sure it captures purpose, identity, and values.

- Engage teams to re-articulate values and purpose that will be easy to communicate down through the ranks and out to multiple stakeholders. Use outside facilitators if necessary.

- Identify and role model elements of culture as a part of your larger narrative.

- Develop a dashboard to select and track key metrics that will support the story you want people to tell.

- Coordinate the interaction of all story components—vision, mission, values, culture, strategy—around your singular purpose.

- Make sure your business plan and budget derive from—rather than drive—your narrative.

CHAPTER 3

LEADER OF TEAM ZERO

Stalling When You Let Your Team Splinter

"A noble person attracts noble people and knows how to hold on to them."—JOHANN WOLFGANG VON GOETHE, *Torquato Tasso*

"It's a terrible thing to look over your shoulder when you are trying to lead—and find no one there."
—FRANKLIN DELANO ROOSEVELT,
recounted in Samuel Rosenman's *Working with Roosevelt*

Leaders in organizations both big and small will, in private moments, complain about the people who work directly for them. This is no surprise. Often a leader's team members work at odds, clashing over goals or style, putting their own priorities over the common goals of the enterprise. We even hear from leaders who have essentially thrown up their hands and adopted a laissez-faire philosophy about their teams: "What am I supposed to do about their lack of collaboration? I'm not a marriage counselor."

Or we hear things like, "These people are experienced and getting paid a lot. They should step up—why don't they execute better together and innovate more?"

We infer from such complaints that leaders somehow feel that the people who work for them, who in turn lead other people, should lead themselves. When we hear such comments in our work as board members or consultants, we often detect uncertainty over who should be taking responsibility for this lack of teamwork and execution. That's why, if asked to facilitate offsite meetings with an executive team, we often use some simple exercises to help people assess and create a better understanding of where the teamwork problem lies.

As an example: To kick off a meeting with a team, we sometimes ask all the members to introduce themselves, describe their roles, and describe their team. Everyone follows instructions and enthusiastically describes the function or business they lead and the organization they are responsible for. "I'm Sally, and I run the finance group." "My name is Tahir, and I head up marketing."

We're setting a trap, and almost everyone falls into it: When talking about "my team," almost none of these managers refers to the most important team: the one sitting around the table with them at that moment.

We use another exercise to determine how well the team is aligned with the organization's most important goals and priorities. Each team member fills out an index card answering the question, "What are the three most important priorities for this organization over the next year?"

We're setting another trap, and almost everyone falls into this one, too: The team members almost always list different priorities as their top three.

In organization after organization, this same script plays out. It doesn't matter if the organization's headcount is 10 people or 10,000. After doing alignment exercises such as these, a warning sign flashes to each executive in attendance: This team may not be a team at all. Team members don't have the same goals. They don't work together or to the same ends. They don't work via the same means or models. Worst of all: They have all been complicit in suffocating their un-team-like behaviors in silence, even as their behavioral problems scream for attention.

The reaction of the leader? Too often, it's an abdication of responsibility. Amid clashes of goals and people, the leader defaults to a hands-off philosophy: "Let the chips fall where they may! These people are bright and capable: Let them wrestle their way to collaboration on their own." We have even seen leaders who seem to relish the resulting melee, as if a *Lord of the Flies* competition will yield both entertainment and results. (One CEO was known to take a "jump ball" approach to decision-making and accountability on his team.)

You could argue that this approach is not unreasonable. After all, most senior executives are seasoned and capable. They lead teams of their own and should know intuitively how best to perform in a group. The more senior they are, the more you could expect them to self-organize. But experience shows that if you think you can let nature take its course with a team, you will lose control of it. And the more accomplished and prestigious your team members, the harder you'll have to work to bring them back into cooperation. You will stall.

A senior executive we'll call Rebecca, head of a major business unit of a Fortune 100 company, asked us in to help improve her team's performance. We started, as we usually do, by interviewing each team member in the days before an offsite meeting. Doing so allowed us to uncover people's unvarnished opinions of the unit, its opportunities, and its challenges. All commentary was made in confidence, and as we usually do, we summarized key themes in a document to share with the whole team to frame the offsite conversation.

What did we hear? When asked, "What do you think is going particularly well for this business?" the responses were glowing—and probably what that leader hoped to hear: "Rebecca is recognized as a truly amazing leader, both in this company and in the industry. She's energetic, smart, and really committed to results. Communication, collaboration, and camaraderie are all exponentially better than a few years ago. People are committed to the strategy and believe in Rebecca. She has pulled together a talented top team made up of smart, experienced, and committed people."[28]

In other words, Rebecca hadn't racked up a lot of failures. She was a star performer, lauded for producing profits, in part by developing strong followership and respect for her capabilities. Her team universally credited her with "tremendous strategic vision."

So why relate this story? Because when we went on to ask, "What do you feel isn't going so well for the business or for the senior team?" we heard feedback that was quite different: "This leadership team doesn't work like a team. We lack sufficient amounts of trust and there's too much territorialism. Members of the senior team don't speak up or share their ideas. We have problems with tension among team members. Rebecca doesn't come across as open or receptive to the team's ideas."

Although Rebecca sensed all was not well, and understood she was facing barriers to taking performance to the next level, she hadn't fully grasped what her team was struggling with. From her point of view, she deserved to be the one most frustrated, because her team wasn't picking the ball up and running with it.

So what was the real problem? Rebecca wasn't having trouble with the challenges of complexity in her job: She had streamlined her organization chart, added talented team members to reflect changes in the business, and transformed strategy and operations to align with changing customer needs. She knew the business better than practically anyone in the industry. She was doing the right things.

Her challenges resulted from not deploying more sophisticated leadership capabilities that could help her and her team perform even better: setting group expectations, establishing norms, managing behaviors and holding people accountable, spurring the right conversations, and fostering the skills and mindsets that bind a team together. Her own leadership, not just her team members' followership, needed to evolve. She was stalling from a lack of thinking, behaving, and guiding her team in a new way, essential to reaping higher levels of performance *as a team*. So the question was, how could she—and how can you—foresee this kind of stall in the making?

When you're frustrated or angry with your team, how can you understand that *you* may need to do something different? How can you learn and deploy the sophisticated leadership your team needs? Even if you have a virtuoso's record of results, if you don't see how to reinvent yourself as your organization grows or changes, you risk seeing your team's performance flatline. As you realize your leadership engine may be stalling while your organization outruns you, you wonder, What happens now?

Beware: Team Zero Going Nowhere

If you've spent time in even basic leadership roles, you'll probably empathize with Rebecca. That's because failing to develop your capabilities to get results from a group worthy of being called a team ranks high among the seven most common stalls of a leader. Along with failing to develop and promote a potent and engaging purpose, the topic of the last chapter, you may hit this point repeatedly as the sophistication of your organization and business grow.

We could paint portrait after portrait of leaders in this stall—Rebecca is by no means alone or even an extreme case. Take, for instance, Michael Barnett of InGo, the trade-show networking software company profiled in the last chapter. Barnett struggled to avoid this stall when his team's leaders wanted to go in a variety of new directions to create growth instead of better executing the existing strategy—which was already yielding subscriber growth of 300 percent a year.

The good news is that you can get past this stall. The main obstacle at the start, as with Rebecca, is a shortage of situational awareness. The first step in troubleshooting is learning what the stall looks and feels like. What are the hints and cues that you're in one? Why are your team members not aligned? Why are they not collaborating? How do you realize you need to check your own growth as a leader to see if your team-leadership software is causing the misfiring? Are you the trigger for your own travails?

Twisted Alignment

The first hint is simply that the people on your team, not having a strong collective view of priorities, clash. They feud during conversations, avoid productive conflict, or shut down and resist passively. Once people break the weekly huddle, they don't seem committed to milestones, don't earnestly shoulder responsibilities for executing strategy, and don't seek each other out to innovate or collaborate.

You may have demonstrated the ability to spur a swirl of healthy energy, innovation, and competitiveness among capable people—and that's a good thing if the result is bonanza of productive teamwork. But it's not if the team delivers less than the sum of its parts: Dysfunctional teams won't perform better based only on locker-room pep talks and enthusiastic cheerleading. This is what CEO Trevor Boyce found, in the story in chapter 1. As you'll recall, for a time at Microbac Labs, Boyce's equation for team output was $1 + 1 = 0$.

If the solution for Boyce amounted only to his changing structure and systems—org charts, reporting systems, pay-for-performance, appraisal systems—he could have fixed the stall overnight. Like a contractor rehabbing a house, he would have swapped out parts (people) and installed new wiring (organizational systems)—and eventually he did so. But the most pressing challenge for Boyce was that team breakdowns came from how he and the team handled personal, interpersonal, and political challenges.

You know you are bogged down in a teamwork stall when you're struggling to manage the sophisticated challenges of fostering collaboration, motivating people, building relationships, and engineering effective decision-making. You'll hear not the roar of organizational acceleration—where your team operates according to the magic of Boyce's ultimate equation, $1 + 1 = 6$—but instead the sputter of a sidetracked team impatient for you to lead them in a new and better way.

As one of Rebecca's team members said, "Our strategy is sound, but the internal tension is killing us. We need to come together and agree on how to prioritize and drive change together and get past the egos." Another said, "One of our biggest problems is senior team dynamics. Are people willing to play for 'us' and not 'me'?"

That internal tension on teams bedevils a lot of leaders. Boyce, if you recall, had long run operations where lab managers did everything—acting like owners of their operations. They were "the heartbeat of the company," he says. And yet to grow, Microbac needed company managers who created efficiencies through an integrated and collaborative system. That required Boyce to do some hiring and firing, reorganization, change in meeting formats, and other mechanical repairs—all the challenges of new complexity.

But it also required a different kind of realization from Boyce: He had to better define a new reality in which job number one was celebrating integration and damping autonomy. His vision was to grow with a team focused on and committed to integrating science, purchasing, IT, finance, and every other part of a company growing quickly via acquisition. And Microbac had to be tuned to serve a national customer base with a full repertoire of testing services, ISO-sanctioned quality, and world-class reliability.

"All of a sudden, I'm saying we have to operate differently if we're going to grow," he says. "Our age-old mantra that drove our culture of autonomous labs was not good enough." So he spent three years trying to handle the sophisticated task of getting his team aligned around new priorities—and all for naught at first. His team members simply did not buy in. "I was personally in a state of being too kind to the senior team because of all the good things they had done for me," he says. "I tried to reshuffle them. And it failed miserably."

In team after team in growing and changing organizations, leaders are more prepared to deal with the structural challenges brought on by their teams' handling of organizational complexity than with the sophisticated political and interpersonal demands. The leaders we work with often find it far easier to reassign executives or reorganize to avoid conflict than fix the teamwork breakdown. If sophisticated, they would realize they must spend emotional energy, precious time, and political capital getting big egos aligned around common purpose.

One of our clients in a mid-size company complained to us, "My people are too myopic and focused only on what they personally lead rather than working as a true team to deliver the best outcomes." He described the attitude of his senior team members as essentially, "I run this portfolio of businesses, and therefore I'm spending my entire time focused on this portfolio with no regard for other businesses or functions, and that's just the way it is."

A stall is not merely inevitable if you believe a team running in this fashion will deliver top performance: The stall can become interminable. The solution demanded isn't one of rehabbing or updating the team machine—expressing frustration at direct reports who can't get along—but rehabbing and updating the driver. Reinventing yourself as a leader requires shifting your attention from your systems of spreadsheets and reports to people's unsystematic styles, psyches, and relationships. It requires taking your eyes off the levers for controlling the business and shifting them to the nature of the people running the business.

Alphas on the Run

A second hint that you may be headed for a teamwork stall is when your team is populated with managers whose egos balloon out of proportion to their roles. The bigger the organization you lead, and the more experienced the leaders, the more often you will be challenged by outsized egos that trigger and prolong stalls. When you hire and promote high-performing people, many naturally have confidence that can veer into cockiness. But as you let the cream rise to the top, you can't let it sour the performance of the whole.

If you're a fan of the Olympics, recall the 2004 Athens games. To the chagrin of many Americans, the US basketball team lost to Puerto Rico in the first game and never even got to play for the gold. Unthinkable and embarrassing! Those results weren't because the team didn't have big-time players, among them LeBron James, Allen Iverson, and Carmelo Anthony. It was because the American all-stars hadn't practiced as a team, didn't think like a team, and didn't play like a team. And it was because the other teams had practiced a great deal, and did think and play like teams on offense and defense.

The US lost three out of seven games, getting bumped out of the gold medal round by Argentina, 89 to 81. Of course, the competition had gotten much stiffer since previous Olympic games. The rest of the world had discovered basketball and nurtured stars. Look at the roster of any NBA team today, and note the many countries of origin of the players. And then, too, the US players had probably also become complacent, never having had to work too hard to win the gold after professionals were allowed to play. But the point is that individual skill was not enough to win. While the US took third place by beating tiny Lithuania (still at a remarkably close 102 to 96), Argentina, playing Italy, won the gold.

The explanation is simple enough. Top people display characteristics to help them triumph personally: They are confident, action-oriented, trailblazing, just-do-it types who often exude charisma and courage. You may be like that yourself. But if you are leading a team of equals, in which people need to shine not alone but together, you have to check your ranks: Do you have too much "alpha" behavior that may result in a team of betas?

When he was CEO of Sotera Defense Solutions, John Hillen, this book's coauthor, had a brush with this problem. In the fast-growing company, he gradually focused his time and energy away from the company and onto the wider marketplace, including outside stakeholders. To free up time, he recruited a talented team of all-star executives, several of whom had run bigger operations at top-ranked rival companies. Within two years, Sotera was able to go public, buy and integrate four other companies, and eventually be taken private at a huge premium to its stock price—all during the recessionary 2008–2011 period.

In leading his team, Hillen gave people room to run and trusted their judgment, and he tried to be the kind of boss that he liked to report to himself. In essence, he ruled over his team with a policy of benign neglect. But even as he was lauded for executive talent—Sotera won a company-of-the-year award in 2012—he learned the same lesson we've seen executives learn over and over: A well-functioning team does not form and manage itself.

The upshot at Sotera was that within a year of Sotera's new owners taking the company in a different direction, five of Hillen's six senior team members moved on. Like many members of top teams, they had big egos and big talents. But even so, when the direction of the company changed, they needed—but were not getting from Hillen—the active care and nurturing to harness those talents to deliver even better results to the overall organization.

As the leader of any team, you must ask yourself, have I let the "Alpha Dog Problem" develop on my team? And do I have it myself? Is either behavior pulling me into a stall?

The Frozen Grip

A third hint that you're in a teamwork stall is when you fear relinquishing work, responsibilities, and decision-making authority to others. At one dot-com we worked with, the CEO couldn't let go of anything but minor tasks and decisions. He was so dogmatic about being the boss that he would commandeer the whiteboard at team meetings even when he had delegated the session to someone else. He alienated the talented people who worked for him, micromanaging them and generating mistrust. Worse, he unintentionally obscured his own poor performance by not hiring stronger people, lest they upstage him.

If you're a leader with a talented team but you think nobody can do the job as well as you can do it—and thus you do the job yourself time and again—you are certainly due for a stall. Comments from the subordinates of another senior leader we worked with shed light on his ability to relinquish the steering wheel. His people told us: "People on the senior team behave differently, including shutting down, when he's in the room." And, "I'm not being fully empowered and not feeling like I have his trust. I don't know if he realizes how hard he can come down on people." And, "I'm worried that if he can't get out of the details, he won't be able to step up and take on a bigger and broader role, which the organization really needs him to do."

Does any of this sound familiar? We chose just two case studies out of many we have come across. They point to the same conclusion: The inability to delegate and give up control is one of the biggest risks for leaders as their jobs get bigger and demand a more sophisticated kind of leadership.[29] Are you risking a stall in this way?

Static in the Conference Room

A fourth hint that you're in a stall comes when the harmonious vibe of collaboration in your regular team meetings breaks into a static of disrespect. Do your team members' tenor and behavior seem out of line, whether actively or passively? If you have lost control of your team, your team members will almost always broadcast attitudes and behaviors of discord.

You can see it easily in people's conduct in meetings. Do people work on email on their laptops, dial into meetings instead of attending them, routinely arrive late, or make a habit of cancelling because of other "pressing priorities?" Do you allow these behaviors? How effective are your meetings, really? You could be forgiven for reading such signs as symptoms of "healthy" conflict, "focused" leaders, "busy" people, or "innovative" minds at work. You might even think you've headed your team in the right direction.

But maybe you shouldn't. When you're going into a teamwork stall, your people reflect the worst of your own behaviors. They arrive late if you tend to arrive late. They become absorbed in their email if you don't shut off your own devices and focus on the dialogue. They write off meetings as meaningless if you've been subjecting them to meaningless meetings.

When you're outside the meeting, what do echoes of the meeting in the hallways tell you? What do people say about your team or organization? Are they looking for scapegoats? Are they talking about trading stars and hiring new talent? What are their decisions when you're not around? People take their cues from the culture you create by your own behavior. If you poison the well of culture and teamwork, everyone drinks that tainted water.

Extensive research over decades demonstrates that three sets of factors govern culture.[30] The first are factors inside the organization: hiring specifications, policies, training, performance management systems, internal communication. The second are factors outside: industry practices, competition, the organization's geographical or national location, and market conditions. And the third set are behaviors exhibited by the organization's leaders. And which set matters most? The third one: An organization's culture is *most* influenced by its leaders' behaviors, especially those of the top leaders.

It's an old truism that people don't do what you say; they do what you do (or believe you would do). What do you value and what do you reward? What do you punish or refuse to tolerate? How do you treat people, from business partners and clients to employees and support staff? Do you hire people who both fit the culture and propagate it? Are your own actions in line with your espoused values?

Culture is the boss when you're not around. So when you observe how your team members are acting, you may well be seeing a reflection of how *you're* acting. Do you see low levels of trust, commitment, or accountability? Do people routinely put themselves first, alpha people spurring beta results? The causes of dysfunctional behavior may be hard to see, and you may be biased by advice from people who hear only your side of the story. To pull out of a teamwork stall, you'll probably need to take a harder look at yourself. Maybe the organization has run a few laps ahead of you—and it's time for self-reinvention as a more sophisticated leader.

WARNING: YOU'VE HIT A TEAMWORK STALL

You lead strong-minded people whose own priorities often prevail over those of the organization. People clash more than they collaborate. You don't spend time actively developing and managing your team members under the assumption that they will and should manage themselves. Disgruntled remarks leak out in hallway banter. You hesitate to hand over more responsibility, and you wonder: Am I riding this bronco or have I been thrown off?

Assess: Your Team Stall

If the dynamics of the human mind seem forever unfathomable, and often untamable and untrainable, so too the dynamics of the "team mind." That unfathomability makes the assessment of a stall harder than you realize. If you sense something is wrong with your team, it's time to make sure you're gaining the right situational awareness to know where and how you need to change.

Let's assume you've mastered the questions of complexity related to running an effective team. You've dealt with issues of organization structure, lines of authority, reporting protocols, hiring, firing, formal team processes, performance appraisals and compensation, and so on. That leaves the sophisticated team-leadership capabilities. It doesn't matter if you're growing, transforming, or moving the organization in a new direction: If your team demands sophisticated leadership, you can't fall back on lists of "do's" and "don'ts" typical of many management books.

We like the way Patrick Lencioni describes the five "dysfunctions" of teams, or the traps that any team can be prone to falling into:[31] 1) people don't trust each other; 2) they shy away from conflict or honest conversations; 3) team members lack commitment because they are not committed to the same team goals; 4) people don't hold each other accountable; and 5) individual team members are unable to put "we" before "me."

To assess and understand whether these dysfunctions apply to you, engage in a troubleshooting analysis. What practical approach do you take? How do you go about an inquiry? What questions should you ask yourself? What mental exercises and probing will tell you how to recover? We have three favorite approaches, and if you feel you're stalling, you should probably undertake these sooner rather than later. Without your commitment to "own" this troubleshooting—a job you can't give to someone else—the teamwork stall will stymie you.

Ask the Key Questions

Every team at any level in any organization must be able to answer three simple but critical questions:

1. Where are we? (What's the current state of our business? What's working well and what isn't? What does the competitive landscape look like, and where are the disruptors? What are our strengths and weaknesses as an organization and as a senior team? Have we done an honest assessment and do we have agreement?)

2. Where are we going? (What's our three-year vision? What are the most important near-term and longer-term strategic milestones to achieve it? What are the critical questions we need to address or problems we need to solve in light of our longer-term strategy? How will we measure success?)

3. How will we get there together? (What do we need to do as a team and as individuals to achieve our short- and long-term goals? What might get in the way of our achieving our objectives? What is the roadmap, and who's accountable for what? How will we hold each other accountable? What do we need to commit to perform as a team and not just a group of talented individuals?)

How would you reply to these questions? How would the members of your team reply? If you don't dedicate time, resources, and effort to address these questions—and not just when they become problems splitting your team—you will run into trouble. Have you actually spent time to assess whether everyone on your team would have the same answers?

As a trouble-shooting exercise, write the name of each of your team members at the top of a page. In columns underneath, write down how you think *they* would answer these questions. And then go ask them. Talk through the questions with each team member individually. What does this one-on-one sleuthing tell you about your team leadership and each person's alignment?

The purpose of this exercise is not merely to see if everyone can articulate the organization's purpose and values in the same way. The purpose is to understand why members of the team might not be sharing the same objectives and path forward. This is not only about clarifying your organizational purpose and narrative, the subject of our last chapter, but discerning disconnects among team members to reveal whether they are interacting and collaborating as well as they need to.

We know from experience that the items you may think are on each team member's mind often are not. In many cases, team members fail to buy into each other's views from the start. In meetings, you'll pick up body language that shows people disagree with each other. You may also perceive from the actions you see people take that what they say and what they believe are different. In other words, you already have some inside knowledge of a problem, and the purpose of this exercise is to give you a simple framework to assess the lack of alignment.

Our experience repeatedly shows that if you are not gathering your team together at least twice a year to address and talk through these questions deliberately, the minds of your team members are likely not meeting at all. You must dedicate time and collaborative effort to improving how your team works, distinct from your standing weekly or bi-weekly meetings. If you don't, you'll risk the organization outrunning you, hitting a wall, or failing to get to the next level of excellence.

We attribute the failure of many leaders to engage their teams regularly in these fundamental questions to many factors: The demands of running the day-to-day business are pressing. Talking about the business in these ways feels too "touchy-feely." The answers to the questions seem obvious. Overconfidence leads to benign neglect. And the powers of procrastination simply get the better of you.

We hear excuses from leaders: "We're all super-experienced—everyone on the senior team knows and understands our strategy—we just need to do it." Or, "Yeah, we should probably make the time to do something like that, but we're so busy." Such excuses may be another warning sign that you're testing positive for a stall.

What Kind of Team Are You Leading?

In their classic 1993 article about teams, Jon Katzenbach and Douglas Smith found that what people call "teams" should actually be distinguished into two entities: *teams* and *working groups*. Working groups are made up of people who work on separate tasks, often with their own goals and purposes, to deliver necessary output that is dependent on what each member can produce on his or her own. Teams, in contrast, are made up of people who work in concert, with shared goals and mutual accountability, to deliver performance that none of them could alone.[32]

Teams are not necessarily "better than" working groups. Each operates in a different way to a different end. A basketball team is a team by Katzenbach and Smith's definition. The goal is to win the game. A track team, on the other hand, is a working group. Its goal is to deliver superior individual results, which in turn may result in their winning the meet.

In Trevor Boyce's math, working groups operate according to the simple equation $1 + 1 = 2$. That's not a bad thing, if that's what you want. Some organizations—for example, sales functions in early-stage companies—work perfectly well with this model. But a working group cannot beat the performance of a team as the organization and business grow.

Some leaders believe they have a great team because each member excels at specific, assigned tasks. But such a team is just a collection of talents. A collection can be a great asset, but it can't work to its potential unless it works as an ensemble. Ten people rowing their own boats simply cannot go as fast as ten rowing the same one.

Our experience is that a working group model gives teams in organizations subpar performance—and yet in many instances, if not by design, "teams" do often operate as working groups. As an example, we once worked for a financial services company where a newly hired leader could see early on see her team had no sense of urgency. Team members worked to clear a low bar. From the team members' point of view, success meant, "I did what I was supposed to do." The team leader could see that, although the team diagnosed organizational or strategic problems well, it did not solve them or take responsibility for results. "My team," she told us, "manages to mediocrity via ambiguity."

This mediocrity, unfortunately, is what can result from "teams" operating as working groups. If this is the kind of team you run, you will likely see other problems as well. Your team may meet largely for updates on operations (aka "death by PowerPoint"); people will debate individual priorities (aka "can't see the forest for the trees"); or the team as a whole will fail to focus on adapting to new circumstances (aka "if it ain't broke, don't fix it"). These maladies highlight the importance of the second troubleshooting question: Have you decided up front what kind of team you want to run? Is that the kind of team you *need* to run? Is it living up to its potential?

If you've abdicated making a decision about what kind of team to run, you're probably not delivering the performance you should. Be clear about one thing— creating a high-performing team demands significant investment, on the part of both yourself and the team. You'll need to devote more time and effort in a different way—a more sophisticated way. That might mean listening, being honest and vulnerable, and coaching the team to create its own unique greatness. It's a big job, but you can't lead an organization competing at the top of its game if your dominant model is the working group. A well-led working group may excel in producing strong track stars, but only a well-led team wins the overall gold medal.

Does Your Team Share Priorities?

One of the easiest ways to assess a team stall is the one mentioned at the start: the index card test. At its simplest, you ask each team member to write out clearly, without acronyms or jargon, the answer to the following question: "What are the three most important things for this company over the next year—the most pressing objectives to accomplish, issues to address, questions to answer, problems to solve, or results to drive?" You will already have asked yourself this question, but by asking the team you get explicit evidence of whether you've stalled.

We have conducted this exercise scores of times over the years, working with teams at offsite meetings or strategic planning sessions. We have never seen an instance where every member of the team came up with the same three things. Not even close.

To facilitate dialogue, improve team alignment, and establish a clear path forward in these team meetings, we go on to use the cards for a prioritization exercise. After collecting the cards, we start to build a collated list on a whiteboard. The list usually includes clusters around eight or ten general ideas. It also tends to include a dozen or more one-offs that are not mission-critical or relate only to the agenda of a single executive, not to the enterprise. If the team isn't aligned around what really matters for the business, how could anyone lead it effectively?

Given that your team members are also leaders of their own teams, it's a good time to remind everyone about the parable of the blind men and the elephant. You probably know how this goes from grade school:

A half-dozen blind men are led to an elephant and asked to describe it based only on their sense of touch. The first man grabs the trunk and says, "An elephant is like snake!" Another places his hands on the flank, and says, "An elephant is like a wall!" A third embraces a leg, and says, "An elephant is like a tree!" And so on.[33]

The parable is a way to remind people that too often leaders and managers focus only on the parts of the business they control, and they don't work together to consider the enterprise as a whole. And that's dangerous. As we said in the opening of this chapter, the managers are thinking only about the teams they lead, not the team they're a member of. As for you as a leader, the parable can hit you like a comeuppance. Your effort to lead a team may have not produced a team at all, at least in one of the most important ways—having a clear set of common goals. If so, you have work to do to recover from a stall.

How you conduct the index card test doesn't matter much. As an alternative, you can break your team into several groups and have everyone ask the same questions. Or you can ask people to engage in the "middle-of-the-night" test: "If you were shaken awake at 2:00 a.m. and asked the single most important priority of this organization, what would it be?"

No matter the form of the exercise, if you've stalled with how you are building and leading your team, you'll get the same suboptimal results. That's what we've found with organization after organization: Senior leaders cite issues to tackle as numerous as items on a menu. We hear "Our strategic plan has 37 priorities for next year." The reality is, if you have 37 priorities, you probably don't have any, and your leadership is unlikely to lead to meaningful results.

On the bumpy road of organizational growth, if you're going to avoid stalling, you must work on team dynamics *all the time.* You'll get top grades for team leadership only when you endow the team with clarity of objectives, authenticity and trust, honest communication, a voice for everyone, results orientation and accountability, and continuous learning and feedback. Your prime task, from the start of your reinvention and ongoing, is to create alignment.

Recover: New Math for Teams

One mistake leaders can make when they face a teamwork stall is to call in a consultant to help with social interaction to spur teamwork. That isn't a bad thing. It aims at helping people "to get to know each other" or "to work together better." But such exercises don't usually help you in your ability to align teams or create teamwork. Even if necessary, ice-breaking games and bonding exercises, though enjoyable and spirit-building, aren't sufficient to create a high-performing team. Instead, you need to focus on ways to change your own mindsets and behaviors so that you, by virtue of your authentic actions, instill in the team the direction, motivation, and energy to get results together.[34]

A myth persists that teams made up of experienced managers should "self-manage." As we've mentioned, our experience is just the reverse. Top teams don't manage themselves any more than fighter pilots land their jets on aircraft carriers all by themselves. In so-called self-managing teams, you may get 1 + 1 = 2, but that's the best result you get. If you want 1 + 1 = 6, you have to lead and guide team members in changing their own mindsets and behaviors.

If you think you can do so merely by means of structure, think again. George Schultz used an exercise to demonstrate this when he was US Secretary of State, one of the most structured of any organization. He would meet with new US ambassadors and ask them to show him on the map "their country." Ambassadors would invariably talk about the country to which they were being posted. After letting them go on for a while, Secretary Schultz would offer a gentle rejoinder: "No, your country is the United States."

By starting with this exercise, Schultz set the perspective of the meeting in the same way we do with the exercise at the start of this chapter: The team whose performance most mattered—the team Schultz was leading—was the team sitting around the table. The US team, which coordinated America's diplomatic missions, was intended to accomplish the most on behalf of America.[35]

Changing everyone's mindset to that effect is a sophisticated job that structure alone cannot perform. Structure, of course, can raise its own challenges. For example, when you recruit new people to a team, you change the composition. Every time you add a new ingredient to a drink, as the saying goes, it's a different drink. Chemistry and complementarity count. But the bigger hurdle is shaping and nurturing others to create group action. And you can only stimulate that action through practice and deliberate attention.

If you don't take actions to recover, you will probably default to the hub-and-spoke model of teams. That means you will stand at the center as the strong boss connected individually with each of your team members. That model might sound effective, but it will constrain your ability to manage meaningful growth and change. You become the bottleneck and single point of failure, and the model is not scalable. If you want to build a team that scales up with the organization, you must create active and sophisticated connections among the spokes. You will then have enabled each team member to accomplish more by working with and through the rest of the team.

Suffice it to say that you can't program your team with a fixed set of features and let it run like a piece of software—not with the pace of change and uncertainty organizations face today. We have a shortlist of tools to help you recover if you have let your team drift off course. These tools can guide you in institutionalizing high-performance teamwork. You can't get top performance by letting the chips fall where they may—even if you are a charismatic leader who knows the business better than anyone. You have to practice running your team, and you have to practice it regularly, or it diminishes with lack of use. You'll know you've succeeded when interpersonal rivalries and feuds dissipate because the team is focused on the same common goals, agenda, and commitment to each other.

Go Deep With the Index Card

When you recognize you've hit a team stall, the first tool you can use to recover is an extended version of the index card exercise. Start with a dedicated, offsite meeting, not a normal weekly or bi-weekly meeting—and certainly not a meeting scheduled on the fly. Set aside separate time, ideally in a different location to help people think differently about the big picture.

We are often asked to help design and facilitate these kinds of meetings. The value of bringing people away from the office is to snap everyone's attention back to enterprise goals and the collective path forward. If you've allowed people to become absorbed in leading their own business or function at the risk of the organization overall, you now have a chance to practice the reverse mindset.

When we do the index card exercise, we get similar results almost every time: The leader almost instantly sees a lack of alignment on priorities, underlining the need to improve and maintain team members' focus. For example, leaders often find that chief financial officers are focused on closing the books and getting their finance teams to deliver numbers, not on using their finance capabilities to help understand where the market and industry are going and how the organization needs to adjust its strategy. Getting narrowly focused CEOs to shift energy and focus is a great way to start on the road to nurturing a higher-performing senior team.

Facilitating your team members to commit to a collective set of goals and outcomes is one of your most important jobs as a leader. That's why the index card exercise has so much power in changing your team-leadership approach. The same is true of the earlier troubleshooting exercise in which you wrote down how you thought each of your team members would answer the "three key questions."

In both exercises, you can ask people for more detail. For example, ask people to complete their cards answering the question about the most critical priorities for the business over the next year, eighteen months, three years, or whatever timeframe makes the most sense.

This question about priorities helps uncover collective goals and answers to the second fundamental question, "Where are we going?" You can also ask related questions: What is our desired future state? Can we describe it in a detailed and meaningful way? How will we measure what success looks if we achieve it?

Back up, and then have the team process the first fundamental question in the context of the second, namely "Where are we now?" What is the status of the business and our processes? Where do we sit in the competitive landscape of our industry? What do we see as our strengths, weaknesses, opportunities, and threats? Do we have a clear and consistent assessment of ourselves as a team?

Finally, come together to answer the third question: What is the gap between where we are today and where we want to get to? What, specifically, is our path to get there? How can we establish clear steps to execute—and milestones to ensure we're making progress? What do we need to make sure we're doing and also *not* doing? Then, in the context of this path forward, how are we working together as a team? How can we collaborate better, make decisions more effectively, have more productive dialogue, manage through conflict better, and provide each other with more support and feedback?

Go into depth with each of these questions. The deeper you go, the better you get at the sophisticated task of aligning your team. Seek mutual insight by having everyone weigh in honestly and consider the issues systemically and holistically. Challenge unchallenged assumptions, and encourage reticent team members to speak up. Be sure nothing important goes undiscussed—and that's much easier when you schedule the meetings outside workdays. You want an environment conducive to training yourself and your team to have conversations that really matter.

A new kind of collaborative thinking and communication, fostered by the index card exercise, should help you better learn how to guide your direct reports in moving from favoring their own priorities to the organization's priorities. The exercise also allows you to winnow priorities and to-do lists in a way that generates agreement and commitment. An index card seems like an awfully humble tool to help you remake your leadership capability. But you'll find it always catalyzes engagement and dialogue to spur a rethinking on your part, and in turn, on your team's.

To your chagrin, you may realize that *you're* the culprit in teamwork malfunctions. You're the one who has let your people take ownership of only one part of the elephant. With a more sophisticated set of leadership behaviors, however, you can learn to help them take ownership and tame the whole beast together. Interestingly, you'll often find that seasoned members of your team have more trouble than new ones. Accustomed to delivering heroic results, they may have to work themselves past ego, ingrained habits, and the momentum of history.

Obviously enough, the index card exercise provides a big benefit beyond helping you recover from a stall as a leader. You and your team end up identifying the handful of items everyone needs to address as soon as the meeting breaks. You've answered not just the big questions but many tactical ones—and you've clarified the importance of the tactics in the context of the broader strategy. What are we committed to doing starting Monday morning? What are the specific deliverables? The timeframe? Who is accountable? You are ready to get rolling immediately with aligned, collaborative work, organized around a manageable number of priorities.

Don't let the index card exercise remain a one-time trick in your bag of leadership tools. Use it regularly to reset your mindset, leadership behaviors, and team alignment. Bake it into your team-meeting processes. Many of our clients use this exercise in their standard planning, monitoring, and operations oversight, which helps embed alignment in their habitual thinking.

Craft Your Rules

Another tool for recovering from the teamwork stall is asking your team to devise explicit "rules of engagement" or "rules of the road." What are the ground rules for how your team meets and works together? Teams that assume these rules are a given or tacit will run into trouble especially when the pressure is on.

You might at first think you can impose rules, but imposing rules often doesn't work, because team members with big egos may behave as if your rules don't apply—after all, what do smart people like to do more than break rules? Instead, use this exercise as a way to help the team create for itself a set of behaviors and norms they are all willing to be held accountable for.

Drafting rules of engagement can sound like an exercise in etiquette, not leadership. But when you turn the exercise into a deliberate and conscious group task, it forces people to think in a more sophisticated way about their minute-to-minute behaviors and their accountability to each other for acting in line with them.

Not surprisingly, we invariably find that teams list roughly the same half-dozen behaviors or values: be honest, speak now not later, listen attentively and be fully engaged, don't disrespect others, limit the group to one conversation at a time, stay on-agenda and don't wander into rabbit holes, keep digital devices closed, and so on. The rules themselves are not always novel, but if the team members create them together in their own language, it's much more likely people will take ownership of them, and adapt their behaviors accordingly.

As an example, Hervé Sedky, president of the Americas unit of Reed Exhibitions, the global event-management company, took over in 2014 at a time when there was a perception that digital marketing was disrupting face-to-face marketing. His team confronted a monumental strategic challenge: to bring together the best of face-to-face and digital marketing in the live event settings that Reed operates.[36]

Sedky, eager to make sure his team came together around a new plan to reshape the business radically, asked his team to develop rules of engagement that in the end included the following:

Respectful honesty and candor
> *Don't express opinions as facts*
> *Be comfortable challenging*

Step outside your role
> *Don't be defensive*
> *Be open*
> *Think team/enterprise*

This is a safe zone
> *Trust*
> *Celebrate*

Assume positive intent

Encourage participation by all

Once we agree, execute

Be fully present and listen

When you establish rules of engagement with your team, you've taken an important step to move beyond your team leadership stall. You may also find a bonus in gaining new, unexpected leverage. When you're the leader who asks the entire team, together, to produce rules of behavior and etiquette, you are then empowered to say, "I'm going to hold you all accountable for following the rules—and I'm going to ask you to hold each other accountable."

If you conduct this exercise at an offsite or dedicated meeting, you should ask the team to assess itself as the session concludes. As a group, assign grades for each rule—a B for listening, a D for putting devices away, an A for honesty, and so on. And then have an honest conversation about why the group did or didn't do well and how everyone can get better. Ask yourself, too, where you could have better exercised team leadership.

You'll then realize you also have a second point of leverage. Ask your leaders, "Should these rules apply only when we are off-site—or in our day-to-day work as well?" Everyone will agree that the rules should be taken back to the workplace. (How else could they respond when they just came up with rules for working together effectively?) Engaging in this simple exercise is a powerful way to deepen the team's social contract and performance in an ongoing manner.

Draft This Charter

As you can see, if you take our approach to avoid a team-leadership stall, you'll end up creating what we might call "ties that bind." Ask yourself in all your contacts with your team, "What are the ties I can put in place to hold the team together, to keep everyone focused on executing on the team's chosen priorities?" These ties can take many forms, but when you coax your team to adopt new norms and frameworks, and when the team honors them, you will be leading a team that moves forward together, with resolve, confidence, and strength that is unmistakable.

Here's an illustration. On the deck of an aircraft carrier, during night flight operations, fighter jets take off and land one right after another. Flight teams on deck wear color-coded uniforms: yellow for aircraft directors, green for catapult, purple for fuel, and so on for seven teams.[37] There is little ability to communicate verbally amid the roar of engines—just hand signals as people move constantly and planes shoot off the end of the ship every four minutes. That's when the crew culture and training allow everyone to work as a genuine team. All the pieces fall into place because, if you're on that flight deck, you can practically feel those ties binding the sailors together.

The biggest surprise with the sailors conducting this aircraft-handling ballet is when they come off the deck. They remove their gear and it's suddenly obvious that most of them are eighteen- and nineteen-year-olds. They are so young you wonder if, in another context, you would allow them to valet-park your car. And yet they operate as players within a perfectly aligned team, executing perfectly with only light supervision and almost no direct verbal communication.

So what are the ties you can create to help your people work together in their own kind of joint ballet? What are the ways you can institutionalize teamwork on your team? We offer one additional exercise, the team charter. After you have your people work with the index card and rules of engagement, deepen your collective work by having them address the fundamental components of any effective team (Table 3.1) and create a charter together. Far from subjecting them to a "busywork" exercise, you will be encouraging a collective investment that can bind the team together and help you execute as never before.

Beautiful Culture

In the same way that you can make yourself a culture warrior to reinforce purpose, as in the last chapter, you should have an active hand in affirming or re-affirming culture as a way to lead your team. John W. Rogers, Jr., founder and CEO of Ariel Investments, the $13 billion money-management firm headquartered in Chicago, with offices in New York City and Sydney, has set a standard of team behavior that has served him well since the firm's founding in 1983. He demonstrates how leaders who have reached a high level of sophistication can even use culture instead of other tools to recover from teamwork stalls over the long term.[38]

Rogers played basketball at Princeton in the 1970s. This was a time when the legendary Pete Carril coached the team. Carril, Rogers recalls, "drilled into our heads" that thinking about your teammates first was the most important basketball lesson at Princeton. "Every coach talks about teamwork and sharing the ball, but very few are able to effectuate this change with their players," he says. "Coach Carril was the best teacher I ever had, because he was able to bring about this change in his team."

When a team first forms, there is minimal trust, no shared goals or history of past performance, and roles are unclear. Despite this lack of clarity, members are eager to jump into the task at hand. The single most critical success factor for high-performing teams is having a shared understanding of **why** the team exists, **what** it is trying to accomplish, and **how** it will work together. The chart below proposes some of the most important questions a team should address together and agree on to become a functional team and deliver better results faster.

Table 3.1 Creating a Team Charter

Key Topics	Questions for Each Topic
Purpose and Key Responsibilities	• What is our purpose? Why do we exist? • What are our core responsibilities as a team? • What are others counting on us to do?
Vision	• What do we want to accomplish, achieve, or create as a team? • What will be the impact of our collective efforts?
Values	• What are the most important values that we will adopt to guide our actions and decisions as a team? • What are the specific behaviors that describe each value?
Goals	• What are our shared goals and deliverables? • How will we measure our success?
Roles and Responsibilities	• What are our individual areas of responsibility? • What are the "borders" between our responsibilities, and how will we manage them? • How do our individual skills and accountabilities complement each other?
Mutual Expectations	• What do we want and need from each other? • What could negatively impact our working relationships? • What is the best way to give each other feedback?
Operating Procedures: Meetings	• How often will we meet? For how long? When and where? • How will we develop meeting agendas? • Who will lead or facilitate our meetings? • How will we keep track of our decisions and execute on our agreed-upon actions?
Operating Procedures: Communications	• What is the best way to communicate with each other and keep each other informed? • How quickly do we agree to return phone calls and e-mail? • How and what will we communicate to our key stakeholders?

(Continued)

TABLE 3.1 CREATING A TEAM CHARTER *(Continued)*	
Key Topics	**Questions for Each Topic**
Operating Procedures: Decision-Making	• What should our primary decision-making method be? • What decisions will we make individually? • What decisions will require agreement among all team members?
Operating Procedures: Conflict	• How will we resolve disagreements? • How will we hold each other accountable to follow through on our agreements?
Operating Procedures: Reflection and Improvement	• How and when will we evaluate our team performance? • How can we get useful feedback from outside our team? • What will we do to continue to get better?

Carril's philosophy was a revelation to the competitive Rogers. "It was such a freeing epiphany," Rogers says. "Your main focus on the court was how to help your teammates. And that was simple, straightforward, and uncomplicated. In the past what was going through the back of everyone's mind was how to position oneself to score points or win accolades. But with Carril's approach, you could breathe easily, enjoy the game, and have fun being a part of the group."

How did this work during a game? When setting a screen to get a teammate open, Carril would show how, if you freed up someone else, the opposing players would chase after the new open man, and that would leave you as the one setting the screen free to get the ball and make the basket. "The right play for the team ends up being the best move for you," Rogers says. With that approach, he led the Princeton Tigers in 1980 to sharing first place in the Ivy League championship.

Carril would stop play to scold players who didn't get his message. "He could be brutal if he saw selfishness," Rogers recalls. "And Coach Carril was very clear what these values stood for. Eventually everyone on the team came to understand his philosophy, which was beautiful to behold, because everyone on the team played better. No one who was selfish played all four years."

"It was as if a transformation came over me," he says. "We all came to the realization that if a teammate was struggling, our first priority was to help him."

Rogers believes Carril made him team captain when he was a senior not because he was the best player, but because of his hard work, determination, and team effort. Every chance he had, Rogers demonstrated to his teammates the importance of looking out for one another, to help everyone be successful. "I also learned that if you help your teammate succeed on the court, your teammates will look up to you as a leader," says Rogers.

"That is exactly the leadership style I have tried to instill at Ariel," he says. That's not to say Rogers isn't competitive. Outside his career as an investor he achieved a reputation as a formidable athletic opponent: He is the only player at fantasy basketball camp to defeat Michael Jordan in a one-on-one competition.

Still, Rogers remains focused on how he can help his teammates at Ariel be successful in their careers. "How can you help your colleagues realize their potential? How can you enable them to share in the profits, have a stake in the ownership of the company, and partake in decision making? Asking these questions is essential to my leadership style."

Rogers founded Ariel Investments, the first African-American investment management firm with publicly traded mutual funds, in January of 1983 when he was 24 years old, with $200,000 from his friends, family and former clients. Today it has over 90 employees and is consistently ranked among the top tier of firms in long-term performance, using a patient Warren Buffet-style value approach to investing in small and mid-cap domestic and global stocks. "Slow and steady wins the race," as its motto says. At over $11 billion in funds under management, Ariel remains the largest African-American-owned investment firm in the country.

Another sign of the success of Rogers's leadership approach? He jokingly says he has so often urged journalists and broadcasters who sought to interview him to interview others at Ariel instead that now the broadcasters only occasionally call him. For example, Charlie Bobrinskoy, vice chairman and head of investment group, now often fields the calls. As on the basketball court, so in the court of investment opinion, Rogers says, "I'm going to share the ball."

And that mindset has helped Rogers avoid stalling as a leader of teams for thirty-five years. Indeed, he has been called upon to work on teams well outside the borders of his own company. Chicago leaders have asked him to join a host of civic and nonprofit boards. He has served as board president of the Chicago Park District (including 580 parks and museums) and as board member for the University of Chicago, Rush University Medical Center, and the Chicago Symphony Orchestra. Corporate leaders have asked him to join boards such as Exelon and McDonald's. "When I walk into a board room, I am going to bring my values with me. I am going to always be thinking of ways I can help that team succeed."

Team leaders like Rogers who might be heading for a stall—but want to avoid it—don't abdicate the responsibility of developing a strong team. They don't suggest their team members need a "marriage counselor." Nor do they merely complain when members of the team aren't stepping up as true teammates. When they feel these kinds of knee-jerk emotional reactions arising, they reject them. Instead, they view failures in teamwork as helpful warning signs and cues to self-development: You win if you reinvent yourself to refocus deliberate effort on leading others to overcome the challenges of sophistication, as we sum up in our breakout summary on the next pages. That's when your teambuilding math goes from $1 + 1 = 0$ to $1 + 1 = 6$.

~Reinventing Your Leadership~
A Teamwork Stall?

Become a True Team Captain.

Beware of Danger

- Team members act like freelancers, concerned mostly about their own organizations.

- Team members can't agree—explicitly or implicitly—on enterprise priorities or strategic execution.

- Team members resist team rewards and accountability.

- Team members can't seem to collaborate without you as an intermediary.

- You don't believe you need to actively manage all-star team members.

- Team members have low mutual trust and commitment.

- Team members shy away from difficult conversations in team meetings—and/or try to have "backchannel" conversations.

- You feel uncomfortable delegating to the team.

Assess & Troubleshoot

- Employ the index card test to assess team alignment on priorities.

- Generate honest (and ideally anonymous) feedback from the team on how everyone sees the team's—and your own—effectiveness.

- Query each team member to weigh their viewpoints:
  Where are we? Where are we going? How we will get there . . . together?

- Explore those three questions as a team to identify gaps or traps.

- Give your team the "working group or team" test to measure separately performed tasks vs. collaboration and cooperation.

- Examine your incentives. Do they support team or individual goals?

Recover & Reinvent

- Hold frequent strategic meetings or off-sites to ensure alignment of the team around shared goals. (Minimum twice per year.)

- Create team "rules of engagement" and require team members to hold each other (and you!) accountable to them.

- Deploy the index card exercise to drive understanding of, and agreement on, fundamental questions and the path forward.

- Collectively draft a team charter and ensure commitment from the team to its goals, processes, and principles.

- Be explicit about the culture that ties the team together, and relentlessly model the behavior of that value system.

- As a cultural warrior, call out dysfunctional behaviors and reward team approaches or behavior.

- To prevent leading only a working group, create useful dependencies, shared work, and rewards for team collaboration where you are not always the "hub."

CHAPTER 4

ASLEEP AT THE STAKEHOLDER WHEEL

Stalling When You Neglect Your Stakeholders

"One person with a belief is a social power equal to ninety-nine who
have only interests."

—JOHN STEWART MILL, *Representative Government*

"Who shall set a limit to the influence of a human being?"

—RALPH WALDO EMERSON, *The Conduct of Life*

Leaders spend much of their careers communicating and interacting
over two managerial channels. The first one is telling people who
work for them what to do. The second is telling people who don't work
for them what they want to hear. In other words, in the first mode they
give direction and orders to employees or vendors, and in the second
they act attentive and responsive to customers, prospects, or bosses.

But what happens when the relationship challenges get more sophisticated? As your organization and responsibilities as a leader grow, two
broadcast/receive channels will no longer suffice or get you the results
you need. One reason is that you no longer deal with just a handful
of constituents. Nor do you deal only with people you see regularly.
As you rise, you gain a host of new stakeholders: regulators, investors,
boards, the public, the media, political figures, and even rivals in your
organization. And these new stakeholders simply don't interact with
you through either of those two communication channels.

That's why some leaders, once they are in the driver's seat of their
organization, can suddenly seem asleep at the wheel. They haven't
made a point of building relationships with new stakeholders to drive
performance at new levels. Nor have they realized the sophisticated

capabilities needed to manage stakeholders at a higher level. We often hear from leaders who have not gained broader stakeholder influence, "I'm too busy. I wish I had the time to spend talking with people."

That's one of the great lies leaders tell themselves: that the people whose work they control or oversee should take the majority of their time, and the people whose work they cannot control should wait until next month, or next year, or forever. This lie comes back to haunt them, because after such protests, the predictable then happens the next week: The people they can't control take control of their work.

You've read the news stories. Regulators shut down factories, lenders call in the company's debt, the media pans year-end performance, or an investor co-opts the game plan. That's when, if you're that leader, you get a terrible sinking feeling: You're bent on controlling your destiny, but you've just lost control—all because you didn't build the right relationships with the right people in a growing and increasingly sophisticated stakeholder universe.

How can this happen? When you're busy, it's easy to convince yourself that your critical focus should be chain-of-command relationships with core constituencies, namely your employees, customers, and funders. But that thinking won't survive an encounter with reality: As your organization grows and changes, you're likely to be caught off guard if you continue to view stakeholders in an insular way and don't develop higher capabilities to engage them.

We know of what we speak. John Hillen started as CEO of GTEC (Global Defense Technology & Systems) when the Northern Virginia-based company was privately held with $140 million in sales.[39] In his first few years he concentrated on managing people in his three most critical stakeholder groups: employees, customers, and the owner. With employees, he developed an elite corps of high-tech professionals in national security. With customers, he championed the benefits of GTEC's best-in-class technology, along with the expertise of authorities like John Brennan, former head of the CIA's counter-terrorism center and later director of the CIA. With the company's owner, he preached investment growth through expansion into an unfilled corner of the market for national security services.

By focusing on building relationships with and influencing just these three stakeholders, Hillen helped GTEC grow to over $200 million in sales within 18 months. But then the rules of his leadership game changed, because GTEC needed an injection of new capital to grow faster and realize its market potential. In 2009, GTEC sought to go public to raise funds. That's when Hillen, who thought of himself as a best-in-class pitchman and relationship builder, began to feel out of his element as the range of stakeholders he had to influence suddenly expanded.

Hillen, a former US assistant secretary of state, had a stellar track record of successful persuasion. He had helped talk presidents, kings, princes, prime ministers, generals, and scores of foreign officials into working more closely with the United States on a range of high-stakes national security issues. A Wall Street veteran, he had closed scores of deals with customers and government agencies. But now he was out of his comfort zone, and at first he didn't know it.

In preparation for the IPO, Hillen went to New York for a dress rehearsal of his pitch. He faced a much more sophisticated—and entirely new—crowd of listeners. In a Manhattan high-rise, he stood before cameras streaming his entire twenty-minute pitch to a new Wall Street constituency. He knew that the story of GTEC's vision for its place in the high-tech government contracting market was compelling—it practically told itself. Moreover, the company was highly successful. What could go wrong?

Hillen had practiced the pitch at least a hundred times and felt he could recite it in his sleep and win everyone over. He profiled for the Wall Street group the company's most prestigious contract, which was to create key systems for the FBI's Terrorist Screening Center—high-tech, mission-critical, expert-intensive. And when he finished, he thanked the listeners warmly, feeling as if he had just done a great job.

But the audience of twenty-five bankers and analysts, along with others watching on video link, expected more. "You may think you know your business, but you don't know how to talk about your business to us," he recalls bankers, stockbrokers, industry analysts, and investors complaining. They didn't want to hear about the company in the same way he talked to employees or customers—cool tech, cool mission, committed high-security-clearance employees. They didn't want him to replay that old tape, the one that had always snapped his traditional stakeholders to attention. They wanted to hear about how an investment in GTEC could create wealth for their clients, GTEC's potential investors.

Hillen stalled because he hadn't addressed the nuanced interests of parties who could make or break GTEC's future success. His presentation was sweet candy for employees and customers. But at time of a severe recession, it tasted like stale bread to these new stakeholders. "I spoke intelligently and accurately," he later recounted, "but in completely the wrong way for my new audience. They probably thought, 'How did this idiot ever become an assistant secretary of state and CEO—he can't understand or influence anyone.'"

"This was a real aha moment," he recalls. "The great influencer had been exposed."

He was exposed because he had not grasped the sophistication of the stakeholder network in which he, a soon-to-be public-company CEO, was being called to manage. What did these constituencies value?

The answer required a new way of thinking. Shareholders valued evidence of steady revenue growth, business development, and a hot market. Analysts valued a predictable business model that they could explain to investors. The media valued a fresh story, at a time of an IPO drought, about a growth company in Washington, DC. Bankers were looking for a story about a company that could make waves in the market and might one day become a hot acquisition target. In his new universe, Hillen was not reaching or influencing the constituencies that could make or break the company's success.

Every leader needs to understand and effectively engage the universe of people with and through whom they and their organization will accomplish their objectives. However, in our experience of working with scores of executives, we have observed that leaders hoping to perform at the next level often ignore the people they most need to reach. These may be people who speak the same language and embrace the same values—your employees, vendors, and often customers. But they might also speak a different language and have different values, for example if they are investors, regulators, the press, competitors, politicians, community leaders, and advocacy groups.

Stalls can happen in both cases. In the first, you are challenged to manage "down and in," that is, largely down through the ranks and inside and across your organization. In the second, you are challenged to manage "up and out," where you increasingly must manage relationships outside the organization with people beyond or above your normal circle of influence. In Hillen's case, he didn't at first grasp that his "up and out" stakeholder world had grown so quickly and in such an elaborate way. At the time, he had fourteen direct reports who had long demanded most of his time. But they were now just one group of stars in a wider constellation of stakeholders—and in fact the easier ones to manage.

A new insight dawned on Hillen: "One of the reasons it's lonely at the top is because you don't control your own future."

The truth is, the higher you go, the less control you have—at least directly. And when you don't build a network of influence, you also lose indirect control—and you will stall.

Of course, as your stakeholder network grows, you can restructure to exert control. In your organization, this might mean adding new reporting lines, a matrix organization, steering committees, work groups, and so on. Across your industry or sector, it might mean adding structural elements to coordinate everyone's work. But trying to manage a growing and more complicated stakeholder network only with structure will yield diminishing returns.

Instead, you must think about developing sophisticated capabilities to deepen relationships. Your down-and-in network might include people you need to touch daily, or week-in and week-out, to be successful in achieving your outcomes. But the more strategic network you likely need to invest more time and effort in is your up-and-out network. It will include people who can shape your future but might not affect your day-to-day operations.[40]

In Hillen's case, he had started to build a strategic network of industry analysts, press, and others: the people who control allocation of investor capital or influence opinion. But he stalled because his longtime focus on minding people down and in the business initially blocked him from grasping the change. His and GTEC's success was now tied more to influencing the new up-and-out stakeholders. He had not adapted his thinking to understand the new stakeholders that day in the conference room in Manhattan.

Like Hillen, you will stall if you don't see that your stakeholders will change—and probably quickly—as your job changes. You will need to understand each of these new people and invest in meaningful dialogue with them. And you will need to deepen relationships and exert influence not via conventional management communications channels but rather with the sophisticated capabilities of a leader adept at stakeholder management. As our friend Sid Fuchs notes, if you wait until you need that network to build it, it's too late.[41] That's when you're left asking, "What happens now?"

Beware: Adrift in the Stakeholder Universe

In our experience with leaders, the idea that you need to wield influence where you don't or can't wield control is not news. But many leaders mistakenly believe that the conventional tools of management are all they need. They get frustrated when they can't just pull the strings on organizational marionettes to get stakeholders to act. We hear leaders lament,

"I wish I could just tell them what to do." Or "I wish they would listen better." This is the first and most obvious warning sign of a stall and a need to reinvent yourself as a more sophisticated leader.

An example of that kind of frustration can be seen when some leaders shift to civilian life from command positions in the military. Dawn Halfaker, CEO of Halfaker and Associates, founded her Arlington, Virginia, firm after her military service was cut short by a serious injury. Caught by a rocket-propelled grenade in Iraq, she woke from a coma in the US, stunned to find she had lost her right arm. She understood her command of a platoon was over, but she was determined to "continue to serve," so she launched a firm to provide, among other services, medical and health IT solutions focused on saving lives on the battlefield.

Halfaker recalls how different from the military her leadership role felt as her 2006 startup grew from five people in one room to dozens in many offices.[42] "What I didn't appreciate was that in the military if something was wrong, I could bark an order, or I could have a platoon sergeant reprimand private so-and-so for doing whatever," she says. This dovetailed as well with her experience as a Division 1 college basketball player. "As an athlete," she says, "I was very much in control of what I was doing. I was a good player. I knew I was a good player. I knew I could score."

But knowing how to put up points in her new leadership role was different. During her startup phase, Halfaker and Associates ran easily under her control because everyone was located together. But that control became more tenuous as the company expanded to serve a range of agencies in the government, from the Departments of Defense and Veteran Affairs to the Departments of Transportation and Agriculture. The challenge was that in supplying new cyber security, data analytics, software engineering, and IT infrastructure to her customers, Halfaker and Associates not only had to please the direct customer but also the federal agencies that regulated how they worked with the government.

Halfaker's most recent challenge has been meeting hiring quotas for veterans. As a wounded warrior, she sought out the opportunity to help others similar to herself find employment. In fact, she has been a proponent of that cause in several roles, including serving as chair of the nonprofit Wounded Warrior Project. But delivering on that promise meant shouldering the challenge of building the right relationships and influence with people inside and outside her company in ways she had never done before.

"It's a very nuanced question," she says of her work in trying to develop new skills that have nothing to do with giving orders. "Dealing with so many stakeholders, it's about having a flexible mentality, automatically reacting and thinking through what this person is trying to accomplish, what's motivating them, reading that, and then figuring out how do I make the situation a win-win." Without that sophisticated set of capabilities, she couldn't be the supportive leader she wanted to be in a company of young, civilian professionals. She admits that she still struggles with this role.

Another warning sign of a stakeholder stall is when you realize you're spending a lot of time with people in your organization whom you like and feel comfortable with. What about the senior people in your organization whom you choose not to deal with because they have different points of view or agendas, or because they don't always tell you what you want to hear? Or because they're not supportive? Or because you're worried they'll hijack your agenda? Are you spending time with the people whose confidence you need to advance your future? Do you even know who these people are?

We like the story told about Dick Parsons, former CEO of Time Warner, when he reacted to activist investor Carl Icahn's campaign to get him to spin off Time Warner Cable and buy back $20 billion in Time Warner stock. Most CEOs lock the doors when outsiders like Icahn storm the castle walls. They stall completely in exercising skills to influence a stakeholder whom they believe is likely to hurt or impede their ability to advance their company's goals.

But Parsons asked Icahn if he could visit.[43] The two didn't come to agreement when Parsons dropped in on Icahn for a forty-minute chat, and Icahn's bid was hostile and ultimately failed. But the point is, if you can't remember the last time you sat down with a stakeholder entirely out of your comfort zone—an industry competitor, if not a shareholder activist—you may be avoiding the sophisticated challenge of developing the relationships with the biggest payoffs.

Often the most critical stakeholders are not the ones you think they are—even if they are right in front of you. As an example, a chief executive we once knew believed his organization needed a fundamentally new strategy. He had been the architect of the company's prior strategy, a highly successful global reorganization, and he was lauded across the company for his commitment, intelligence, and strategic capability. To develop this new strategy, however, he essentially locked himself alone in his office for the better part of eighteen months. When he finally unveiled his work, he was addressing a gathering of the company's top 120 executives at a posh conference center. What do you think happened?

Launching into a PowerPoint presentation of his vision, he got only as far as slide 3 when he was assailed by criticism. No matter how smart his thinking—and on paper the strategy was indeed brilliant—by disappearing into his office for a year and a half he had locked critical stakeholders out of his zone of influence. He had barred the doors rather than gaining input and support. He should have recognized this behavior as a warning sign of a stall of his own making. Unable to do so, he held an ill-fated meeting that toppled him from his position of influence. Within a year he was no longer running the company.

How could a brilliant CEO, of all people, not see this folly? Because he was relying entirely on his intellect. He was the smartest guy in every room, with degrees from the world's best universities. But he had not seen the handwriting on his office wall: You are not going to win without reaching out to your most vital stakeholders to understand, appreciate, and meet their needs. What if, instead, he'd taken even 20 or 30 percent of the time he'd spent devoted to crafting perfect slides and invited the sixty most influential and challenging of his senior colleagues to individual lunches, sketched a few ideas on a napkin, and said, "Here's what I'm thinking—I'd love your thoughts and input?"

One final warning sign of the stakeholder stall is the one we opened the chapter with. Feeling overworked, you say, "I'm too busy." Too busy to invest time in meaningful dialogues with key stakeholders or groups. Too absorbed in the daily grind to have big-picture future-looking conversations with customers or investors. Too rushed to eat lunch with board members or visit peers in sister organizations. We hear the "too-busy" complaint all the time. We lead workshops on how to build strategic networks and effectively manage stakeholders, and at the end someone will always mutter, "This is great stuff—I wish I had time to do it."

We feel empathy for such people, because we've made the same mistake in our thinking and behavior. Earlier in his career the coauthor of this book, Mark Nevins, was global head of people development at consulting firm Booz Allen Hamilton. He had been lucky enough to adopt the firm's general counsel as his mentor, and they had lunch together three or four times a year. As the coffee was being poured at the end of one such lunch, his mentor noted, "You and I have these great lunches every few months. I have about twenty or thirty fellow senior partners in this firm—how often do you have lunches with any of them?"

Nevins didn't miss a beat: "I'm too busy to have that many lunches—I have so much to get done." Even as he responded, he recognized the lameness of his excuse. The general counsel looked at him with a wry smile, "Those lunches are probably the most important work you can do."

So when you say, "I'm too busy," don't be surprised if you find yourself in a stall. Leaders who make this mistake often later tell us, "Why are my stakeholders not on board? I sent them the information. Didn't they get it? I don't have the time to sit down and explain it to each of them—I'm trying to run a company for crying out loud!"

The same leaders complain they haven't gotten any "real" work done because they're getting waylaid by the demands of stakeholders—investors or analysts or the press or their industry association.

Beware if you have concluded, even unconsciously, that conversations with stakeholders are distractions from your "real" work. With every passing month as a leader you will need to depend on people you didn't depend on before. The web of support required from stakeholders grows inexorably—and so it should if you're leading a growing and changing organization. You must learn to appeal to the values of all your stakeholders, become adept at adapting to their needs and perceptions, and spend meaningful time with them to look at your business and the world side-by-side while developing open and trusting relationships. Merely sending out missives without sending yourself out to engage with key stakeholders will accelerate your stall.

WARNING: YOU'VE HIT A STAKEHOLDER STALL

You wish you could still give orders to get things done, but the people who determine your success are increasingly outside your direct control. You want to influence them, but they all seem to have other agendas—and you're so busy you neglect the task altogether.

Assess: Are You in a Stakeholder Stall?

How do you discover for yourself if you have stalled in exercising influence through your stakeholders? How do you know you need to reinvent yourself to tackle this growing challenge? You do so by exploring whether you understand the people with whom, and through whom, you'll accomplish your most important objectives. Doing so requires answering some questions that are at the core of more sophisticated leadership: How does influence flow? How can engagement with others help?

With whom could meaningful dialogue lead to improved outcomes in your work both today and tomorrow?

How's Your Cartography?

The best way to start this exploration is by creating a stakeholder map. Many leaders resist drawing one, because they believe they have an intuitive grasp of their network of influence and have already connected the dots between themselves and the others on whom they depend. A stakeholder map sounds fairly basic—after all, it's taught in entry-level project management programs. But experience shows that although a few people seem to manage brilliantly by intuition alone, the majority don't really understand their network.

When you hold yourself accountable to sitting down and drawing a stakeholder map, you will almost certainly realize that your tacit assumptions and mental models are not accurate, complete, or up-to-date. That's why you should go through the mapping exercise from scratch. On a blank sheet of paper, list all your stakeholders, an inventory of all the players and how they relate to you and your objectives. Then configure the names into a graphic you devise on a 11- by 17-inch sheet of paper, depicting the network of stakeholders in whatever way makes sense to you.

There's no standard template for a stakeholder map, because there's no standard way in which people visualize or illustrate the universe of people with and through whom they will get things done. The exercise helps you discover your own personal cartography. Your map might look like a flow chart, a spider graph, a 2 × 2 matrix, a series of concentric circles, or something else altogether. One of our clients even drew his map as the petals of a flower.[44]

There are only two rules for drawing your map. First, don't draw a standard organization chart. Org charts lie. They may capture the structure of a hierarchy, but they don't capture the sophistication of relationships or patterns of collaboration. Those relationships differ markedly from an org chart's boxes and lines.[45]

Second, put specific people on your map, not just categories of players or groups. When you form relationships, they are with people—not institutions. Which individuals can help you win? What is each individual's agenda and objectives? Who may oppose you? Who do you need something from? Who needs something from you? Who is affected by your team's work? Who can, and will, influence outcomes? Or stand in the way?

Don't lapse into drawing boxes that merely highlight people's organizational roles or jobs. Make your map a people-centric view of your relationships. When John Hillen was an assistant secretary of state, his staff members would sometimes say, "The White House is against that." Hillen would quip that buildings are not for or against anything. "*Who* in the White House is against it?' he would then ask, "Let's go talk with them to find out why."

Once you've drawn your map, assess each of your stakeholders. Do you see eye to eye with them? Can you collaborate with them effectively? Do they return your calls? Do you like them and trust them—and vice-versa? Do you spend enough time together? Grade the quality of your relationship with an A, B, or C. Or mark strong and productive relationships with a plus (+) sign; neutral ones with a 0; and sketchy or troubled ones with a minus (–) sign.

We expect you'll be surprised at what you discover and learn as you draw your map. Almost all executives we've worked with who have resisted this exercise as "busy work" come back somewhat amazed at how creating the map made them think differently about the relationships they needed to achieve results. They recognized they had a *lot* more stakeholders than they thought; that they weren't spending enough time with the right people or on the right topics; and that they were avoiding a handful of critical influencers. Their maps made them think more honestly about soured relationships that threaten to trip them up.

With the map in hand you should start to think about action items: "There are important relationships at my peer level that need work—I'm not spending enough time with Luis or Kathy." Or, "Three or four influential senior leaders or board members probably don't have a good enough idea of how I see the future of our business." Or, "My network of relationships is smaller and more internally focused than I expected—I have gaps I need to fill or bridge." Or, "I have really comfortable relationships with Stephanie and Joel—am I spending too much time with them?"

Keep your map updated. Treat it as a living document, because your network evolves as quickly as your organization. If you don't freshen up the map periodically, you risk letting established lines of authority mislead you about the real lines of influence. You also risk not pinpointing key stakeholders with whom you need stronger relationships.

When Hillen stalled before the sophisticated crowd in that Manhattan high-rise, it wasn't because he didn't have the skills to persuade people. It was because he had not mapped the new connections explicitly, and in turn had not inquired deeply enough to know the terms of conversation that would resonate with people in the new court of opinion. When he cited the Terrorist Screening Center contract without indicating why outside stakeholders might value it, he revealed his mindset as a CEO of a private company.

The stakeholder map he held in his head came from formerly managing mostly employees and customers. Both constituencies prized the contract because they were battling on the front lines to protect the homeland. They were reminded of this lofty purpose daily, as they regularly passed through the Terrorist Screening Center headquarters entrance way, where a monument was erected from bent and burned steel girders from the September 11, 2001, attack on New York's World Trade Center.

The twenty people listening to Hillen had different goals and motivations in mind. These new and powerful stakeholders wanted to hear about how GTEC's sensational contract mattered to them in *their* jobs. "None of what I said really appealed," he recalled later. His mental rendering of stakeholders had many lines leading down and into the organization, but too few up and out. He lacked a perspective that would have tipped him off to the blank spots on the map that he needed at the higher level, as the leader of a public company. He illustrates why a stakeholder map, updated regularly, can be so revealing. It can alert you to the parochialism of your mindset, and it can indicate how you may be misallocating time among both known and overlooked stakeholders.

Who Has Power? And Interest?

Another way to evaluate whether you have stalled in adopting the right mindset to manage your stakeholders is to use the classic power/interest grid shown in Figure 4.1. This grid encourages you to sort stakeholders into four quadrants, classically called "Players," "Context-Setters," "Crowd," and "Subjects"—and in doing so helps you to answer some basic questions: Who has the power to affect outcomes I care about? Who has interest in what I am doing? Who has both? Or neither?

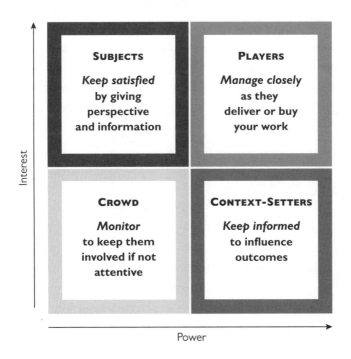

Figure 4.1 The Power/Interest Grid

If you organize your stakeholders into the appropriate boxes on the grid, you'll be able to determine even more clearly if you risk stalling by not appropriately investing the right efforts with the right people:

» *Players* are people with high power and high interest whom you should engage, understand, collaborate with, and satisfy—regularly and always. These are your most important stakeholders.

» *Context-setters* are people with high power but low interest whom you may tend to give short shrift to. That's dangerous, because they can hurt your results or shut down your work. You should work to deepen relationships here and find ways to increase their levels of interest.

» *Subjects* are people with low power and high interest whom you should keep in the loop. They may not control your results, but they are often inclined to be supporters, evangelists, and your eyes and ears to understand how other stakeholders are thinking.

» *The crowd* includes people with low power and low interest whom you're inclined to ignore—after all, they don't care and they can't wield influence. But monitor them, because as things shift, they may gain more power and/or more interest.

What insights might you glean once you plot your stakeholders into this grid? You probably have a good idea of how to handle people like your boss and peers. But what about others? Have you overlooked an operations head who will determine your success in a supply-chain initiative? Or a board member whom you think has no interest in your work, only to discover later that she won't advocate an investment you have a lot riding on? Or a Wall Street analyst whom you could have reached out to before he criticized your financial results in the press?

What does the grid tell you about the sophistication of your approach to engaging the people who can most affect your success? Or how you can reduce the amount of resistance or antagonism from people who oppose your priorities or philosophy? Who can best help you achieve your objectives? Remember Hillen's experience: People with no previously apparent power may suddenly have all the power that counts at your next turning point.

Where's Your Horizon?

Another way to assess a potential stall in managing stakeholders is to diagram what we call your stakeholder horizon, as shown in Figure 4.2. The horizon line delineates which stakeholders are "down and in" in the organization and which are "up and out."

Figure 4.2 The Line of Control

The stakeholders below the horizon line are those you can control, at least to some extent. The stakeholders above the line are those you have to engage and move via influence alone. If you're a rising leader, the diagram often depicts existing stakeholders as below the horizon, and new ones above. It reflects the range of people who might be relevant as you operate in a more sophisticated stakeholder environment, where invariably you're going to have to dedicate a bigger share of your time to stakeholders above the horizon.

The difference between the two hemispheres, when it comes to how you think about influence, is pretty stark. Below the horizon, or line of control, you can often manage organizational change and growth by applying more of the methods and tools of complexity: new information systems, new forms of organization or structure, new processes, new reports, new meetings, and so on. Above the line, you have to apply a more sophisticated mindset and behaviors: dialogue, questioning, more open-ended conversations, and really listening to understand. That's the only way you can connect with people whose view of creating value differs markedly from yours.

Now that you've put your stakeholders on a map and in a grid, locate them at the right point above or below the horizon. Note that as you go farther above the horizon, few of the people who affect your destiny contribute directly to short-term value in your organization. As a result, we often hear managers and executives protest, "But they have their own agenda—they don't work for me." True enough. But if you are trying to manage your organization only by managing people down and within the ranks, you're likely in a stall.

Ask yourself: When was the last time I looked up? How much of my time is spent influencing people on the organization chart versus not on it? Be honest: Which relationships are most critical to your success and the success of your enterprise? Wouldn't you benefit from shifting from command-and-control based on processes, reports, and data to command-and-influence based on culture, relationships, and leadership?

In growing companies, one of the most common triggers for a stakeholder stall is the effort to go outside to raise money—often humorously referred to as OPM, "other people's money." That's when you become accountable to new, demanding constituencies who require intensive management. When you're dealing with OPM, you have to serve above-the-horizon constituencies in a new way. The same is true in government and nonprofit enterprises when you're accountable to the public and politicians. If you deal with OPM and you think you might have stalled, ask yourself whether you have actively managed relationships with your above-the-line stakeholders.

How Do You Dialogue?

One further way to test the nature of your stakeholder stall is to reflect on how you connect with others. How do you engage in conversations that really matter? Whether you're working over or under the horizon line, how do you initiate dialogue? Do you have the capability to engage people and get them to open up to you to assess problems and opportunities and create solutions together?

When clients call us, whatever their level, they often hope we can help lubricate the squeaky wheels of their stalled organization. They usually don't believe that the rusting parts causing the squeaks come from their own stall—they are thinking they come from malfunctioning organizational machinery. These leaders are often mistaken, as we usually find the bigger problem is with how they are engaging and dialoguing with their stakeholders.

So what kinds of dialogue are you fostering in the service of managing your stakeholders to your organization's benefit? As an example, recall Dawn Halfaker, CEO of Halfaker Associates, and her challenge to hire more veterans. Her commitment to mainstreaming veterans into civilian business was initially a social-minded personal commitment. She then made it a way to differentiate her business. Once she put new goals for veteran hiring into her firm's strategic plan, and set new targets, she had to reconsider whether she was reaching the right internal stakeholders to achieve those goals.

That effort became especially urgent when her government customers, attracted by her strategy, made veteran-hiring percentages a requirement in Halfaker Associates contracts. Halfaker recognized she had to ask herself the same question all leaders must as their ambitions grow: Am I having the right conversations with the right people in my company? Says Halfaker, "I can't just sit in office, send email, and pound my fists and say, 'Hit the target, hit the target.' I have to get out there and work with folks to find the win-win."

Halfaker had work to do to sell her initiative more broadly to internal stakeholders. One of her stakeholder groups was her recruiters, another was operations, and another was finance and accounting. She eventually determined that the recruiters were critical but overlooked. She went to her company's lead recruiter and initiated a dialogue: "Here's what we need to do," she said, "How do you think we should go about it?"

That was a conversation that mattered. It led to the recruiter developing a veteran-hiring initiative in which Halfaker and Associates recruits veterans as interns straight out of military service—veterans entirely new to civilian jobs—and rotates them through different parts of the business. Though Halfaker exercised her leverage as a boss, she demonstrated that success in building relationships with stakeholders often has little to do with lines on the organization chart. "The win-win," she says, "was that people were excited to take on the challenge, being entrepreneurial in coming up with solutions, and having incentives to meet targets and feel good that they're doing something important in our society." That all happened because she adopted a new way of approaching stakeholders.

Having the right conversation may not be easy if you are an assertive problem solver. That's because you may have to loosen up on your "just do it" approach. That approach, so common in top performers, may in and of itself cause you to stall. Are you fostering dialogue to generate the views needed to identify the best options? If you're the bull that drives the herd forward without looking left, right, or back to stakeholders, you're likely to break some china.

If you have doubts about whether your capabilities in handling dialogue are up to the task, ask your direct reports. Better yet, ask your spouse or significant other.

Meanwhile, test how your approach is working on multiple levels. Check both in your organization and outside, below the horizon line and above. Where aren't critical conversations happening? How can you enable them? Don't find yourself like that CEO who didn't present his vision, engage in dialogue, get input and buy-in—and was later shot down in a group session, grandstanded by 120 top leaders.

Recover: Getting Your Stakeholder Bearing

If your assessment suggests you're stalling because you haven't, or can't, identify, schedule, and engage in the right kinds of conversations with stakeholders, we suggest a few specific actions for reinvention. Each one focuses you on adapting the way you think about managing your most important stakeholders. With a level of intent and deliberateness, you can think and act in more sophisticated ways to markedly expand your range of influence.

The Touch Agenda

Hierarchy, organization charts, chains-of-command, reporting relationships—they all have a place in your life as a manager. As your organization grows and becomes more complex, more moving parts are required to keep everything working smoothly. But as you mature as a leader, you'll have to turn more to informal networks for insight and influence, and you'll have to develop the sophistication to have these most important conversations. The sooner you change, the more effective you'll become in managing the stakeholders you do control and those you don't.

To cultivate this sophisticated capability, create a stakeholder management plan: Using your stakeholder map as a guide, schedule regular conversations and work sessions to build and deepen relationships. Use your plan to establish a habit of figuring out people's positions, perceptions, and expectations—deepening trust, collaborating better, and influencing outcomes. We call this a plan, but you should consider it a commitment to investing in deepening the relationships with the most important people identified in your map, power/interest grid, and line-of-control diagram.

Leaders need to make a habit of building strategic networks to help see stakeholders, understand their assumptions, and respond to their values. As you go about reaching out, determine the questions you must ask to foster better dialogue and gain collaboration and support:

» What do these stakeholders most want or need from me? What are they afraid of or worried about?

» What interest—political, emotional, financial—do they have in what I'm trying to do? Are they supporters or detractors or competitors?

» How can I best engage these stakeholders? In what ways/ styles do they want me to engage?

» Do they understand what I'm trying to accomplish? Can my efforts help them achieve their objectives?

» Do they have a strong relationship with anyone I need to get closer to—and can they introduce me or advocate for me?

» If these stakeholders are resisting what I'm trying to do, how can I turn them around?

One of our clients, a leader who ran a business unit at a prestigious financial services company, spent little time on any of these questions.

Nor did he make much time to reach out to his key stakeholders inside the business. He was whip-smart, innovative, and committed, but he didn't have a relationship-building mentality, to the point that he worried the company's board members. When the CEO told him that other company leaders wanted recognition and attention from him, he still didn't get it. "We're all aligned with our strategy," he claimed, "What's the problem?"

As serendipity would have it, he answered the question himself. As we were talking one day, he opened the top drawer in his desk and pulled out a handwritten note he had once received from another CEO, the celebrated leader of his prior company. He had kept the note as a memento, an inspiration, from his own "best leader ever." He turned to us, showing a new awareness of the motivating power of reaching out to others, and said, "Well, I guess I need to build a 'touch agenda.'"

"A touch agenda." We've used that term ever since. To change the way you think and behave when it comes to stakeholder management, one of the most potent tools is to manage a list of people you must go out and "touch"—build a deeper and more meaningful relationship with, one based not merely on transactional matters. Some leaders do it naturally, but this particular leader was stalled in an old mindset: "Another day, another dollar for the company." He had to work a bit to shift to a new one: "Another day, another dialogue with key stakeholders."

Your touch agenda should highlight how you will invest in the most important relationships in your stakeholder map and power/interest grid. You won't succeed with the mentality that you win at the leadership game by being the smartest person in the room and giving orders to others. You have to ground your relationship-building effort in trust, intimacy, persuasion, and dialogue—the only tools you have when your success depends on people you can't control.

We don't mean to suggest you change your personality. But you do have to change the ways you think and act. Your efforts can't be mere add-ons to your leadership work: You must make them behavioral reflexes, even if they're not natural to you. Depending on your personality, you can tailor your approach. (For example, if you're more introverted, think about focusing on one-on-one interactions—which give the biggest returns anyway.)

Most of us do a lot of our work in meetings, such that we can forget that we dedicate the bulk of our time to managing ourselves, sometimes artificially, in groups. When getting together one-on-one, on the other hand, we all tend to be more relaxed and willing to share. You can better sense how people feel about your ideas. You're also more likely to uncover facts or emotions for enhancing the relationship.

When you're working one-on-one, don't wait for people to come to you. Go out and engage them. Create a personal relationship. Meeting people in their own environments sends a powerful message: I value you enough to go the extra mile. You set the stage for success because people are more comfortable in their own spaces: behind their desk, in a position of dominance, surrounded by their own stuff, relaxed and open. If they need to show you something, they have it right there. They also have personal items on the wall and desk: totems, awards, photos of family. Personal cues help you to better understand them and establish bonds through personal stories and shared experiences.

What happens if you expect your stakeholders to come to you? They may never come at all, since you'll be projecting the impression that you're more important. Or they may be put off and not bring their best self to the conversation. The result is that you get less interaction and miss the chance to strengthen the relationship, and meantime people think you are sending a message that you don't value others.

Similarly, if you seek mentoring, mentors usually feel good about giving help if you approach them openly. People like to be consulted and give advice: It makes them feel included and inclined to support and collaborate. We all have egos, and if you show respect, you encourage connections to flourish, whether during a five-minute meeting, troubleshooting chat, or hallway catch-up. However you reach out to others, recognize that there really is no "efficient" way to do it. You just have to put in the time to build strong relationships. Without them, without enduring relationships with people who know you, understand you, like you, and trust you—you may never get the "real" work done.

Lift and Shift

For thoughtful leaders, a touch agenda can be a helpful prod to look for the best ways, and the best times, to "lift and shift" your gaze to new stakeholders. If you were to highlight your stakeholder map with a marker, you could turn it into a heat map. It would show where you're too warm with people and where too cool, and in turn show where you should refocus your engagement with others on your power/interest grid.

If you're a rising leader needing to lift your attention to people above the horizon line, you'll have to change your "sight picture," a military expression for lifting your gaze across a bigger landscape. Many leaders we work with remember all too well cultivating a new self at this juncture. They recall finding themselves not just looking out the window to the layout of the organization, but across a panoramic landscape extending into the future. They refer to it as "the day every-thing changed."

That's how John Hillen recalls that day in the Manhattan high rise. He was soliciting OPM, and he had no choice but to change from look-ing down and in to up and out. He even recalls going overboard after this revelation. He placed so much emphasis on up and out that he spent much of the next year out of the office. Unintentionally, he neglected his senior managers, who essentially had to self-manage. That meant he again had to fine-tune his sight picture to recover.

Of course, you can't tune every relationship so that it meets A+ quality. That's what Hillen learned. But you can seek high marks across your portfolio of relationships as long as you take a balanced and holistic approach. Hillen recovered by recalibrating his sight picture both inside and outside the organization, taking back into account relationships he had to manage down and in. He shows that at a certain point in your career, if you become a top leader, your real work will be spending most of your time with stakeholders you cannot control. That shift is manageable, because you can delegate many down-and-in management tasks, even while you cannot delegate up-and-out relationship building.

John W. Rogers, Jr., from the last chapter, is a leader who lifted and shifted throughout his career to found Ariel Investments, an investment-management firm based in Chicago, and now with offices in New York City and Sydney. Inside the company of over ninety people, he long ago delegated most authority to President Mellody Hobson. He now takes pride in her growth as an industry leader. She hires her own team and they work collaboratively, but independently, to make their own decisions, keeping Rogers informed about major initiatives.

"I am not always or necessarily involved in the process," he says. "The ability to be autonomous and make decisions provides Mellody with the confidence she needs to create the platform to execute effectively."[46] Rogers's time-tested managerial and investment philosophy are responsible for superior investment results. His long-term track record has been acknowledged within and outside the industry. One such example is his being listed among other greats in Magnus Angenfelt's 2013 book *The World's 99 Greatest Investors*.

Rogers's approach to the larger civic, business, and philanthropic stakeholder community dovetails with those lessons he learned at the feet of Princeton coach Pete Carril in the 1970s. Rogers views his stakeholder world as a set of interconnecting teams. Where these teams intersect and help each other succeed he sees potential in helping his firm achieve success as well.

"The way I've conducted myself in building those relationships has always been to again position myself as a really good teammate who will fight for what is in the best interests of each organization," he says. "The spirit of my involvement is to always think about my team first."

On the one hand, Rogers reaches up and out as part of the African-American business leaders team. That helps him fulfill one of Ariel's corporate values, to promote minority-run businesses. "If we can create more African-American business leaders and more African-American businesses," he says, "we are going to realize higher employment in urban communities, help close the wealth gap in urban communities, and create role models for young people." Among other initiatives, he cites as most successful the founding of the Black Corporate Directors Conference, a group now fifteen years old with a membership of 190 African-American directors attending the 2017 conference.

On the other hand, he reaches up and out as part of the value-investing community. "It is important to keep your eye on the prize—working as part of the group you respect and believe in, striving to make a significant contribution and learning at the same time," he says.

As a routine, Rogers seeks a seat on the investment committees in charge of managing the endowments of various institutions—for example, the University of Chicago, the Chicago Symphony Orchestra, and nearby Rush Presbyterian Hospital. Rogers's involvement has enabled him to meet many investors who are responsible for managing all types of investments from different asset classes, including those who compete with him in value investing. This, in turn, has often led to sharing best practices.

Rogers has also cultivated good relationships with other investors in visits to Omaha, where followers of the Warren Buffett school of investing gather each year for the Berkshire Hathaway annual shareholder meeting—which Rogers has attended for the last sixteen years. "Over time, there's a mutual respect that develops, and you are drawn into this larger group of investors," he says.

Rogers believes it is valuable to keep a stakeholder map in the forefront of his mind. In recent years, he has made his selection of relationships from a stakeholder map in which he puts the University of Chicago at the center. He grew up in the Hyde Park neighborhood of Chicago, attended the University of Chicago Laboratory School, and lives in downtown Chicago. Rogers's parents met at the University of Chicago on their first day of law school, and his mother became the first African-American woman to earn a law degree from the university. Guided in part by his affection for the school, he declined the opportunity years ago to join the board of another prestigious Chicago university. In time, he was offered a board seat at the University of Chicago, where he could serve both the institution he had grown to love as well as the business needs of Ariel.

"I started with the place closest to my heart, but it wasn't lost on me that they had this extraordinary finance and stock-market expertise, and being part of the University of Chicago family is a real blessing." The association with a world-renowned brain trust of professors in economics and finance has aided Rogers in raising the level of insight at Ariel, all as part of seeing the University of Chicago as a hub for his interconnecting teams.

Today, Rogers reaps the rewards of this practice. He brings in professors to coach Ariel employees and speak on the latest research in finance and behavioral finance. He in turn speaks to University of Chicago students, from entering high-school seniors on up through its law and graduate business schools. He also hires talented young professionals, most recently eight from University of Chicago's Lab School, and seven research analysts from its Booth School of Business. "Our ties with the University of Chicago help burnish our firm's reputation and Ariel's brand," he says.

Rogers's story also illustrates that the most senior leaders should expect to spend 80 percent of their time managing at or above the line of control. Counterintuitive as it seems, that 80 percent more than compensates for time lost managing below the line. For many leaders, this mindset is hard to grasp, especially as their stakeholder universe expands like Rogers's to industry and society as a whole.

One CEO we advised, who headed a firm with $120 million in revenue, had long worked down and in almost exclusively. He even edited sales proposals and worked on pricing for every contract. As the company grew, he hired a new CFO, promoted the president to replace himself as CEO, and brought on an advisory board. He then focused on his duties as chairman. With so many of his former duties taken over, he felt the honeymoon of extra time wash over him. He remarked, "I have no idea what I'm going to be doing with my time now."

He would soon learn better. "Don't worry," we responded, "You'll be busier than ever. You're now important as a leader in your industry and not just in your company. Why don't you go have lunch with the CEOs of similar companies that you encounter all the time?"

Still, he was nonplused: "Those are my competitors!"

We responded, "No, they're also your partners!"

As an industry-leading CEO, he was now on a common journey with his industry peers. He needed to exercise his leadership at a new level—still for the good of his company, but now advocating for the interests of the whole industry. His success at this inflection point depended on his ability to navigate in a much bigger and broader landscape. You yourself may never deal in such rarified circles, but the principle is the same at all levels of leadership: As you rise as a leader, you'll hurt your chances for success if you retain a fixed mindset about working with one stakeholder or another as a hindrance.

How About a Fresh Style?

The main capability you need to develop to get over the stakeholder stall and grow as a leader is to foster dialogue in a more sophisticated way. If you think of this as a complexity challenge, you'll assign the task of relationship building to someone else, to public relations or marketing or engineering. But that job of relationship building is and must be *yours* as a leader.

We suggest to clients that they keep track on a calendar, or even create a dashboard, of the time they commit to meaningful stakeholder interaction. The biggest challenge comes from keeping up with outside stakeholders, who are unlike employees or vendors or an owner. You cannot command them to do anything. But you need their support to advance your organization.

The most critical capability required for building these relationships is learning how to balance advocacy and inquiry. Advocating means *telling*, usually pressing for a particular position, course of action, or set of principles. When you advocate, you are persuading or arguing for a point of view or conclusion. Inquiry, on the other hand, is about *asking*. It enables you to see the other side's view and position, rather than driving to change minds or opinions.[47] Most people have a natural "default" preference for one style or the other, which may be a personality trait but could also stem from education or professional training: Law and higher education often teach advocacy, journalism and social work inquiry.

You get the best outcomes when you consciously balance the two. Start by asking, honestly, "What is my natural or preferred style? Is it asking or telling?" If you have doubts, ask others. If you tend toward one style, adopt the other more often. If you feel the urge to draw conclusions, ask open-ended questions. If you usually ask questions, take a stand and push for closure by making a declaration. You'll end up having a much more adaptive style and more success in stakeholder relationships.

One good approach for high-intensity advocators is to pause, suspend your own assumptions, and ask questions to understand what the other person believes: "Before I share my point of view, I'd really like to understand how you see things." You may have to work hard to bite your tongue and hear the other side out. And later, once you have laid out your reasoning, encourage others to challenge it: "Here's my thinking and here's how I have arrived at this conclusion. How does that sound? What makes sense and what doesn't? Am I missing anything?"

Conversely, if your natural style tends more toward inquiry, it may be helpful to take a position more quickly and firmly and see how others respond. Be aware, too, that you may unintentionally come across as opaque if you only ask questions—people want you to share the thinking behind your questions and pull them into building an answer or a new way of looking at things along with you.

Changing your style to be sure you bring out your best self and have the best conversations in the best way ranks among the most sophisticated of leadership capabilities. You are having a dialogue with people you don't control, partners and outsiders among them. We call these "non-transactional conversations." How often do you engage in non-transactional dialogue with your key stakeholders?

The more senior you are, the more non-transactional relationships you will have, and the more your business will depend on these conversations. These are situations where you and your stakeholders can be honest and vulnerable, explore questions without pat answers, and even share concerns and worries. You may not wake up every morning thinking about non-transactional conversations—instead, you're probably consumed by the list of the day's tasks. But you'll know you've gotten past this stall when you start to dream in the language of sophisticated relationships.

Sights On New Stakeholders

The challenge of getting through a stall in stakeholder management brings up a question we suggest you ask throughout this book: "Where are your eyes?" What are you looking at? As your organization gets more complex or runs in a more sophisticated environment, where should you place your focus? What data should you watch and why? What parts of the organization and its processes should you attend to most closely? Which stakeholders should you invest in, and why? In answering those questions, you learn what it means to establish a whole new sight picture.

A few years after GTEC went public, it was taken private again in a private-equity buyout, after which it almost doubled in size over three years. Hillen's sight picture changed again, as he became chairman of the industry trade group. Part of his job now was working on behalf of 450 government services contractors, ranging from smaller firms to giants like Lockheed Martin. He was an industry figure and spokesman, and head of an executive committee with twenty CEOs and a board with seventy CEOs. He was meeting with the secretary of defense and the head of Pentagon procurement on a regular basis.

Obviously, Hillen had to influence at a whole new level to benefit his firm (renamed Sotera Defense Solutions). He needed to let go of many of his longtime company tasks, as he exerted more influence than he ever had before. And once again he had to think differently about his role as a leader, focusing much more on the sophisticated skills required when you can't get results by simply telling people what to do.

And this is the nature of all stall points: Just when you think you have the finer aspects of leadership nailed, you get nailed yourself as circumstances change and you're challenged to press forward in unfamiliar terrain. That's what makes stall points so maddening. You can't tackle increased sophistication with an off-the-shelf response. This approach may work for managing the complexity of an organization, but for dealing with sophisticated challenges you have to evolve to a new and different kind of leadership that's outside your historical sight picture.

And when it comes to stakeholders, you are in a position where you must learn to see a landscape of relationships you didn't or couldn't see before. You have to cultivate relationships in different ways to achieve new levels of success. This is a time when you need to run ahead of your organization in the way we show in our breakout summary below. If you succeed, you will accelerate to a lead position not just with your foot on the performance accelerator but with your hands comfortably controlling the stakeholder wheel.

~Reinventing Your Leadership~
A Stakeholder Stall?

Amplify Your Reach and Influence.

Beware of Danger

- You get frustrated when you can't just give orders to make people perform.
- You have not built a strategic network of influencers.
- You don't see engaging in open-ended inquiry and dialogue as core to your role as a leader.
- You avoid people you don't like, even those who are critical to your success.
- You wish you had the time to talk with stakeholders, but you have too much "real work" to do.
- After some bad press or a run-in with a regulator, you complain about your lack of control of stakeholders.

Assess & Troubleshoot

- Draw a stakeholder map—a depiction of the people with and through whom you will accomplish your objectives. What insights or surprises do you see?
- Assign each of your stakeholders to a power/interest grid. Are you spending enough time with the people who have the biggest effect on your outcomes?
- Draw a horizon line and assign each stakeholder to a position above or below this "line of control." Where has your focus been?
- Ask yourself honestly how you go about fostering dialogue with people. Are you appropriately balancing advocacy and inquiry?

Recover & Reinvent

- Create a stakeholder management plan. Who will you put on your calendar regularly? What kinds of conversations should you be having with them?

- Actively develop a strategic network of stakeholders who exert control over your success but whom you don't directly control.

- Create a lift-and-shift plan, reallocating your time to people with the right levels of power and interest to ensure your success.

- Tune your lift-and-shift plan to include stakeholders you don't control, but who control your future.

- Create a dialogue-tracking system or dashboard to keep yourself honest in your commitment to deepening stakeholder relationships.

CHAPTER 5

"NOBODY GETS IT!"

Stalling When You're Failing to Lead Change

"If you cry 'Forward' you must be sure to make clear the direction in which to go. Don't you see that if you fail to do that and simply call out the word to a monk and a revolutionary, they will go in precisely opposite directions?" —ANTON CHEKHOV, *Note-Book of Anton Chekhov*

"The great enemy of communication, we find, is the illusion of it."
—WILLIAM H. WHYTE, *Is Anybody Listening?*

"**W**hat are the pillars of your strategy?"

That was the question we posed to kick off a leadership development program with the senior leaders of a top-tier professional services firm several years ago. We had come to the firm just as the top partners were implementing a new global strategy. And we wanted to get the conversation about leadership grounded with a review of where the company was going.

Naturally we assumed every partner knew and understood the CEO's new strategy. "Okay, let's recap the key points," we began. "We can then anchor our discussion on what you as leaders will need to do to help the firm move forward in this new direction."

We expected nodding heads and quick bullet-point summaries. Instead, twenty leaders stared back at us with blank faces. This was puzzling. "You are the leaders of this firm," we said. "You *do* understand the strategy, right?"

Finally one wise guy piped up: "To be honest, emails from the CEO are the first ones I delete. We're all thought leaders and rainmakers, and we're way too busy serving clients and driving revenue to read internal memos."

Nobody was listening to the CEO. Should that be a surprise? Maybe, but it happens more often than you'd think. And it's an urgent warning of a stall if you're a leader who sends those kinds of memos. As for this CEO, it confirmed that he had run into what we call the leading change stall.

Whose fault was it? The CEO could point to the organization, a common reaction—"my people aren't listening!" But he would have been pointing the wrong way. *He* was the one who wasn't successfully making his message of change stick. *He* was the one lacking that critical sophisticated leadership capability.

To his credit, the CEO had crafted a great story, very much in the way we described in chapter 2. With input from multiple sources he had neatly framed the strategy and grounded it in a meaningful purpose for both clients and the firm's own professionals. His memo elegantly and concisely recapped the new company narrative. But, as we often say, he had not understood that "transmission is not communication."

Even though the CEO had developed a great story and purpose, he was not delivering his message in a way that people could receive and do something with. He should have been wondering: "Why aren't my senior leaders putting in the effort to understand our new narrative and take ownership? Why aren't they following my lead in communicating this story to all the people they touch?"

The problem was that the CEO's signal was getting lost in the noise. This problem is so common it prompted one of our colleagues, Ron Jones, to coin the "Rule of 100." When it comes to communicating a new strategy in a fast-growing and changing organization, he asserts, "you have to say it one hundred times, in a hundred different ways."[48] Or else nobody listens.

Jones was dumbfounded himself when, in the early 2000s, he was head strategist for Veridian, a high-tech firm later sold to General Dynamics. His strategy had guided the growth of the firm through the dot-com era from $250 million to nearly $1 billion in revenue. And yet at the start nobody knew the basics of that strategy. Now a veteran of strategic makeovers at four high-growth companies, he observes: "People don't get it the first, tenth, or even twentieth time."

Worse, people keep acting in line with the old strategy. "We had strategy sessions, meetings, but people were not taking to it," says Jones. The strategy was to build a firm that delivered cyber security, systems engineering, and related national security work. The aim was to spur growth through acquisitions, to create a midlevel high-tech juggernaut serving government customers.

Jones had stalled in figuring out not *what* to tell people but *how* to deliver the narrative so they cared enough to become believers—indeed to become devotees, disciples, and evangelists. He needed people who lived and breathed the strategy, along with its related values and culture. To lead that effort required change in thinking and behavior. "Not a lot of people were looking for a breath of fresh air," he says. They would just as soon stick with the old strategy, their old behaviors, and a set of realities they were comfortable with.

When your organization grows and changes, it's easy to take one thing for granted: that you can communicate easily, just the way you always have, and that people will "get it" and change. Email, company newsletters, town halls—that's all you need, right? If you think that way when you need to lead change, the sophistication of your growing organization may have outrun your ability to spark people's engagement and catalyze action.

Surprising as it may be, with each new tier of growth and shift in direction, many leaders who expect their people to get with the new program instead can't wait to get behind closed doors to vent their frustration: "Nobody gets it!" We've heard leaders rage about the immovability of their people time and again. They are exasperated when their followers don't buy into what they feel is a clear explanation of purpose, direction, and required change.

The Rule of 100 is a bit tongue-in-cheek, because repetition plays only a partial role in making believers and actors out of people. In fact, repetition is not that sophisticated a skill. What's necessary on top of it is the capability to deliver communications with the right thought patterns, demeanor, and style. That's the activity that will induce organizational change at every level. When you stall without those capabilities, you may have created a meaningful story (chapter 2), aligned your team (chapter 3), and succeeded in influencing stakeholders (chapter 4). But you may not have developed the mental and behavioral repertoire to communicate change as an effective leader in an increasingly sophisticated organization.

Especially during wrenching or dynamic change, you can't get by with just a sound story straightforwardly broadcast. You must also cultivate one of the hallmarks of the sophisticated leader—the ability to hear and speak to your people on *their* terms, not yours, in a way that motivates them to execute.

Many leaders continue to think of communication to drive change as a question of handling complexity. Give the marketing folks the story, they think, and tell them to make it stick. Prepare a public relations blitz with email, press releases, and tweets—and kick it off with a town hall meeting. Print banners and wallet cards and posters, and distribute batches of them to every office. Build training programs and hold retreats.

Albeit necessary, none of these moves to rev up the communication engine can fully have the intended effect, because, typically, they don't elicit your people's *reception* of the message.

You're then caught in the most common of breakdowns to successfully drive change. You're transmitting but nobody's receiving. You may be a practiced organizational emcee, accustomed to being on the organizational soapbox, but you're unable to capture your audience's attention.

Hitting this stall is easy and common. That's because in the past you probably led fewer people and they worked closely with you, often in the same office. To transmit, all you had to do was lean over the cubicle or stand on a chair to shout out the message. Your passion alone charged up your loyal listeners. Alternatively, because change was incremental, you operated like a sports team captain whose athletes work in synchrony. You relied on everyone being attuned to each other's moves: "We play this same game every day—no need for anything but a 30-second huddle." Everyone was on the same wavelength.

But as the organization got more sophisticated, you instituted more dramatic change to take on new, more sophisticated challenges. Although people still heard your words, they didn't always understand or buy into your priorities. You may have had the right story, at the right time, for the right people, but you couldn't figure out the secret to getting people to truly hear your message, or own and act on it.

And you stalled, outrun by your organization. And that's because you were short on developing the capabilities of what we refer to as the "chief explaining officer" of your organization. Those capabilities don't come just from practicing your story again and again—although that's not a bad idea. They come from learning to understand the different ways your followers think and feel, and then speaking to their heads and appealing to their hearts in ways they appreciate, resonate with, and feel energized by.[49]

No matter your level as a leader, *you* are the chief voice and face of the organization. Your followers see you that way. To ensure that your finely crafted message from chapter 2 is received, you must deliver it in a way that's compelling, evocative, repeatable, and spreadable—enough to spur the change you desire. And you have to deliver it simply enough that your followers can deliver it to their own followers in their own voices. Only if people down through the organization hear and embrace the story will they help realize the future you envision.

What's surprising about this stall is that so many leaders let it go on as long as they do before realizing they need to reinvent their leadership approach. As with other stalls, they often endure prolonged pain from poor performance until the crisis of the stall crescendos toward disaster—just as in that professional services firm that wasn't tuning into its CEO's new strategy.

You can't wait forever to ask that fateful question, "What happens now?" When you stall at leading change, you can't see the solution merely as providing more communication more of the time to more people. If you just see your job as rolling out a new communications campaign, you will fail in your aspirations for change. Instead, you must reinvent yourself as a sophisticated leader—the chief explaining officer—and one who cultivates high-voltage two-way communication.

Beware: When People Just Don't Get It

Once again, we know firsthand of what we speak. When Hillen stalled during his difficulty in influencing outsider stakeholders when he was the CEO of GTEC, he also struggled to get his story of change to take hold. Hillen found himself saying just what the CEO at the start of this chapter was probably thinking: "They're not getting it—I thought I'd explained this to them pretty clearly and they're not getting it, and they're not doing things differently."

A leader in three companies previously, Hillen considered persuasion his forte. He was talking to a workforce that certainly had the intellectual capacity to understand what he was talking about. The company's employees included over 1,200 intelligence analysts, IT specialists, engineers, scientists, and others, most with top security clearances. And his pitch was simple: Merge with other similar firms, differentiate services, win new work as a combined team, and move upscale to make more money for everyone.

The narrative didn't take. He explained it more clearly: We're going to merge with other companies, we'll differentiate ourselves as a mid-sized company in an area where usually smaller vendors compete for government business, and we'll then solicit higher-margin business—and bigger jobs—as a prime contractor on more complex projects that customers value more.

Still, the employees and leaders from six different, merged companies were not embracing this new narrative. No matter how Hillen laid

out the rationale, he often got that same blank stare about the path forward. He was seeing the first warning sign of a stall in leading change.

The problem was partly due to the fact that many employees had
more affinity with the government agencies they had served for years
than with the employer who now signed their paychecks. That's the
nature of loyalty for many professionals in the US capital: People often
feel their first allegiance to their national government, the US Navy, or
the National Security Agency. They are mission-driven, after all, doing
good for the government and American people.

But that wasn't the whole explanation. Hillen was challenged to
help people see that becoming protagonists in the new story for GTEC,
the Herndon, Virginia-based technical services contractor, would make
life better for them personally. Hillen not only had to convey his company narrative, but convey it in a way that made people feel excited to
be part of a new, elite corporate force in a competitive market—so elite,
competitive, and thrilling that their allegiance shifted to GTEC.

On one occasion Hillen drove to Maryland to speak with the professionals in an acquired firm, experts in disciplines treasured by the
National Security Agency, such as crypto-mathematics. In a ballroom
packed with 150 employees, he itemized the strategic advantages to the
government. Among his points were that GTEC would offer enhanced
capabilities to customers, and employees would benefit from growth.
He also discussed the opportunity for promotions, the ability to share
in bonuses or equity, and the market influence of a bigger company.

But what he got in return was largely a lack of response. Most people liked what they were doing already. They didn't *want* to hear about
change. They didn't *want* to indulge this new boss. They did understand the virtues of a well-managed growth company—and Hillen got
them to admit as much in a follow-up question-and-answer session.
He also reassured them that GTEC would not smother their beloved
small-company culture with an impersonal bureaucracy.

So what was Hillen not seeing? He was focused mostly on what he
personally found exciting: the power of the strategy. GTEC, eventually

renamed Sotera Defense Solutions, was going to shift its offerings to a blank space on the map of the government-contracting industry. The company would then thrive by having that space all to itself. Hillen pointed to a few graphs that showed how this brilliant "blue water" play would differentiate GTEC and create fresh and profitable projects for everyone in the new, bigger firm.

Despite Hillen's passion for the strategy, however, people just kept on staring. He was trying to energize people for a higher-order existence, but at best he could get no more than polite, crossed-arm silence. He wasn't overly serious. Nor did he try to bludgeon people with his rationale using data or charts. At one point, to inject levity, he played a movie clip from *Jaws* where the shark breaks the surface for the first time to show its Tyrannosaurus-size mouth. Police chief Martin Brody (Roy Scheider) is surprised and wide-eyed.

"You're gonna need a bigger boat!"[50] Brody says to the fishing-boat captain.

Hillen thought this would be a home run: "We [Sotera] are the bigger boat!" he told everyone.

Still, blank stares. Finally, by the twelfth time he pitched to people in the companies GTEC was acquiring, the audience began to resist actively. People were suspicious of growth, suspicious of new pieces of work as being too big and demanding, suspicious even that the company name was showing up in the newspapers. Hillen felt as if people wanted to run up to him and scream, "You're turning the place into a bureaucracy!"

Five months had passed. "I'm losing them, not winning them," he thought. "I'm telling them they'll have better salaries, better promotions, more room to grow. . . and they're not buying it. They don't even seem to care." Wracked with frustration, he made the ninety-minute drive from Columbia, Maryland, to Herndon. That's where Ron Jones, the former executive at Veridian who now served as GTEC's chief strategist and sounding board, greeted him: "How did it go?"

Hillen was vexed. "They just don't get this!" he said, slamming his briefcase on a table.

"How many times have you told them the story?" asked Jones.

"A dozen times!"

"Well," said Jones, his Veridian experience in the top of his mind: "You have 88 times to go!"

And that's when Jones once again reaffirmed his Rule of 100.

That Hillen was 88 times short was not the entire point, of course. It was that he was blaming his audience for the lack of reception. He would reason, "They just *can't* get it."

Of course, Hillen's attitude was a sure sign of a stall for him as the leader. He couldn't even get people to receive the basic message, let alone raise their pulse rates about a better future. If you've hit a leading change stall like Hillen's, you'll see that this is what typifies transmitting without communicating. People may follow the train of your logic, but they don't put trust in your plans and ideas. You think your passion will electrify the room but nobody seems abuzz. If anything, people just resign themselves to following your orders.

Hillen realized belatedly that corporate strategy sounds brilliant only to strategists. As for the workforce in his growing company, many people already had what they wanted out of their professional lives. Hillen's passion for an amazing strategy came across as simply a threat to what they most valued. He realized he wasn't interpreting upcoming changes in a way that showed people their share of the opportunity. His story, to them, was actually un-fascinating. "For me," he recalls, "the warning sign was, here's a CEO practicing his number one skill and the scoreboard is registering zero."

WARNING: YOU'VE HIT A LEADING CHANGE STALL

You are frustrated because people don't seem to understand what you're saying—or they don't change their behaviors because of it. Followers seem disrupted by change. They dislike the idea of it and remain geared only to the status quo. You blame your people for not understanding, getting excited, or acting differently.

Assess: Where Communication Goes Flat

How do you know if you've developed the capability, approach, mentality, and behaviors to communicate change in a way that truly engages people and moves them? If you can't get your people to join in your enthusiasm when you tell the story, you're not doing your job as a sophisticated leader. You are trying to transform your audience of employees into actors simply by wielding position-based power as their boss. The time has come to consider how you can reinvent yourself to communicate with your audience in ways so people want to receive and act on your message with commitment.[51]

Have You Thought About a Plan?

You can start your assessment with the most basic question: Do you have an intentional and explicit communication plan for yourself as a leader? If you're just depending on conventional or ad-hoc efforts to inform and inspire, you're probably too complacent and at risk of stalling. That's because transmission of even a clear story to distracted recipients has little chance of getting a hook into their minds, especially if you're transmitting through a noisy medium.

One of our friends, John Hassoun, former CEO of Vistronix, a Virginia-based technology services company with $200 million in sales, likes to contrast his success in communicating the new vision for his organization during the 2012–2016 period with the mediocre results he achieved when he was the boss of a unit at Veridian in 1998.[52] In the Veridian case, Hassoun was running a division selling a technology to inspect aircraft engine blades. With this product, Veridian eliminated the need to swap out blades at regular, predetermined intervals, saving money from the scrapping of perfectly good blades.

The technology used "eddy current" capability to detect cracks in the blades of F-15 and F-16 fighter plane engines. The system was saving the military millions of dollars, but competitors were beginning to offer cheaper solutions. Hassoun figured Veridian's market position would be overtaken within two years. His vision was to restore the unit's profitability by moving more into logistics and support and less by differentiating itself only on technology.

Hassoun recalls that his first task should have been to better explain to his people that the business couldn't keep running the same way it had been. His engineers, who remained dedicated to refining old technologies, didn't grasp that the company's customers cared more about getting grounded jets back in the air than using any single inspection technology. The engineers, based in Dayton, Ohio, did acknowledge that they had to cut costs, but they didn't take to heart the feedback the operations people in Oklahoma City were passing on from jet mechanics.

"The engineers didn't want to stop research," says Hassoun. "But the client had a mission—maintaining airplanes so they wouldn't be grounded—and the engineers with their research focus were not sensitive to that."

Hassoun needed a plan to bring everyone around. He was a technologist himself, and engagement and persuasion were not high on his personal comfort list. He felt that facts should be enough to persuade people—and that not conveying the facts strongly enough was causing his stall. "The engineers said, 'Screw that, we know what's needed,'" he says. "And I was saying, 'We're here to look after the client, and the client will dictate the new iteration that will help with our sales and opportunities for people'."

Hassoun did eventually guide the unit to profitability by pushing his new vision, and he doubled the unit's revenues to $14 million. But he didn't get the growth he wanted, and the unit hasn't grown much since he left a number of years ago. He cites among other factors that he didn't pull people in to work with him to create the vision (see chapter 2), didn't educate people enough about the needs of the customer (see chapter 4), and didn't make sure they supported the new strategy before rolling it out (again chapter 4). As we shall see, the lessons he learned from these stalls helped Hassoun avoid another and a much bigger stall when he came to run Vistronix.

If you don't have a communication plan, one problem you'll often find is that you may not be connecting the organization of today to the one of tomorrow in ways that matter to your followers and stakeholders. What is the transition roadmap from where you are today to a future state people will energetically embrace? How will the current organization evolve so that everyone wants to be a part of it? What steps will it go through, and have you conveyed to people the changes required along the way? If you haven't, you may not have owned up to the real job of leading change yourself—in which case you will stall.

Have You Surveyed Quality and Quantity?

Another way to assess whether you're in a stall when leading organizational change is to take stock of the quality and quantity of your communications. To start, ask others for feedback. Do some management-by-walking-around. Hold yourself accountable to delivering the story in a way that gets people to sign on as protagonists. Have you followed the 100x rule? Are your leaders and followers taking initiative to make the story come alive in their own work and the work of the people they oversee? Do you have a routine to generate feedback to get a regular reading of how the change is going?

Transmission is measured on the receiving end. Are you hearing anything back from people? Check performance reviews, executive assessments, 360-degree evaluations, and other survey instruments. What do they tell you about people's understanding of the story you're trying to communicate? Are they inspired enough to act on it? Can you infer the quality of your capability in having your message received?

As for quantity, in our work with executives we've have never once heard a leader criticized for *over*-communicating. Having had a chance to review hundreds of executive assessments, performance reviews, and 360-degree feedback reports, we've seen just about every possible communication sin: failing to communicate clearly, vagueness in strategic intent, lack of conviction, failure to address what's most important, dishonesty or obfuscation, and just plain not communicating enough. But we've never seen "communicates too much" as a criticism. "Paula doesn't have to keep talking about the strategy so much—we all get it and we're on board" never comes up.

Getting feedback is a direct measure of whether you've been communicating enough. The feedback can show whether you've completed the communication circuit: transmission and reception in one direction followed by transmission and reception in the reverse. Have you cycled through the feedback circuit—maybe even cycled several times? Do you ask for feedback and actually get it? Have you nurtured a feedback-rich organization? As the traditional Prayer of St. Francis says, "O, Divine Master, grant that I may not so much seek to be understood as to understand."

The ultimate measure of whether you're communicating the message of change effectively is whether you're spurring ongoing conversations. Do you trigger a give-and-take that guides people in fitting the organization's story into theirs, giving them enough time to reflect on it and to embrace it as their own? Do people "get" the story clearly enough to be able to reframe it in their own terms, summarize it, and tell it back to you? If people don't see their work as a compelling episode in the saga of their own lives, they won't have much energy for coming to the office every day.

One way to dig more deeply into whether you're succeeding as a chief explaining officer is to conduct a version of the "honest conversations" exercise popularized by Russell Eisenstat and Michael Beer at Harvard Business School.[53] Ask a group of high-potential people down through the ranks of your company to tackle a tough organizational problem: an innovation conundrum, a growth challenge, outdated cultural behaviors, or a roadblock to success or profitability. Give that team the authority to talk with *any* employee who might have a useful perspective. And then demand that the team report back what they find—no holds barred.

Like good detectives, your team of investigators will come back with many observations and insights related to opportunities to take a giant step forward. They'll also point out impediments to success. Usually their observations will be points of view that will surprise you or force you to challenge your own assumptions about how well you're getting through to people.

As a matter of protocol, when your people are reporting back at an honest conversations roundtable, you may only *listen*. You're not allowed to debate or qualify or "correct" the team—and that's what makes this technique so powerful. You will end up hearing things you didn't want to hear, that make you uncomfortable, and that perhaps you doubt are true. You may learn about unclear strategic direction, poor execution, confused teams, lack of morale, and a workforce uncertain about what's going on. Your puffed-up notions of how well people have received your messages and how they are acting in response may be deflated.

This exercise obliges you to face your stall without getting sidetracked by barriers to honest feedback. One barrier is flattery from people who won't break silence about problems that everyone knows exist ("elephants in the room"). Another is hesitancy to address emotionally charged issues that can block forward motion ("hot-button topics" or "sacred cows"). A third is your limitations in executing the cycle of transmission and reception ("blind spots"). An honest conversations exercise, though it may feel uncomfortable, will help you understand how to change. You probably need to reinvent yourself to influence people to accept change and keep them committed, even though *they* may feel discomfort.

When Hillen was CEO of Sotera, Nevins guided an "honest conversations" exercise for the company. Nevins was convinced that, however simple the concept, it would help Hillen see that his narrative wasn't getting through as well as he thought. At the time, Sotera was running radio ads about having the best people in the industry. Hillen himself believed in the organization's distinctive behaviors, capabilities, and results. But young up-and-comers didn't seem to be buying into Hillen's conviction about the unique strategic position the company held in the industry.

Hillen chose twenty-five of his brightest young managers for the "Honest Conversations" exercise. When they reported out their findings in the follow-up round table, he remembers one shock above all others: "Nobody thought we were special." People felt Sotera was pretty good at what it did, but they thought other companies were just as good. Nobody saw how Sotera had differentiated itself. Hillen had not successfully communicated even to his own people the company's unique industry position. "We don't believe our own radio ads!" he recalls thinking.

If you send off a hot-shot team of people into your organization to look into why things aren't working, prepare for just these kinds of surprises. When people seat themselves at a table facing you and your senior team, and you promise them the license to be honest, you'll be amazed as they describe what they heard in their investigations. Some of the feedback may be painful to hear, since it will expose how you've stalled as a leader in effecting change. However, being willing to listen honestly will help you learn what you can do to get yourself and your organization back on track.

Do You Know What People Value?

Another way to assess whether you've stalled in leading change is to look into whether you've adequately understood and appealed to what your people care about. Are you someone who values strategy above all—even though your people don't? Are you able to speak to them on their terms? Do you even understand how their terms differ from yours? Do you know what they care most about? When you need to spur change and people yearn to put a firm foundation under their feet, you must be able to tap into precisely the benefits that appeal to them.

When we talk about what people value, we aren't referring directly to the values that are embedded in your organization's culture. Your grip on that culture, and how it fits in the narrative, may help you develop the best terms in which to communicate and partly informs your message. But people need or want many improvements in what they value in *their own* lives in addition to a plan for bolstering the organization's values and principles.

At Sotera, Hillen should have plumbed what his new employees valued early on, and again with each new acquisition. Had he done so, he might have avoided more than a few frustrating days trying to get his communication to stick and resonate. What was it about Sotera's strategy that worried people? What could Hillen highlight to reassure people that the big company culture was not going to squash the small-company ambiance? How could he allay fears that he was going to create a bureaucratic mire and suck the fun out of their jobs? How could Sotera offer a promise of a better life for the likes of a PhD crypto-mathematician?

Bruised by earlier rebuffs, Hillen did some soul-searching to examine whether he had been seeing the strategic benefits through his people's eyes. When he posed the question of what people valued, the answer was sitting right in front of him. The problem was not the strategy or even his general narrative. It was the particular elements of the story he was stressing, as well as the lack of stressing the right things enough times, or not stressing them in a way that demonstrated he understood what his people wanted and needed. He was enamored with the big, industry-level cleverness of the company's strategy. But that didn't matter a whit to his people—especially the new high-tech whizzes who had come aboard via acquisitions. They already felt they were fulfilling their goals by helping their government customers with key missions and deploying powerful technologies.

Hillen realized he needed to respond to nuances, not just big-picture strategic building blocks. People needed to know "How is this change going to affect what I have come to know, love, and be comfortable with?" He would eventually pledge to people a new kind of deal: You will get to work with cool tools, in cool places, with cool top-secret insiders. "How would you like to work in a building within a building within a building at the NSA?" That story would, in the end, resonate like no other.

Our friend Gary White, the former CEO of Gymboree we introduced earlier, had to go through a similar learning curve. He would find out not just how to better run a specialty retailer for moms, but how to better connect to the moms who worked in his San Francisco headquarters.[54] Along with stumbling in getting the story right as he transitioned from to Gymboree from Target, he missed the part about changing his behavior to show he knew what people valued.

Just two weeks after he started, his assistant gave him a hint: Go out and join the daily, thirty-minute afternoon gathering of all employees in the lobby. It's called "recess," she said, and people eat kids' snacks and socialize, just like children in daycare. It doesn't sound all that serious, she said. But, you'll see, you'll learn something.

And true enough, after White started to have ice-cream sundaes at 3:00 p.m., he learned about a lot more than just Gymboree's daycare breaks. He mingled with people from all parts of the company, because during these "recess" gatherings, designers chatted with finance jocks and IT nerds with operations people. The break erased barriers between departments. It allowed communication to flow more freely and more informally and helped business decisions move faster. In many ways, these gatherings allowed White to conduct a one-man honest conversations exercise.

By going to the breaks routinely, White learned how to better communicate company policy and identify what perks really mattered. For example, Gymboree couldn't give out the goodies offered by neighboring Silicon Valley companies. The well-funded tech companies lured employees with stock options and gourmet meals. White learned from working groups at Gymboree that he could offer other things that his people might value even more. Ninety percent of the employees in the corporate office were women, often with children of their own. "Celebrating childhood was the banner of the company," says White.

So he focused on that notion. He fully supported a narrative that stressed the needs and wants of moms. He was able to give women who would become mothers a pager when they were pregnant, and Gymboree was an early adopter in providing private areas for new mothers who were nursing. The company joined campaigns for the March of Dimes for fighting birth defects and supported neighborhood elementary schools by allowing employee volunteers to help teachers. "These were our ways of participating in the communities that people valued," he said.

Nursing rooms, pagers for expectant moms, clothing discounts—these apparently little actions allowed Gymboree to communicate more about the nature of working for the company than any number of strategy discussions could. He thereby communicated that his people worked in a special enterprise that put children, not stock options, at the center. "They wanted an organization that represented quality," he says, "because they weren't working just for the money. We found ways to make it enjoyable for them to be part of a company that was having success."

White's story raises the fundamental question: Are you reaching people in a way that they *can* be reached? And *want* to be reached? Too many leaders abdicate their responsibility to answer these questions honestly. Even as times change and your organization grows, you may be tempted to stick with the same attitude: "This is who I am and how I work, and I'm not going to change." If you feel this way, prepare yourself to live with the consequences. If you set the parking brake on your willingness to grow and develop as a sophisticated leader, your people will hit their own accelerator and head out in a different direction, and you're the one likely to have trouble restarting a stalled leadership engine.

Recover: The Elements of Change

To become an effective chief explaining officer of a changing organization, you need to adopt an approach and mindset committed to engaging and connecting with others constantly. You will probably have to practice new kinds of communication more than you think. Can you make sure you're more self-aware of how you communicate? How you come across to others? How you elicit responses that engage people to join you? Or will you let your organization drive around, or over, or past you?

Build a Strategic Dialogue Plan

If you're going to reinvent yourself as a maestro of change, one way to start is to create a communications plan to genuinely drive change. This is not a plan you would produce for product marketing or publicity, where your focus is on message transmission. It is one that aims to create connection, influence, and feedback—essentially a "dialogue plan." If you don't generate a dialogue plan, you won't train yourself to communicate in a way that takes you out of your stall and catalyzes the change your organization needs.

We advise leaders to embark on the quest to become a chief explaining officer with a four-part plan:

1. To stimulate conversation

2. To focus on your listener

3. To choose your communication channel

4. To choose your medium

In the first part, you describe how you plan to have a conversation both to advocate and inquire. On the one hand, you want to inform, sell, and champion. On the other, you want to ask good questions, have people ask questions, verify what your people understand, and have them inquire as to what you mean.

As with stakeholder management in the last chapter, how can you mix both modes to get a cyclical flow of communication going? Contrary to what you think, the behaviors you model to communicate effectively are counterintuitive—talk less to be heard more; know less to be trusted more. Sometimes you may want to pause: "Does this have to be said? Does this have to be said by me? Does it have to be said right now?"

The second part is understanding your listeners' styles and needs. This means understanding the different "currencies" of communication. People respond to different subjects of interest. Do you talk about the challenge of the job, the meaning of the mission, the brilliance of the strategy, the prestige of their position, their relationships with people, or the value of their being needed? Which currency do they most value in receiving your message? People alternatively prefer a payoff that appeals to their head or their heart, or to the present or the future. Your job is to tender the currency they put the highest premium on.

The third part is learning to transmit on three different channels. One is facts: the logical, objective realities of the situation and the roadmap for the way forward. What detail can you give to people who need you to appeal to their intellect and want logical arguments? A second is emotions, which you can broadcast with humor, encouragement, empathy, honesty, and courage. How can you show you care for others, relationships, and harmony? The third and perhaps the most powerful is symbols: metaphors and images that make a story memorable.

Mohandas Gandhi famously used a spinning wheel and salt as symbols to inspire the people of India into relying on themselves and gaining independence from the British Empire. Martin Luther King employed a powerful metaphor ("I have a dream") to achieve incredible levels of social change in the 1960s in America. More than a few companies have used a light bulb with its allusion to Thomas Edison's inventiveness to highlight their quest for innovation. What kinds of symbols can you use in your own communication to lead change?

The fourth part is choosing your medium, or rather many of them. Communications experts talk about a spectrum running from "lean" to "rich" communication. Each type requires a different investment and delivers different results. On the "lean" side are email, mass mailings, and posters—cheap but not that effective. Slightly less lean are podcasts or group emails. The point is that the lean vehicles, including town halls and even personalized individual emails, offer limited opportunity for direct engagement and dialogue.

On the "rich" side are small-group meetings and one-on-one conversations. If you want rounded, relaxed, earnest dialogue, then interactive team meetings or individual visits are the way to go. Rich communication is resource-intensive, of course. If you have 3,000 people to reach, you can't possibly meet with each of them one-on-one. But you *can* and should sit with your most important stakeholders.

Don't get too caught up in the structure of the way you put this planning onto paper. The point is to practice a new communications mindset and behaviors. Find the techniques that work best for your own style and objectives. A rigid system isn't necessary to become a chief explaining officer. Simply adopt a syllabus of your own for practicing the appropriate ways to spur dialogue.[55] And remember that rich dialogue of the right kind will move people from mere listeners—receivers—to collaborators and advocates.

That's not to say that you should always plan to communicate just what your people want to hear. Sometimes you have to explain that they are *not* going to get what they want, and why, and that they should feel okay about their future nonetheless. As one of our colleagues once said, a leader has to be part detective and part psychologist: detective to uncover what people want and need, psychologist to provide what they need in a way they will accept. Note that you have your own style preferences, so your natural style will be suitable for some people but will benefit from being adapted to reach others.

One form of a dialogue plan is what Harvard Business School professors David Garvin and Michael Roberto call "the persuasion campaign."[56] This approach is what John Hassoun used when he was CEO of Vistronix, having practiced the technique over the years after his difficult work at the engine-inspection system unit of Veridian. At Vistronix, Hassoun worked to integrate six new companies into one, demonstrating his success most visibly when, in 2016, ASRC Federal acquired the company. This time Hassoun approached the job in a way that worked.

For starters, he made sure that when he accepted the role he went out and talked to people about developing a new vision. He made others part of the process. He took feedback from different types of stakeholders and wove it into a strategy integrated into the new narrative of where the business was going.

"I did a lot of out-of-the-box brainstorming with people," says Hassoun. "I asked, 'What do you think about this?' And 'What do you think about that?' I got a lot of feedback around the specific strategy that would resonate with people. I didn't pretend I had all the answers."

Hassoun's "persuasion campaign" began well upstream of where many leaders might think it should. "When you talk about a persuasion campaign, it's not just you persuading the people," he says. "It's them persuading you as well. So it's bidirectional. And that's what leads to the overall vision and strategic intent for the business. Once you decide that, then everyone can speak from one view and agree on what needs to happen. And that's how you become successful, everybody buying into that. So it's really a wrapper around change management."

Hassoun notes that he did lots of presentations, town halls, and one-on-one meetings, but in each case tailored them depending on how the change affected those particular people. He doesn't like presenting slide decks, because he feels people read too much into them and can take them too literally—and in some cases exactly the wrong way. So he prefers talking with others in a give-and-take fashion, in his case always focusing on how individuals will gain in the new integrated culture.

Overcommunicate!

We said earlier that Ron Jones's Rule of 100 was partly in jest—but only partly. His thoughts reflect those of John Kotter, one of the gurus of change leadership, who argues that you must go through your dialogue in as many ways and as often as possible, using every possible vehicle to communicate the vision. That's because, if you are to succeed in leading change, you must convince at least 75 percent of your followers that the status quo is more dangerous than the unknown future.[57]

We like to say that just at the point when you are getting almost physically sick of telling your story your people are finally *starting* to understand it.

Unless information is sensitive, share it widely. When people understand what is being done and why, what is expected of them, how the change will affect them, and how the change supports the vision and strategy, then and only then will they come along on the journey. They will feel like collaborators and actors, not victims. When employees don't have information, they may resist or even sabotage change efforts that threaten their personal stability and security. They often assume the worst: No information means bad things are happening.

Based on his experience at Vistronix, Hassoun notes that a good communication plan is an "endless dialogue." He says, "When we talk about a persuasion campaign, it's not something you start and end. It's ongoing. You're always working on it." For Hassoun at Vistronix, that meant engaging in this dialogue for over four years until he sold the company. He says the most crucial parts of his work as a leader involved collaborating with people, educating them, and mentoring them. That's what's necessary to get yourself thinking and acting like a chief explaining officer.

Recast the Change Agenda

Another means to recover from the stall of leading change is to practice recasting the change agenda in your employees' terms. If you saw yourself when we talked about leaders failing to speak to what people value, how can you change your communications approach to better appeal to your followers? The bigger and more sophisticated your organization, the more you need to work at finding out what matters to people. On what terms will you best initiate and conduct the most important conversations?

You may have that big vision and strategy in your head, but now that you've assessed how you appeal to what people value, on what terms will you move ahead? Do you appeal to needs for money, stature, and recognition? To helping them realize the mission and ideals of the organization? To their professional principles and work ethic? And how do you go about showing through your behavior that you're reaffirming or recasting the change agenda on these terms?

William Shakespeare's *Henry V* offers a good example from literature. We like to highlight the scene in which the king disguises himself and sneaks into the soldiers' camp. It is the night before the battle of Agincourt, a battle in the Hundred Years War in which Henry's men are hopelessly outnumbered and outclassed. He wants to hear what the common soldiers are saying: What are their hopes and fears? He listens, he engages, and he shows empathy—all incognito. And he does so in a balanced manner even as his men question the king's (i.e., his own) motives and decisions.

Henry's late-night visit to his troops allows him to craft the "Crispin's Day" speech—one of the most motivating speeches in history. The speech works precisely because it taps into what his men want out of the enterprise, not merely what he, the king, wants. With the men believing they are doomed, Henry exhorts them to think of their legacy. In today's words, he essentially says, "Hey, if you want to go home, feel free; I won't stop you. I'll even pay for your ride! But, boy, you're going to want to be here today, because from now until the end of the world, on this feast day, you'll be held up as a shining hero—and everyone who's *not* here today will wish he had been."

As for you in your organization, you may not play to such stakes amid such drama. But as with Henry, while you think globally you still have to initiate a dialogue on local terms. That's what John Hillen learned at Sotera. He couldn't motivate his employees the same way he wowed investors. After wrestling with what people wanted, he found several openings to connect more meaningfully. The main idea that appealed to his people was that if you work for a prime contractor you get more interesting work and enjoy more status. Most industry sub-contractors don't even get to talk to the customer or end user, and getting to leap that barrier had a lot of attractiveness to top tech problem solvers frustrated by their isolation.

If you're the boss, of course, you have the right to dictate direction by fiat. But our experience is that authoritarian leaders won't retain the best followers for long. As a chief explaining officer, on the other hand, you can deeply connect the change story to what people care about, as well as the values and purpose and DNA of the organization. This is particularly true in today's democratized, emotionalized, and egalitarian management environments. You have to discern the connections that matter and tie the benefits of change to what matters to people. Otherwise, followers won't own the change.

In other words, you need people to help you coauthor the change. You, as the chief explaining officer, then act as a chief dialogue officer as well. When you cast yourself in this role, you more naturally frame change in terms of how each individual you engage with is affected. Change is always personal, so you must practice communicating in terms that make people want to become advocates. And make sure to be transparent with people about the implications of change at the same time. Benefits rarely come without risks, effort, or discomfort: "no pain no gain." Your dialogue must also allow a safe space for negative reactions to be surfaced and addressed, not hidden or repressed.

Adapt and Accommodate

Once you recast the change agenda, you are on your way to recovering from the leading change stall by using another method, which is adapting to and accommodating the style of others. If in your dialogue plan you outlined different styles and channels for communicating, now is the time to take ownership of them. If you're used to appealing to people's intellects, think about their emotions. If you normally appeal as a financier, appeal as an engineer. If you typically win the argument with data, try persuasion through expressing enthusiasm and using metaphors.

Be sure your claims are well-supported; use graphics convincingly; anticipate questions from your audience; take command of details; assess implications for engaging in productive dialogue. These are basic executive competencies, and you'll find you create the most value and engagement by avoiding a one-way static presentation. Slide decks, strategy blueprints, and MBA-style analytics are means to an end, not ends themselves. One finance leader we worked with brilliantly quipped, "Feelings are not facts!"—but when it comes to the right style of connecting with someone, they sometimes can be.

Don't revert to a communications style simply because it worked before, especially in another organization. Remember that, like politics, communication to effect change is local. Gary White, star of our Gymboree case study, at a later stage of his career helped engineer a turnaround at Wet Seal, a clothing retailer for young women. Tottering on the edge of bankruptcy and working through a rash of store closures, everyone knew the company was fighting to regain its competitiveness. White looked for ways to connect with his almost-all young and female retail staff to increase his employees' commitment to sales and customer service.[58]

White tapped into the technology integrated in the cash registers to deliver congratulatory messages in a style that thrilled his audience. When the winning clerks booted up their cash registers in the morning, a tape would roll out with a message from White—affectionately nicknamed "G-Dub:" "You were my top ten go-getter from yesterday! Absolutely outstanding! Exciting!—G-Dub." The local Starbucks would then show up with lattes and scones for everyone—just the way people liked, because district managers were instructed to know how everyone took their coffee.

"These people loved Starbucks," says White. "And here it was early in the day in retail, and you're resetting the store, getting your banking done and merchandize ready, and everyone is surprised with coffee at 8:00 a.m." To young women, the dazzling, early-morning celebration was a hit. "Having fun was always on their agenda," he says. "They absolutely loved it."

Related to White's insight, consider how you might adapt and enhance your communication style, as well as that of your leaders, by means of a behavioral measurement system. Recall Michael Barnett, CEO of InGo from chapter 2. Barnett worked hard to crystallize InGo's story and purpose, but with that done he still had to figure out how to push his and his leaders' communication behaviors to realize that purpose, especially in building relationships with clients.[59]

Always the philosopher, Barnett reminded his team that "communication" stems from the Latin word "to share" or "to make common," and sharing with clients has to be done in person. "You can't share anything by email. Text messages are convenient but meaningless," he says. "So the question for my team was, 'How many people did you *truly* communicate with this week?'" That is, how many people did his team speak with live and educate about InGo's unique trade-show social media service?

"And 'educate' means 'to bring forth from within,'" he adds. "So these efforts were about pulling information out of clients. Our market has more to do with asking the right questions than giving the right information. And you just can't ask the right questions by email. It's better in sharing communication to ask in person." So to be sure that they know the right dialogues are taking place, InGo tracks how much people "share" with the client through live conversations. Tracking this way enables powerful communication to happen, ensuring the feedback loop is closed.

Practice More Mindfulness

Perhaps the most important way to recover from a stall in communicating in a way that drives change is to become more mindful of both your own basic motivations and those of others. Don't let your motivations become an impediment—they should work for you.

Nevins's colleague Kristina DiStasio developed a simple tool that illustrates what we mean: motivation cards. The cards comprise a deck of 52, but they're not playing cards. Rather, each illustrates a human motivator, and the cards can be tailored for different organizations. Some cards list motivations related to appreciation ("a personal note from my boss") or mastery ("certification in a new skill"). Others relate to recognition ("being rated a top performer"), development ("being part of a new cross-company initiative"), or just plain old perks ("a gift card to a store of my choice").

Users of this card deck are instructed to sort the cards into three piles: "very motivating," "somewhat motivating," or "not motivating." They must then set aside all but the highly motivating ones, and choose and rank their top five. The choices and ranking can be surprising. For most, money is not the top motivator. It doesn't matter what level in the organization people come from. Financial rewards tend to come well behind recognition, the chance to learn new things, or having the opportunity to share ideas with top management and be coached by them.

What do these kinds of responses tell you about how to remake the way you think about communicating and motivating people to change? The levers you tend to reach for—"increase their bonus target"—may not be as motivating as you think. And as it turns out, if you simply ask people what motivates them, they aren't very good at telling you. They don't actually know, and often neither do you. So a tool like motivation cards can help you be more mindful of where you're coming from, where others are coming from, and what you can do to connect with and motivate people more powerfully.

Dialogue to Die For

We believe that the ability to encourage dialogue is one of the most critical competencies of a leader. In fact, it may be the king of all executive competencies. Communicating effectively to drive change sounds overly basic only because people define that capability so narrowly, leaving out dialogue altogether. That's why so many leaders fail to reinvent themselves and lead change effectively. All they are thinking about is broadcasting or transmitting, which explains why, in our experience, at least 80 percent of employee surveys and 360-degree evaluation reports of leaders cite some aspect of communication as wanting.

The dialogue critical to the communication that catalyzes change can be challenging because change invariably ignites conflict. Conflict in goals, interests, desires, principles, or feelings. You can't remove conflict from relationships, and you wouldn't want to even if you could: When managed productively, the differences that generate conflict can spur innovation, enhance learning, improve insights, create new perspectives, jump-start performance, and even deepen relationships. Think of someone with whom you hit an impasse and then worked through that conflict together for a win-win outcome. How much more trust and rapport do you now have with that person?

Don't let perceived conflict stand in the way of reshaping how you communicate change. Work instead to embed a discussion of conflicting issues in the dialogue you use to engage people; meet them where and how they need to be met; and inspire them to do the right thing. If you look at the careers of leaders who have been outrun and sidelined by their organizations, their inability or unwillingness to spur dialogue and honest conversations led to their fall. Their dialogue gap manifested itself as not appreciating the needs of constituents; failing to see the broader strategic landscape; shutting down critical feedback or input; mistaking collaboration opportunities for competition; and projecting a hubristic persona of not needing others to succeed.[60]

Almost any time there is a problem, failure, or stall in an organization, it can be traced back to a conversation or dialogue that didn't happen. Or didn't happen in the right way. Or with the right people. Or at the right time. You don't want that to happen to you or your organization because you stalled in the sophisticated capability to create dialogue.

And that's why you need to develop yourself into a genuine chief explaining officer, as shown in the following breakout summary. You must reckon success by whether or not people own the change, and whether they lead their own people in that ownership. Do they become chief explaining officers themselves? When you spread the word with that kind of leadership sophistication, your people will look forward to reading your emails. They will even reread them to others. And unlike the busy partners of one firm we know, they won't send those emails into the trash folder.

~Reinventing Your Leadership~
A Leading Change Stall?

Become the chief explaining officer.

Beware Danger

- You can't seem to energize employees to own the strategy or spring into action to tackle opportunities in executing a new initiative.
- You have trouble generating confidence in your direction, and employees seem to act only in response to orders.
- You blame others for their inability to "get" your story and own their piece of it. (You may even get angry or argumentative.)
- You cannot draw a picture of each step in getting from today's organization to the future one in a way that allows people to see their role and the benefits of the change to them.
- You fail to generate feedback on your story, and you don't hear people repeating the story back to you.

Assess & Troubleshoot

- Push yourself: Do you have a plan to communicate in a way that excites people enough to change? Can they articulate the change story accurately in their own voices?
- Have you honestly assessed the frequency and quality of your communications? (Do you try to *over-communicate* to avoid communication gaps?)
- Have you surveyed people, formally and informally, to see if you are communicating in a way that inspires action?
- Consider conducting an "honest conversation" exercise in which star employees report back on the communication or execution snags they see in the workforce.
- Investigate whether what people value and what motivates them matches your assumptions. Are you appealing to what they really care about?

Recover & Reinvent

- Whenever possible, make communication two-way: Achieve transmission and reception in both directions.

- Draw up a plan to motivate people with your words and actions. How can you spur more meaningful dialogue?

- Make a habit of communicating three or ten or a hundred times as much as seems necessary. Never fall into the trap of thinking you've communicated sufficiently.

- Recast the way you describe change in terms your people will value. Appeal to heads *and* hearts. Followers don't always care about strategy—they want to know how their lives will change for the better.

- Practice adapting to and accommodating the style in which different people like to receive a message. Transmit on the right wavelength or channel.

 CHAPTER 6

MASTER OF THE OLD UNIVERSE

Stalling When You Lose Your Authority

"Authority without wisdom is like a heavy axe without an edge, fitter to bruise than polish."—ANNE BRADSTREET, *Meditations Divine and Moral*

"If a rhinoceros were to enter this restaurant now, there is no denying he would have great power here. But I should be the first to rise and assure him that he had no authority whatever."
—G.K. CHESTERTON to Alexander Woollcott,
recounted in *Bartlett's Book of Anecdotes*

Y ou probably didn't have a childhood—one both very good and very perplexing—like Chris Howard's.

Howard, now the president of Robert Morris University in Pittsburgh, was his high school student body president, Honor Society inductee, talented band member, and star athlete. During his senior year in Plano, Texas, as captain of the football team, he helped lead the team to twelve straight wins and a state championship with a 12–2 record after an 0–2 start.

But Howard also had to experience the ugly side of humanity. An African-American who moved to Collin County, Texas, with his family in 1979, there were instances "when people used the N-word like they used the word 'jerk'," he says. "There were even some situations where acquaintances would tell me, 'We don't like black people, but we like you and your brother.'"[61]

Perhaps Howard was inspired by the good. Or perhaps he was galvanized by the bad. But insights into elements of leadership started to come to him, he says, as early as age ten. He learned as a young man that his innate strengths and capabilities would not necessarily endow him with the authority he needed to get others to follow him. He had to build himself up in additional ways—and especially so in a community burdened by so much prejudice.

Although Howard's story is just one of many, it demonstrates how leaders hit circumstances that oblige them to prove their worthiness to call the shots. When you're the leader, all eyes are on you, and you have to say the right things, make the right moves, and get the right results, if you are going to win over followers. Are you up to it?

Here is the fundamental question: How do you as a leader generate followership? And why will you stall if you fail to do so? Why is it that you may suddenly feel stale in your strengths, derelict in your appeal, a has-been in a changing world, a captain without avid lieutenants? What is it about the demands on you as a leader in a growing and changing organization that can suddenly snatch your authority away and cause you to stall?

For Howard, success earlier in life stemmed partly from being smart, athletically talented, and self-assured. He also worked hard and held himself to high standards of achievement. When he was in eighth grade he found himself thinking of others, "Okay, you can be smarter than me, or you can be faster and stronger than me, but you won't outwork me." He decided he would bring his grades from A's and B's to straight A+'s—and he did. "That sense of agency helped affirm me," he says, "and I started believing in myself early on in a way that served me well later."

Merely being an archetypical achiever doesn't enable anyone to radiate a sense of authority in the eyes of followers. On the contrary, most followers will be more impressed by your character than your competencies, more willing to follow you based on your understanding of reality—and of them—than your accomplishments. So what must you do to ensure that you can count on earning the label "leader" from your followers? ("Why would anyone want to follow *you*?")

In the case of Howard, who today leads a thriving university, his evolution as a leader started with the need to understand his unique situation in a majority white community—a process of "sense making," he says. The challenge was to grasp how he was perceived, because he was always "the other": one of 28 black kids in a senior class of 1,300. He had to channel his energies into forming himself in character, judgment, knowledge, and those intangible elements that somehow would define him as someone people *wanted* to follow.

Though your journey won't necessarily match his, Howard did what all leaders must do to avoid a stall: He created a personal syllabus for ongoing growth as a leader. You could assume that as a leader celebrated for delivering results and taking the organization to new levels you automatically establish your authority. But individual performance doesn't translate into leadership authority. To retain authority as you step up a level, you need to upgrade yourself to project what followers require in order to have confidence in you, feel inspired by you, and spring into action.

Failing to tap into a more sophisticated approach to engage people to follow you and your ideas is a classic leadership stall. To be sure, when you exert energy and amass victories in your comfort zone of business achievement, you will always earn kudos. But to earn authority as well you need to broaden yourself beyond the capabilities that drove your ascent in the first place.

We worked with one leader who was his business unit leader's heir-apparent in a major financial services firm. He was passed over by the company's management team only because he lacked the "presence" to gain the followership in his organization. He had a stellar track record as a technical innovator, he knew the business inside out, and he could tell a compelling story about both near- and long-term strategy. He was an executive star. But he couldn't get his peers to envision him as the next head of the enterprise.

You may scoff that this could never happen to you. But this stall is so common that, like others, it is often predictable, if not inevitable.

At each inflection point in your growth as a leader, you risk having others recognize you as an *underdeveloped* leader. How you come across to others, how you manage yourself, how you understand the needs of your followers, how you adapt to those needs, where you focus on generating followership—these all require fresh learning and development at each new level of responsibility. This is not a matter of becoming a chameleon and changing your personality to match the situation. Nor is it a matter of going on a charm offensive to win popularity contests and congeniality awards. Rather, it's a matter of learning and internalizing sophisticated skills and behaviors that will give you gravitas and generate genuine followership.[62]

To establish your authority as you move up or around in a growing organization, you will have to ask, "Am I willing to make a commitment to being a *different kind* of leader?" If you are like most leaders, the higher you rise in an organization the more your followers will care about *who* you are and the less about what you can *do*. If you lead at the highest levels, even if you are a technical master of your profession, people will expect you to lead with wisdom that transcends your business expertise. You might even need to be thought of as the "Chief Philosophy Officer" or the "Chief Values Officer."

Having technical and functional knowledge and competence, whether in finance or engineering, will be expected by your followers as table stakes. But having wisdom rather than just intellectual horsepower, having good judgment rather than just good business understanding, being able to listen rather than just command, being empathetic and responsive rather than just determined and directive, being able to inspire rather than just command—those are the traits that earn you willing followership.

Authority comes from displaying for your followers the character, integrity, and intellectual reach to make the right calls on the toughest choices you face. These choices are often what we call "right versus right" decisions, when no single, correct answer exists, and the best path forward will depend on sacrifices and trade-offs.[63] These dilemmas can be contrasted with "right versus wrong" decisions, when you face matters of factual accuracy or moral behavior, and the best path forward depends on analysis and legal or ethical standards. (These latter decisions are, we hope, not the ones that trip you up.)

If you're like many leaders, the realization may dawn on you slowly: The real work of leadership depends on reinventing yourself with capabilities not just for operating an organization but for guiding a community—a community of people depending on you for direction, security, and their livelihoods. You need to exhibit weight of intellect but also spirit and passion. Your organization, after all, is a subset of society, a microcosm of the world, sophisticated in a myriad of interpersonal and political ways. You continue to lead only by growing in authority as your organization grows in sophistication.

Whether you're the boss of ten people or ten thousand, in a volunteer, for-profit, or nonprofit organization, you must lead with emotional authenticity and visible behaviors that earn the respect, trust, loyalty and dedication of your people. "Hitting your numbers" is necessary but not sufficient, if only because, when the day comes that your organization misses its numbers, you need authority, not just performance, to fall back on.

Your people hold in their minds an idea about what makes your organization great, and that organization upholds a set of values, assumptions, and opinions. You cannot engineer what they consider a great organization with just structural or managerial maneuvers. Leading a human enterprise that people prize being a part of requires that you take regular steps to display a level and kind of authority that your followers will recognize as genuine, uplifting, and motivational. If you don't, you risk getting outrun and stalling.

Chris Howard is a good example of a leader growing and evolving over time. He held successive roles of greater responsibility in the US Air Force, Bristol Myers Squibb, General Electric, the University of Oklahoma, and as president of Virginia's Hampden-Sydney College. He racked up an impressive resume of business skills, experiences, and capabilities along the way. He gained range and perspective. But to deeply understand human organizations, he also had to shelve aspects of his old successful leadership self and create new elements to build his leadership persona. "I've had to remake myself at every turn," he says. Riffing on a quote from leadership guru Warren Bennis, he adds, "Leaders are not made, they're not born, but they're self-made."[64]

Beware: Is the Mastery Ending?

Perhaps no other stall sneaks up on leaders so unexpectedly—or stymies their passage back to high performance more acutely—as falling short on authority. That's probably because almost all managers and leaders, especially in well-organized and codified settings, enjoy a formal source of authority: position in the enterprise, title, rank and status, a formally defined role and responsibilities related to subordinates, and so on. When you're embedded in such a structure, you don't easily see that even in a strict chain of command, neither rank, title, nor position confers on you an enduring source of authority, especially as the world changes and the organization grows bigger and more sophisticated.

"Do it because I said so, and I outrank you!" can get something done this afternoon, but over the long run such commands won't give you what the most admired and successful leaders have: engaged and eager supporters. David Kriegman, former president of SRA, a government systems integration company, put it well: "Leadership doesn't come from position. Rather, you're selected as the leader by peers. How can you get people to follow you? The people who follow you are actually appointing you as leader."[65]

To avoid a stall in your authority, you can't adjust the organization chart, shuffle work teams, or issue bolder commands to project your clout. Nor can you merely hire advisors or a chief of staff. Nor can you just attend an executive course at Harvard or Wharton or outsource prickly issues to consultants or turnaround artists. Engaging in such actions signals that you believe you can treat the authority stall as a challenge of mastering managerial complexity, the organizational mechanics outside yourself. To enhance your leadership brand, to beef up your authority, you can't externalize the solution to this stall. You have to internalize it and reinvent yourself.

Your Expertise and Smarts Go Flat

The first warning sign of a stall in authority comes when you sense your strengths no longer generate a passionate following. If you're like many rising leaders, you have long leaned on your technical or functional expertise or knowledge for authority. Your professional credibility depended on it. Thrust into circumstances that demand a more sophisticated kind of leadership, however, you can't keep playing off your former accomplishments. As your organization grows or changes you will be challenged to go beyond your job boundaries and take on broader issues of the larger human enterprise. If you find yourself shrinking from this task, then you can be sure you're edging toward a leadership stall.

Imagine being in the shoes of Google CEO Sundar Pichai in 2017. In August, a male Google engineer circulated an internal memo about gender diversity (the people in tech jobs at Google are said to be 80 percent male) arguing that the gender gap exists not solely because of sexism but in part because men are biologically more fit than women for technology jobs. Suddenly Pichai was not handling a technology issue but a philosophical and moral one. He fired the employee, citing a transgression of the company's policy not to advance harmful gender stereotypes in the workplace.[66] But all the while, his authority as a leader was on trial.

The issue, and the firing, raised vehement debate and testy interchanges across Google—and indeed across the US business community—that had little to do with superior technology or Google's admired operations. Do tech companies muzzle free speech? May employees use the workplace as a forum for social commentary? When do conversations cross the line from free speech to demeaning or even hate speech? Should companies protect dissenting employees from social media harassment? In many ways, Google had become a crucible for examining heated social issues that transcend the "normal" challenges a fast-growing company faces.

The fired Google engineer wrote in an op-ed for the *Wall Street Journal*, "Public shaming serves not only to display the virtue of those doing the shaming but also warns others that the same punishment awaits them if they don't conform." He was photographed in a "Goolag" T-shirt.[67] He added, "the viewpoint I was putting forward is generally suppressed at Google because of the company's 'ideological echo chamber.'" Suffice it to say, Pichai's authority as a leader was under fire in the public sphere as well as the hallways of his company.

The point here is not what Pichai decided, but that he had to make the decision at all. He was facing a challenge that tested his sophistication as a leader. Whether he liked it or not, he had to operate well outside the boundaries of running a complex and successful company. He couldn't say, "That's not my job" because matters like this weren't in the job description. The implication for him is the same for leaders at all levels, even if you're just a front-line supervisor: You can't avoid the human aspects of work. If you wish to retain your credibility and effectiveness as the boss, you must come across as a leader of people.

Whatever your go-to source of authority, you will sense you're in for a stall when your persona no longer evokes esteem. Being an expert, the most confident and quick to answer, the most assertive, or the smartest person in the room isn't enough. Nor is your technical or functional knowledge, whether you're a lead engineer, a financial analyst, or even the CFO. Eventually, people will resist or challenge you if they don't feel and respect your sources of authority. If your leadership gravitas isn't based in something more than the line items on your resume, followers will disconnect, shut down, or vote with their feet rather than showing their confidence in you.

"You Don't Have What It Takes!"

Some of the leaders we have worked with have seen the warning signs of an authority stall around the time of a promotion. "He's just not the right guy for the job" comes the explanation. Or, "I didn't think she was ready for the next level." Or, as in our earlier anecdote, "He doesn't have the presence." In each case, if you're that leader, the underlying message is the same: You do not have enough of the sophisticated capabilities to convincingly convey authority and gain followership. And that failure shows you have not developed in the way you need to for the next role.

We often hear executives cite a Catch-22 to explain why they didn't get a job: "I didn't get the job because I didn't have the experience, but I didn't have the experience because I didn't yet have the job." It's an old chicken-and-egg excuse that you should probably take as a warning sign. The people responsible for promoting you into new positions, whether office manager or CEO, are looking for the makings of your authority at the next level *right now*. Do you have those makings?

As a way of illustrating what's at stake in the authority stall, consider a tale of three chief financial officers. Each worked, in succession, for John Hassoun, the former CEO of Vistronix introduced in the last chapter. A onetime Air Force program manager and former CEO of three smaller firms, Hassoun started with Vistronix in 2012, when he was charged with moving the company deeper into the fields of cybersecurity, big data, data analytics, and cloud computing. As he built the company through acquisitions, each CFO, in his or her turn, offered just what the company needed at that time—until the job grew more complex and more sophisticated than the CFO him- or herself.

The first CFO was a master of time-and-materials contracting, which was a make-it-or-break-it skill in winning business with the company's traditional customers in defense, intelligence, and health care. She wasn't a finance whiz, but she was an asset in overseeing these kinds of contracts for the $40 million company. "You have to get government approval of your contracting procedures in this industry,"

Hassoun explains, "so creating a process that fits the desired business opportunity is key."

But eventually the company's aspirations for tackling bigger and more sophisticated business opportunities outran her resolve to get to the next level of authority. To continue the company's track record of growth, Hassoun needed a CFO who could oversee all kinds of contracting mechanisms—time-and-materials, fixed price, cost-plus, and hybrid—as well as run the financial numbers. He also needed a senior finance leader who displayed a creative mindset to help win business by applying different combinations of contracting techniques. Unable to elicit those capabilities in his first CFO, he found them in a new executive who had the chutzpah and accounting-systems skills to build the business to $100 million in sales.

"This new CFO could think out of box," says Hassoun, "and she integrated the finance function and set up a finance system to support the integration of the newly acquired companies along with their unique contractual mechanisms."

All well and good. But then, just a year after that second CFO came on board, the company acquired three more companies, and the scale of the job outran her skills and authority, too.

At this stage, Hassoun needed someone who had the intellectual weight and emotional makeup to work with people he was courting for an infusion of capital. The right person would need the skills to handle more complex accounting, rigorous audits, Sarbanes-Oxley regulations, public disclosure of company data, and more. But additionally, he or she would need the behaviors and bearing that bespoke a different kind authority to new investors, lenders, and equity partners. These would be the behaviors that defined the gravitas expected for a CFO undertaking an IPO.

"We needed someone who could earn credibility with outsiders," Hassoun says, "to show we had the processes, people, and tools to grow into a $500 million company." So once again, with the demands of new business opportunities outrunning an existing leader's capabilities and comportment, Hassoun hired another CFO.

A pattern like this one at Vistronix—of managers shuffling through a revolving door that gets bigger at every turn—is common in many organizations, and not just in the C-suite. One of the most difficult challenges for every leader is to create and project authority that other people respond to, and expect, in a changing organization. At every level, at every phase in organizational growth, more sophisticated challenges demand a different and broader authority than you had in previous roles. You may find your intellectual legs are too short, your polish on the pulpit too limited, your outlook too provincial, your reservoir of worldly knowledge of the human condition too shallow. You may, by dint of hard work, come up with new technical skills needed for a more complex operation—but still come up short on becoming the leader your followers want and need.

No surprise that business consultant John Hamm, in studying the "Achilles Heels" of founders trying to build larger organizations, discovered that all of these weaknesses related to a lack of breadth and depth in authority: too much loyalty to comrades, myopic task orientation, stubborn single-mindedness, and working in isolation.[68] You can't blame the founders: Their relentless focus enabled them to get their enterprises off the ground. But their inability to develop meaningful sources of authority, observed among more than 100 entrepreneurs, led to their stalling after the start-up stage.

Your People Don't Trust You

Oftentimes the most straightforward signal that the fabric of your authority is growing threadbare is that people no longer seem to trust you. Maybe you discover this perception in a 360-degree appraisal or performance review. Or maybe your boss tells you. Or perhaps you get blasted by a departing employee or on Glass Door. If people don't trust you to say the right thing, do the right thing, and do right by them, your authority will take a hit.[69]

Back before the financial crisis of 2008, Mark Nevins was called in to coach a brilliant, charismatic superstar performer in a highly regarded Wall Street firm. What Nevins heard, in blunt terms, was: "Look, this guy is making us a lot of money. But everyone hates him. Can you fix him?"

An awkward question. Nevins admitted that the developmental goal was complicated by an equally awkward reality: This executive was receiving huge annual bonuses for making the firm so much money, which meant he was getting one message clearly: "You're doing great—keep it up!" The leader was constantly rewarded, even though people didn't want to work for him and took opportunities to leave his division and even leave the company. All of this probably didn't put the superstar in a position to be very open to a coaching conversation.

During one of their early meetings, the executive suggested that Nevins sit in on one of his team meetings to see how charming and masterful he was. This leader did indeed put on a virtuoso performance, talking the entire time about his ideas, how to do better deals, what the clients "really wanted," and so on. However, throughout the meeting he was also blissfully unaware of the deadening effect of his monologue. The irritation and disengagement displayed in the body language of his team completely escaped him.

At the end of the meeting, he asked Nevins, "So, what did you think?" And Nevins surprised himself with an uncharacteristically blunt response: "Well, if your objective was to alienate everyone in the room, you did a great job."

The client was stunned. A type-A alpha dog, he had never heard an honest appraisal from any of the people around him.

Nevins waited for a response. The leader didn't get angry—he paused, and reflected. And then he opened up to changing himself.

Over six months, the leader worked diligently to better understand what his followers wanted and needed from him. He eased off on behaviors that focused too much on himself rather than his people, too much on his own ideas at the expense of dialogue. He worked hard to substitute a collaborative style for an autocratic one—not an easy or natural shift— and he focused more on developing his followers and less on showcasing his own performance in front of clients. In short, he recognized that he could adopt more sophisticated means to bolster his authority, and that he could do so as effectively as he had advanced his ability to exceed his revenue targets. Within two years, he was successfully leading an even larger part of the business, two levels up from where he had been previously.

You would probably agree that this executive should have seen the warning signs that he had lost his people's trust. But in our experience, if you fail to retain authority by losing trust, you make two key mistakes you often can't see: You cause people to feel so uncomfortable they shut down in difficult conversations, and you put your own interests before those of others to the point that people simply give up on you.

High-caliber followers of course want to know that you're a technically capable and performance-driven leader. But they also want to know that you're going to listen well, engage them, and empower them. To make this point in a lively way, we often point to a clip from the Hollywood film *The Crossing*, a movie about George Washington. The scene we show depicts General Washington and his commanders debating his plan to cross the Delaware River to surprise the Hessian mercenaries in Trenton, New Jersey, on Christmas Day 1776.[70]

General Horatio Gates, a highly accomplished commander, enters into an argument with Washington, who had up until that point been markedly unsuccessful on the battlefield. Gates, far and away the most experienced and successful battlefield leader in the Continental Army, dresses Washington down in front of other officers, telling him the only viable military option is to surrender. And to top it off he bluntly insults Washington by ending his tirade with, "And you, sir, are a damned poor leader!"

Washington's rejoinder is firm, but not in countering Gates's facts or debating military records. Instead he explains why the long-suffering men of the Continental Army would never follow Gates but instead "have put their trust in me . . . and if I, a bumbling Virginia farmer, decided to lead them into hell, they would follow me into hell." Washington then banishes Gates from any command.

Why does this scene make sense? And why, if you're a viewer, does it resonate so much? Why would anyone follow Washington, a serial battlefield loser? Gates was a greater master of the technical elements of battle, and he was arguing from logical and pragmatic grounds. But when watching the film you're grabbed by the fact that Washington *cares*—cares about his men and the cause they're fighting for. His followers trust him in spite of his poor battlefield record. To be sure, Washington is humbled by his defeats, but Gates shamelessly dishonors himself by breaking the trust his men have put in him as a leader.

Washington earns authority by serving others; Gates loses authority through his rational detachment. Gates was a master of the complexity of an increasingly difficult military situation. Washington recognized the higher order challenge of motivating an amateur army wedded to a precarious cause. Doing so posed a far more sophisticated challenge than merely managing logistics, lines of communications, training, and operations. Those battle tactics were all important, but beyond those Washington needed his ragtag army to trust him against steep odds with the future of the young nation at stake. Gates slammed into a stall of authority, in this case outrun by the momentum of history.

WARNING: YOU'VE HIT AN AUTHORITY STALL

Your expertise and smarts don't win you followers anymore. People resist your direction and act uninspired. You miss a promotion because, "You just don't have the presence of a leader." You're not even sure people trust you anymore. You wonder: "Have people given up on me?"

Assess: Your Winds of Your Authority

If you suspect you're stalled because of your shortage of authority, ask yourself a simple question: What *is* my source of authority? Why would anyone want to follow me? Or for that matter, respect me; invest themselves in my vision, decisions, values, or mentorship; or trust my enthusiasm or judgment for getting great things done? Why should I expect people to call me a "leader"—just because of my title or position? Do I project Washington's sense of caring about my people and their values? Or do I (even unwittingly) commit Gates's error of showing disrespect for my peoples' ideals and values?

Okay, Ask the Obvious

We usually find when we talk with leaders that they haven't fully inquired into the foundations of their authority. When Nevins has gotten to know an executive coaching client well, he sometimes gets the question, "What impressions do you have of me?" Or "What have you heard about me?"

"Good question," Nevins responds. "Who else have you asked? What are your peers and direct reports saying?"

More often than not, the response is, "Hmmm, you know I'm not sure—I guess I've never really inquired."

And why is that? If these leaders are trying to be honest, they often start to say something like, "It didn't seem important enough to bother them." Or, "I didn't want to impose my personal needs on a business conversation."

But what's the real reason? A hint often comes out between the lines: "I'm scared of what I might hear . . . and what I might have to do about it."

No matter your leadership position, people ask questions about you all the time, implicitly and explicitly. They ask about your strengths and weaknesses. They question how you are coming across. They wonder to themselves, and they talk around the water cooler. You should probably find out what they are saying. Are people saying they put stock in you because you are an expert, with credible capabilities? Or are they putting stock in you because they value your character, judgment, and appreciation of their needs and values?

As a test, start a conversation. Ask your colleagues at an opportune time for feedback on strengths you can better leverage or on any blind spots you may have. Everyone has weaknesses, even the most successful leaders—and in some cases, especially the most successful leaders. Rare are leaders who cannot bolster their sources of authority by getting feedback from the people most critical to their success.

At Halfaker Associates, CEO Dawn Halfaker, who was introduced in chapter 4, tried to lead her startup with a style learned from the hierarchical organization that is the US Army. In the military, she says, "I was a pretty good leader because I cared about my people and I realized it was about empowering them. But when something was going wrong, how was I reacting? How was I reacting when people weren't perfect or didn't achieve the standard?"[71]

"Having that mentality that it's top-down, holding people accountable, holding people to high standards—that's what I took from the military to the civilian world," she explains. "People obviously reacted very, very poorly. I was overly involved and strict about people needing to be in the office and asking, 'Where are you at this time? Why aren't you here?' And at end of day, I'd ask, 'Did you get this done?' Eventually, people were either fed up with me or upset because there was a lack of flexibility, or because my standards were too high."

And then the realization started to hit her. "It was 'holy cow,' what did I do?" she recalls. "That was a very hard transition for me." The question, she says, was how to motivate civilians who can work for any company in the world. "I had to learn how to handle difficult situations, but do it with a lot more humility and grace and empathy," she says.

Her lesson: "People don't respond to negative criticism. They don't want to fear you. So over time I realized how to communicate the vision and plan and hold people accountable without having to do it in a way that made people feel they were always under a microscope and always had to be in the office. And I realized how to get people to be motivated while also being empathetic and understanding that life happens. Because in the military life doesn't happen. Life is the military."

Halfaker grew more honest with herself. Many leaders do not develop as quickly, whether hailing from the military or anywhere else. They continue for far too long to rely on positional authority to generate a following, even if that following is not so avid. Remember: Followers are not wholehearted followers if you don't have the empathy to show you believe in them and want to make them stars.

Use Some Hindsight

Scan the record of your past. Have you amassed experiences that provide you with the judgment and character that appeals to people? What have you done that makes you qualified to handle questions, as did Sundar Pichai, about the human dimensions of your organization? Is your capability broad and sophisticated enough to conduct capably both the solo performance of your own role and the orchestral performance of your organization?

Do you make a habit of shying from or engaging in the weightier issues of our time? What have you done when faced with issues of corruption, sexual harassment, sales to questionable customers, recalls of shoddy products, nepotism, online privacy, security of customer data, safety of foreign nationals, and—like Pichai—freedom of speech inside a corporation?

These are not always day-to-day questions, but they *are* the questions that, like it or not, can define, sustain, or undermine your authority as a leader. For leaders of major organizations, questions like these may not seem all that relevant until they appear suddenly and with potentially catastrophic consequences.[72] If you doubt it, scan any day's *Wall Street Journal*. The difficulties and disgraces you read about don't happen only to other people. And when they come up for you, they will put your authority to the test of a lifetime.

There is a proverb many leaders will recognize, sometimes with a wince: "You often hire executives for *what they can do*, but end up firing them for *who they are*." Ask yourself: In your years of professional life, have you accumulated the diversity of experience that gives you the wherewithal to lead a human institution for integrity, not just manage a business organization for success? When the winds of crisis blow, will you stand on one leg of principle, easy to tip off balance, or two?

Range of experience matters because you're pressed to deal with cultural, ethical, moral, and philosophical issues that, although they are often unpredictable, are easier to handle if you understand their pillars and parallels in other fields of human experience. We can ask the question, for example, what kind of leader Chris Howard, the president of Robert Morris University, would be without a background in the military, corporate, and educational institutions; with positions in philanthropy, sales, strategy, and other functions; and with a private life lived in the South, the North, and abroad. Howard jokes about himself and his wife, who have moved thirteen times: "We like to say, 'We're good at being the new people.'"

Howard is indeed a newbie in Pittsburgh. But he is a veteran of a broad world that bolsters his authority more than if he were solely a Pittsburgh native. For instance, his professional experiences have forced him to work toward divergent objectives. In business, he notes, you keep score largely by moving the bottom line. In the military, you win by taking land and beating the enemy. In academic administration, you keep score partly by balancing the money coming in and going out and partly by managing the needs, desires, and complaints of a diverse group of intellectuals who don't really believe they report to you. Everyone's values are different, and you gain authority by having the experience to understand them and the mind to bridge them.

Your experiences serving different constituencies contribute to your authority. So does tenure in volunteer and professional capacities unaffiliated with work. Have you invested in networking and attending conferences? Joining advisory boards in other sectors? Leading trade associations? Serving on charitable and government boards? Acting as a leader in your town and city? All the better. Each is a source for building a more sophisticated, authoritative leadership capability, making yourself fit for the next level of challenge and success.

Recover: Back On Your Horse Again

If you were to ask Bob Zoellick, former head of the World Bank, for examples of his leadership that stand out, you would partly hear about loans and grants to developing countries. Or about helping countries grow, build institutions, and expand opportunities for men and women. Those are the important functions of the bank. But you'd also hear about the time Zoellick had to resist South African politicians who wanted him to jettison his corruption-fighting chief because that chief had challenged powerful interests when leading a special-investigations unit in his home country. Or about how he had to protect an Egyptian employee, a leading reformist, who was threatened by score-settling after the Arab Spring. Or about how he had to insist the bank find a way to aid the emigration of a Ukrainian corruption informant whose life was at risk in his home country.

As for the Ukrainian, says Zoellick, "We had, in effect, to create a witness protection program. Some World Bank people said, 'Well, he ran the risk so he's on his own.' And I said, 'You can't do that with people! What message are you sending? And what is your moral standard here?' So we had to help him get out and take care of him and his family.'"

"That was an important moment," Zoellick says. To be sure, performance at the bank would be measured by his work to overcome poverty and spur sustainable growth globally. But his authority to lead did not depend only on his performance or smarts. Nor did it depend on his earlier postings as US trade representative, deputy secretary of state, or White House deputy chief of staff under George H. W. Bush. Or even on making people feel that their work is bigger than themselves—as important as he feels that is.

On top of all those things, his authority depended on asking more pressing, controversial, and difficult questions, in particular, "What's the right thing to do?" "Maybe an obvious question," he says, "but too often it is skipped over. You have to have integrity and be willing to use your judgment to do what you believe is right, even if difficult in certain circumstances."

When asked by our clients, employees, or students how they can enhance their sources of authority—based on wisdom not business smarts, on judgment not data analysis, on character not competencies— we often suggest that they delve into the staples of leadership theory, among them works by Warren Bennis, James O'Toole, Max De Pree, or Daniel Goleman.[73] But we also tell them that they have to create their own defining moments, as Zoellick did. These are moments when you leverage your authority to do the right thing, to be the person other people will *want* to follow.[74] It's not enough to be just the one with the answers, the intellect, or the expertise.

Own the Human Dimension

Another way to boost authority is not to push away, but rather to embrace, decisions about the human dimension of your organization. To do so, like Zoellick or Pichai in our earlier examples, you have to prepare yourself to think through the conflicts inherent in any organization in a sophisticated way. For instance, how do the big human questions intersect with the questions that are most pressing for your people and organizations? How, for example, might you grapple with issues of free speech versus violations of corporate policy? Or the rights of the individual versus the needs of the corporation or the market?

Or let's take a more direct business issue. How, say, might you decide how to divvy up shares of equity when your startup goes public? Who's to say what's "right"? If you take for an assumption that the organization is just one form of a human community, you'll find that people have been thinking deeply about the issue of property distribution for millennia. You're not the first, not by many centuries. You don't have to reinvent that wheel, any more then you need to reinvent managerial fixes like total quality management or lean manufacturing.

The fact that many sophisticated leadership questions will challenge—and validate or detract from—your own authority as a leader is the starting point of the Aspen Institute's executive seminars, where this book's coauthors have long served as moderators. One premise of the traditional week-long Aspen Seminar is that a wide variety of thinkers and writers over the last three thousand years have argued for the different and sometimes conflicting values that shape any good society: John Stuart Mill on liberty, Jean-Jacques Rousseau on equality, Plato on efficiency, Aristotle on community, and many others.

What leaders learn in Aspen Institute seminars, and what you can learn if you undertake this kind of inquiry on your own, is how to employ sophisticated ideas and concepts of great thinkers to consider recurring problems and challenges in your own organization in a new and more fruitful way. Becoming familiar with the intellectual conversations of great historical thinkers can help you to become a more sophisticated leader. As Sophocles said, "Let men be wise by instinct if they can, but when this fails, be wise by good advice."

The root question of the Aspen seminars—How does a leader help create a good society?—is as old as human society itself. The seminars call on leaders to read classic texts in political, economic, and moral philosophy that provide analogues to their own present-day business and organizational challenges. What did John Locke, Jean-Jacques Rousseau, and Karl Marx have to say about the origins of basic human rights? Whether you agree or not with any writer's specific position, their arguments and "conversations across the ages" force you to rethink your decisions while you also develop your own philosophy.

No leader can avoid it: You will be called on periodically to be that chief philosophy officer or chief values officer. You may need answers to tough questions, and quickly: On what basis do you decide who has an equity stake in the firm, and on what different terms? On what basis do your let your workers engage in free speech versus corporate-controlled communication? Do you have the range, the background, to consider issues such as these in a way that speaks to wisdom and not just smarts?

If you're engaged in an ethical decision, do you side with Immanuel Kant, who argues that lying or stealing is wrong no matter what the situation is? Or do you side with a Utilitarian such John Stuart Mill who argues that what is right or wrong depends on the circumstances and what yields the greatest benefit for the greatest number of people?

In reflecting on and debating classic texts, participants in Aspen seminars gain a point of view not only on specific decisions, but more fundamentally on ways to go about making decisions. Rooting your leadership point of view in a set of values informed by great thinkers across the ages enhances your authority because it gives you a more sophisticated way to reason through dilemmas and conundrums. Additionally, it can be both comforting and edifying to realize you're not the first leader to struggle with some of these basic questions.

A classic sign of unsophisticated leaders, leaders who stall on decisions dependent on human dimensions of leadership, is abdicating tough decisions to "experts" such as the legal department, HR, or public relations. While you should tap into expertise, to sustain your authority as a leader you must be meaningfully involved in these decisions yourself. And you also need to ensure that the leaders below you take similar accountability and responsibility, and reason in just as thoughtful a manner.

When we talk with leaders about issues related to the broader human enterprise, we are often reminded of the story of King Solomon (though not the infamous decision about dividing a child). When Solomon was granted a wish for what he most needed to "rule" his people effectively, he did not ask for *power*. Rather, he asked for *wisdom*, the wisdom to tell good from bad and right from wrong. He asked for an understanding and discerning heart—not a big brain or physical strength or a long life. For Solomon, wisdom was the key to being an effective and authoritative leader.

In an age where being nonjudgmental is considered an agreeable social quality, you may be uncomfortable with being the final authority on issues of right and wrong. A large institutional ethics study co-led by Hillen concluded that many leaders felt less anxious handing such issues off to their lawyers rather than accepting them as their own responsibility. But delegating the exercising of wisdom may put your authority, not to mention integrity, in question. In most organizations, unlike in governments that feature a separation of powers, you as the leader have to act not just as an executive, but as judge, jury, and sometimes executioner. Are you prepared? Can you handle this responsibility with wisdom and authority?[75]

We often suggest that leaders invest in serious-minded executive education experiences outside their industry or even outside traditional management disciplines. We always stress a distinction, however: You can raise your authority as a manager of an operation if you *deepen* your knowledge, especially in areas of technical expertise. Doing so helps you tackle challenges of complexity. But you will raise your authority as a leader of the human enterprise when you *broaden* your knowledge and increase your capabilities of sophisticated leadership. As a critical side benefit, you will equip yourself to take a position on issues you are not expert in—by a process of internalizing rigorous, universally applicable concepts to guide yourself in wise decision-making.

In our Aspen seminars, we often leave leaders with a tool developed by leadership expert James O'Toole: "The Executive's Compass."[76] This compass illustrates how, in our social as well as our business lives, we all engage, even if unconsciously, in a tug-of-war between four core but in some ways *competing* human values: liberty, equality, efficiency, and community. The significance of the compass quickly becomes clear for Aspen participants. They can see, for example, if you are faced with a dilemma like the one described by Pichai at Google, that you need to make some awfully controversial tradeoffs. How far should you let liberty (free speech) go? How much should you allow it to threaten the stability of your community?

Often there is no "win-win." Your answer depends on how you value each point of the compass—and on your own powers of philosophical navigation developed through years of experience. What you need in these situations is to think back on your intellectual travels for anchors that moor "right" decisions. Accumulating more of these anchors is a means to increase your know-how in handling sophisticated concepts, even if it's natural to be buffeted by competing needs and values.[77]

Role Model Gravitas and Range

Another useful move in avoiding, or recovering from, a stall in leadership authority is to role-model the sophisticated mindset and practice of the authoritative leader. At its simplest, this might mean demonstrating what former Morehouse College president Robert Franklin called the "five wells": well read, well traveled, well spoken, well dressed, and well balanced.[78] Become fascinated by the world. Try teaching or writing. Travel outside your comfort zone. Speak at industry events and panels.

Experiment with lots of things, but seek balance in the end. Add expertise to your conventional knowledge base, but also add expertise in new knowledge bases. At the same time, be wary of tapping too broad or superficial a base that might be interesting but not decisive. A well-balanced leader is neither head down in the industry nor head up in the clouds with a vague opinion on everything. Ultimately, you want people to say that you're a thoughtful and consistent leader who has *range*.

How do you establish yourself in your organization as a Solomon who can make wise decisions, a Socrates who can tease out the major issues confronting the team that are not obvious to everyone, and a mountain-top guru who is recognized not just for being a business leader but as an industry sage? Among other things, you work through the five wells again and again. You practice. And that practice, as sages such as Marcus Aurelius have noted, can provide insight into solving problems or developing opportunities that you might not otherwise have recognized.[79]

When it comes to reading, we would add that you should also take your cue from serious fiction. It's naïve to think that insights into solutions for the most fundamental leadership challenges are all going to be found in "business books." The most difficult challenges you face as a leader are timeless, so a good way to grapple with them can be to take a more deliberate look at yourself through the lenses of great authors. Pick up a novel to engage and stretch the right side of your brain, the creative, introspective, empathetic side, in the same way your job exercises the logical, rational, analytical left side.

Although we won't plug specific "great novels" (check the internet for classics and prizewinners and choose the ones that appeal to you), we would like to stress that reading fiction can improve how you make decisions, manage conflicts with others, engage and pull people along, and show your followers that you are reflecting critically on your own assumptions and perspectives. Of course, good literature can help you in other ways, too: increasing empathy, expanding your emotional capacities, improving your writing style, and stimulating ideas. In your quest to increase your leadership sophistication, great novels are grist for your mental and behavioral musings.

To Franklin's Five Wells, we would add another: well experienced. Seek a range of experience even if your job has not changed from outside appearances. We very much believe in the phrase that it is better to have ten years of experience than one year of experience repeated ten times. If you are in operations, look to lend a hand in business development. If you are in technology, ask to help out in finance.

As we said earlier, just as you drink from the cup of experience in your own industry, you need to drink widely from cups in others. How many sectors have you worked in? Corporate, clerical, government, political, nonprofit, nonaligned civil society? Each sector wrestles with different dimensions of the human enterprise. The more you wrestle with, the more human you are, the greater your authority.

Embrace Your Strategist

Many leaders have a tough time making the full transition to strategist, by which we mean a systems thinker who sees the whole and the parts at once. Few leaders are born strategists, and as a substitute they think in connected pieces instead. They reason out and justify their moves by connecting one event to another, and then to another (or several others), the accomplishment of which creates institutional movement, which then, with luck, creates waves in the marketplace, causing a new dynamic for competitors and customers, which in turn opens opportunities not previously available.

Yet a strategist's way of thinking is essential for winning not just as a competitor, but as an authoritative leader. In their work studying leadership, David Rooke and William Torbert found that fewer than 5 percent of executives use strategy as their principle rationale for selling or defending their ideas and decisions. Most executives use expertise ("I've got the data; therefore, we must do it this way"), short-term achievement ("We want to get this done soon so it will roll up in the quarterly financials"), or diplomacy ("I think everybody can leave this meeting happy that their equities were protected").[80]

For most organizations, strategic planning is a drill, and one driven less by leadership intent and more by the calendar—"Wow, it's October already! We better get to work on the budget and strategic plan for next year." For greater authority, you need to practice with the mind of a strategist. Strategic thinkers do not think about strategy only at a certain time of the year. They are constantly envisioning the world as an ecosystem of interactions with competitors, customers, and partners. They are always looking for strategic options, and they don't underuse persuasion driven by the logic of strategy.

Strategic thinkers have their eye on the market, obsessing over customer behavior and competitor's moves. When they look inside at their own organizations, they are consumed with understanding the strengths and weaknesses of their people, their technology, and their core competencies—to better understand their capacity for making moves in the market. They not only read widely, but seek out intelligent opinions about the broader forces shaping their marketplace. They debate and test their ideas with their direct reports, their boards, their employees, and intelligent leaders in other industries.

Sophisticated leaders that have internalized strategic thinking are always puzzling over how all the pieces connect and fit together—and if what is happening in the world now and in the foreseeable future could change that fit. They don't consider it enough to be forward-thinking idea generators. They know it's critical to have an eye for implementation and how dozens of pieces interlock: pricing, technology, organizational structure, opportunity costs, priorities, capital, partnerships, talent management, and more. If one component works the wrong way or not at all, a good strategic idea may be all for naught.

The sophisticated strategist's mind is a big one, and you can embrace that mind to develop and demonstrate authority. Strategic thinkers always have a game plan to move the organization to a different place. They think in terms of priorities, trade-offs, dependencies, sequencing, and the allocation of resources. They ruthlessly assess talent to align skills with teams, activities, and goals. They trumpet the core values and purpose of an organization, but they also push to allow for new undertakings that will fulfill the mission in an ever-changing environment. And they keep score!

As organizations become more sophisticated, operating in environments whose levels of sophistication pale in comparison to anything in the past, followers will not continue to revere leaders who demonstrate largely tactical genius—even if that's impressive. They will grant leaders authority when technical and business expertise shifts toward the troops. You as the leader need to exhibit a clear and confident perspective on strategic direction. That's how you make it apparent to everyone that you know where you are taking the organization, as we outline in the breakout summary at the end of this chapter.

Become a Lifetime Student of Self-Discovery

As a final way to recover from a stall due to lack of authority, restart your own learning about the art of leadership itself. Whatever your title, you will benefit from becoming a lifelong freshman in the university of the human enterprise. When you ask, "What happens now," the answer, no matter your leadership level, is always, "Go back to school."

Which brings up yet one more "well" we would like to add to the earlier six: "well reflected." We return once again to the story of Robert Morris University president Chris Howard. Howard makes the case that, to be a truly effective leader over the long term, you need to work on three "PhDs" in leadership. The first PhD is in yourself. The second is in the world around you. The third is in the subject of leadership itself.

Like Dawn Halfaker, Howard didn't learn this lesson during his military career: "The very same thing that will help you succeed as a company commander," he says, "will cause you to wither on the vine as a battalion commander." He cites the old joke from the Air Force Academy, his alma mater, where units are called squadrons and groups of squadrons are called wings. People will ask, he says, "What kind of wing commander is he?" And the answer: "He's the best squadron commander I've ever met."

"That's a real dis," he says. And it's a reminder that, if you've hit a stall, your first step can be simple: Realize you need to start learning again. As Socrates, the ultimate authority on self-knowledge, is alleged to have said, "I know that I know nothing."[81] Sometimes a "know-nothing" is the smartest leader in the room.

Such an attitude will keep you on a perennial journey of self-reinvention—toward stronger emotional intelligence, deeper experience, a broader range of mind, and deeper thinking about strategy. You won't find certifications or accreditations for becoming an inspiring leader. Nor for an empathetic boss, master strategist, ethics guru, or philosopher-king. Indeed, there are no actual "leadership PhDs." But over time you can and must test and re-test yourself as if you're pursuing one.

You must engage in such self-testing or self-certification to enhance your breadth, presence, and gravitas ceaselessly. So that your followers hear you and believe in you. So that people can act and execute with confidence. So your followers, in their growing wisdom, become the kinds of leaders they themselves need to be. So that, in the end, you are not just a captain with avid lieutenants, but a general in whom the troops entrust their future.

~Reinventing Your Leadership~
A Stall in Authority?

Flourish as a Philosopher-King/Queen.

Beware of Danger

- You believe your job title carries sufficient weight with followers, even though their behaviors suggest you need to do more to earn their respect.
- Your technical expertise and smarts no longer impress followers, who judge you for "who you are" more than for "what you know."
- You're called on to answer ethical or moral questions, and you have no idea how to do so.
- You give your people direction but increasingly they resist it or fail to follow through.
- You keep getting passed over for promotion.
- Your evaluations and feedback hint that you don't have the presence or gravitas to lead at the next level up.
- Your people no longer trust you to do right by them, hinting you don't understand what they value or you put yourself first.

Assess & Troubleshoot

- Ask yourself: What is my source of authority? Is it based on my capabilities and intellect? Or character and judgment?
- Ask peers: How am I coming across to people?
- Does your resume show "ten years of experience"? Or "one year of experience ten times"? How many legs does your background give you to stand on?
- Do you overly depend on experts to help you make important decisions about the "human enterprise"? Or do you take responsibility for these decisions yourself?
- Have you regularly engaged in developing yourself in ways that challenge or push you to do different things in different ways?

RECOVER & REINVENT

- Shift your actions and behaviors to come across to followers more authentically and emotionally. Empathy works, and builds character.

- Focus on defining moments that deliver credibility, reliability, faithfulness, and selflessness. Bank the trust you get for later.

- Complete a personal syllabus exploring the universal questions of work and life, tapping into philosophy and literature.

- Own decisions about not just the business enterprise but the human enterprise. (Authority blossoms when you lead your community.)

- Take on a nonprofit board position, a community leadership role, or industry association responsibility to broaden your leadership experience and range

- Role model gravitas with the seven "wells": well read, well traveled, well spoken, well dressed, well balanced, well experienced, well reflected.

- Think and behave as a strategist, a systems thinker. See the parts and whole at the same time.

- Become a master of authority by always remaining a student of yourself. Remember that self-awareness rules.

 CHAPTER 7

HAMSTER ON A WHEEL

Stalling When You Focus Your Time and Energy in the Wrong Places

"He that will not apply new remedies must expect new evils."

—FRANCIS BACON, *Of Innovations*

"I wish it need not have happened in my time," said Frodo.

"So do I," said Gandalf, "and so do all who live to see such times. But that is not for them to decide. All we have to decide is what to do with the time that is given us."

—J.R.R. TOLKIEN, *The Fellowship of the Ring*

Jonathan Bush, CEO of athenahealth, a $5.5 billion healthcare IT services company, still admits having what we dub "the weed-whacker impulse." If you ask him what he'd do if he had a day away from his Boston office, he'll tell you he'd fly to the Bahamas where he has an off-the-grid bungalow. There he would cut weeds and brush to better maintain his solar-power panels.[82]

Bush likes to toil in a T-shirt. But he admits that this impulse is "toxic" when he can't restrain it at work, where he leads an organization of people delivering a full suite of healthcare services: electronic health records, practice management, care coordination, patient engagement services, and mobile apps.

He recalls the thrilling days of 1997 when he started the company with two friends from his early days as a management consultant. Back then, he did a little bit of everything, and he spent a lot of time laboring in the field. "I worked for more than a hundred hours to sell our first system to a four-doctor group. It was a contract for $150,000 a year, and we thought we'd signed the Magna Carta," he says.

"Hitting the road and doing sales pitches for the company was great," he adds. He crafted the marketing pitch himself and put together the pithy presentation slides. "I'll never forget practicing the pitch again and again and again, and going from little rural clinic to rural clinic." He and his team traveled in a 1986 Jeep Wagoneer, sharing cell phones and laptops, and visiting one doctor's office after another to tell their story and try to sign up practices.

Then growth happened. Since 1997 the company has expanded to more than 4,000 employees with offices in six US cities as well as India. athenahealth now serves 85,000 physician practices and hospitals. "All of a sudden, my comfort zone became a no-fly zone," Bush says. "At first the organization was just a small group of people, and if you didn't make the coffee, you were kind of a jerk," he says. That was appropriate, and he liked it that way. "Now if I leave fifteen people waiting in a conference room for me to go make the coffee," he says, "I'm kind of a jerk."

And so, in steps, he came to terms with the downside of the weed-whacker impulse. In one instance about a decade ago, he was taking a turn as a telephone support rep. He messed up a customer account so badly that four of his colleagues had to lean over his shoulder to help him undo the damage. The lesson from growth was clear: He could no longer cut the company's brush. And when he tried to do so, he stalled out in the briar patch.

Bush is by no means unusual in facing the challenge to appropriately focus his time and energy, to do the right work in the right way at the right time. Many leaders find that the weed-whacker impulse can get the better of them. As they try to stay on top of bigger and more sophisticated organizations during dramatic change, the impulse to get inappropriately into the details trips them up again and again. It just takes different forms as they ascend to each new organizational role.

In these situations, whether a leader on the front lines or a new C-suite executive, you may begin to feel drained and overwhelmed, with diminishing returns to show for your efforts. You continue to dedicate the same hours and effort to your organization, but you think, "I'm working like a maniac but not getting anywhere!" Is it possible you're still trimming weeds? Maybe you should instead be addressing the tall trees the organization really needs you focused on.

Time and energy are finite resources, no matter how vigorous your passion for work. Giving an hour of focused attention to X means you're not giving that time and energy to Y. As a leader, you can't afford to burn energy on tasks that don't truly demand your perspective and wisdom as the boss. It's easy to get caught in a weed-clearing tizzy—and find you're rarely chopping big timber or planting new trees. Bush says, "Setting the right balance so the team feels you're making the highest and best use of your time is one of the great challenges for any leader."

When we work closely with executives, we often take the time to walk through their weekly routine. We assess with them where they spend their hours and minutes. They often come to see a disconnect between their biggest priorities and their biggest time and energy expenditures. Almost everyone makes this error, and smart and committed leaders can fall into it often. As your organization grows and becomes more complex and sophisticated, you'll likely see this pitfall repeatedly, in others if not yourself.

Think about the work necessary to resolve the stalls described in the earlier chapters in this book: shifting your time and energy to ensure that your constituents understand your organization's purpose, aligning the team of leaders who work for you, mapping and influencing your stakeholders, engaging people in dialogue to ensure they drive the change agenda, and broadening your sources of authority to be a leader people are eager to follow. All of these critical leadership roles demand a deliberate investment of focused time and energy. If you don't get the focus right, you will stall.

What is the answer to how to spend your time and energy when things have changed? Your first impulse will probably be what it is for most leaders facing any of the stalls we have described: Find a new structure or system or set of processes. You'll seek to free yourself up to do the tasks that you do better than almost anyone in the enterprise. After all, that kind of work got you to where you are.

But that is where you may go awry. Instead of acting like the team manager, you will then be acting like a player-coach and redesigning the team lineup to allow you to do what you do best, even if it's no longer top-priority work for you as the leader. You would perhaps reorganize your leadership team. Or hire a chief of staff to take care of other executive duties or tend to the team. Or, if you're like many executives who think they can better manage their time with more data or different reports, you would consider investing in a new CRM or ERP system.

All the while, you would be thinking you'll gain by deliberately organizing your time to take advantage of your best solo skills from the past. You would be like the player-coach whose forte is shooting three-pointers—redesigning the offense so all you do is shoot long jump shots.

None of these impulses is necessarily bad, but notice how they follow the pattern that contributes to stalls: They attack a more complex operating environment with more complex systems to tackle similar jobs. Meanwhile, they give you a dangerous excuse not to pull back, reflect, and tap into more sophisticated leadership capabilities. In other words, they encourage you to stagnate, to put off deliberately asking, when you sense you've hit an inflection point, "What happens now?"

Check yourself. Maybe you're your own worst enemy, preventing yourself from reinventing yourself to serve as the leader your followers now need. Maybe it's time to deliberately let your old self go. Maybe you should stop thinking you can muscle through by working harder, tapping your historic strengths, and refashioning the organization outside yourself. Maybe it's time to change the way you think, because if you fill your days like you always have, you won't be able to stay ahead of your organization as a sophisticated leader.

Beware: Working Like a Maniac

How do you know you've hit the focus stall? The biggest clue is that you're getting diminishing returns on your efforts. You're gunning the engine and burning a lot of rubber, but you're exhausted. While you're keeping the pedal to the floor, nothing you do seems to drive the organization forward like it once did. The backlog of urgent matters keeps growing. It's not just that you are running like a marathoner all the time—that's not necessarily a bad thing for ambitious executives in a go-go environment—but you find you're losing your energy and enthusiasm for running altogether.

In fact, you get the feeling of being the proverbial "hamster on a wheel." You tell yourself that your endless marathon *is* paying off. The organization is still growing! But in your heart, you feel like you have crossed the line from sustainable aerobic exercise, where exertion gives you a shot of gratifying endorphins, to unsustainable anaerobic exercise, where you will suffer a backlash from overdoing it.

Taryn Owen, president of PeopleScout, the Chicago-based recruiting-process services provider, shared with us some of her experiences related to this feeling.[83] She says that in 2015 she was on a plane almost every day to meet with clients, partners, and employees. She would board a flight in the morning, come home at midnight, and then do it all over again the next day. "I was in a place where I was working thirteen hours a day, hour after hour with hardly a break for water. I sometimes had two to three items on my calendar at a time. I used to have to choose which of three meetings was most important."

One of the reasons she committed to such a crazy schedule was her dedication to nurturing all the relationships she had built. PeopleScout differentiates itself in the recruitment-services industry by its intense focus on client relations and service, starting with the most senior executives in its client organizations. Living up to that commitment in Owen's mind required visiting major clients every quarter for reviews of PeopleScout's service and offerings. Pressed by the competing demands of clients, analysts, her board, her direct reports, employees out in the field, and partners at her parent company, TrueBlue, she started to feel a stall coming.

And right at that point, in late 2015, an attractive acquisition opportunity became available. "It was fast and furious," Owen says. "We bid on the deal in November and closed at the end of December." The transaction was exciting and energizing. She was skillfully guiding the company in fulfilling its growth strategy, assembling a broad portfolio of products ranging from global talent acquisition to recruitment analytics to veteran hiring programs.

"But at the same time, I was worried that things could unravel," she says. "I was trying to do too much. The pressure from the pace made it harder to keep my focus and manage the high stress, even if most of my team or peers would never have known. I needed a new process or solution."

We see impending stalls so often with leaders we work with that we marvel at how easy it is for talented executives to let the work control them instead of the reverse. You have almost certainly experienced this feeling yourself, whatever your role or career, and you've also probably seen warning signs as you approached a crisis: feeling overwhelmed, not keeping healthy, overbooking yourself to the point that your calendar decisions feel like emergency-room triage.

One of the simplest and most fundamental causes for losing focus is rooted in conflicts about delegation of work. For starters, you may feel discomfort delegating your responsibilities at all. In Owen's case, she had personally recruited many of her leaders herself, and with so many people directly under her, the most efficient way for her to better handle delegation was to decrease the number of people who reported to her and have each pick up more responsibilities.

But that raised a concern: "I was worried about losing people because they'd become disengaged if they didn't report into me directly," she says. "These people came to work for me, and I felt I owed them that." Another concern was that the new leaders she hired would not have access to her, which might hurt their morale and performance. "I was hesitant to reorganize my senior team and move people, even though it was the right thing to do, because I knew I was a big part of the reason they were here."

As the acquisition closed, Owen decided to engage a consultant to help design the integration of the acquired company as well as to restructure the organization to make the most of the talents of both companies. She wanted to create a sustainable operating model so the company could continue to achieve industry-leading performance. When she reached out to Nevins to talk about the integration plan, he counseled her to step back and take three to six months to redesign the newly expanded organization and how she worked as its leader. At that point, she had seventeen direct reports.

If you're facing a stall from a lack of focus, Owen's experience may sound familiar. Sometimes it takes hitting a breaking point of overwork to realize you have to change. "I felt I needed to be a superhuman to get everything done," she says. "I never lost sight of the big picture, but with the acquisition I knew that I would not be able to continue to operate at the performance level I expect of myself if I didn't make some strategic changes."

When you reach an inflection point like this one, other warning signs of a stall will likely crop up. One is that your team may complain that you're not delegating enough. They start to grow unhappy that you're making decisions yourself that they could make—and in fact, want to make, and in many cases are in a better position to make. You're the bandleader, but you're holding up the parade because you feel compelled to play all the instruments.

The unfortunate effect is that in the best cases you can demoralize your team, and in the worst stunt the development of the people who work for you. Your people will feel sidelined, disempowered, and frustrated in their aspirations. They may hint that your weed-whacking has put them in dead-end jobs. (And as shown in the next chapter, they may even feel this way if you do hand off roles, duties, and responsibilities.)

Your lack of delegating enough may in turn trigger another warning sign: A pattern of your reacting to short-term crises at the expense of long-term priorities. Whipsawed by endless near-term emergencies, you don't carve out time to think strategically. Do you get a sense of panic if you're not the first responder to every corporate fire? That's when you may be tempted to hire an office manager, chief of staff, or COO to divide up the labor or free up more time for yourself to operate in your old comfort zone.

But falling back on hiring as the solution may miss the point. You don't simply need to divide up the labor, or gain more hours for your old talents. You need to make sure the right people are focusing on the right things, starting with you yourself. Inevitably, this means radically reinventing where you spend your time and how you exert your energy.

To be sure, there is a risk of delegating too much to others and becoming disconnected from the business, its drivers, your customers, or the guts of the operations. But as we sometimes tell executives, you never really perfect the art of delegating—and spending your time and energy on the right things—until you drop one or two balls on an old job or let them go even at the risk of them breaking.

Be wary if you've never felt the discomfort of realizing that the people to whom you're delegating tasks can do the job as well as you can. The fact is, your subordinates may get better results than you. If you don't drop a few balls, you will probably see another warning sign: the inability to pinpoint the few places where you should focus your time and energy to have a decisive impact.

Military leaders talk about the ability to develop a "coup d'oeil." Attributed to Napoleon, coup d'oeil means the ability to view a situation in a glance and know where to act to make the biggest difference.

Do you have trouble with your coup d'oeil, distinguishing the few crucial actions that matter from the many that don't? Or put differently, distinguishing what's decisive and what isn't? Perhaps your sense of focus isn't as sophisticated as you thought.

The ultimate warning sign is that your lack of focus spills over into your personal life. It's easy to rationalize imbalance, and many leaders will choose to make tradeoffs on work-life balance. But are you making these tradeoffs consciously? Or are you deluding yourself? We regularly hear senior executives admit to deferring their investment in family today as a means of bettering family life tomorrow. But have you done the long-term math on such tradeoffs? If not, you may just be developing bad habits that won't make anyone happy at any juncture in your work or life.

WARNING: YOU'VE HIT THE FOCUS STALL

You feel overworked and exhausted, getting less return for more effort. You sense you don't delegate enough work to others, but you're uncomfortable doing so, even as your people ask you to. Crises control your time and dissipate your energy. You've gotten so that you're having trouble enjoying work—and maybe even life.

Assess: Where Are Your Eyes?

If you perceive warning signs that you're stalling, probe further to determine how your habits, schedule, and mindset may be indicators of a coming stall. For a start, we recommend that leaders ask themselves, "Where are my eyes?" Flip back to Figure 1.1 in chapter 1: Are you doing too much of the wrong work—tactical, technical, and delegable—and not enough of the right work, that is the strategic, political, and interpersonal work that only a leader at your level can do?[84]

Time and energy are precious resources, and much like capital and labor must be deployed with discretion and discipline. If, as a financial practice, you calculate an internal rate of return on a capital investment, why wouldn't you estimate the return on your time and energy investments? You should expect and demand a high rate of return and check to see that you get it. Remember that the higher you rise in an organization the greater your leverage should be, especially when you commit to being a more sophisticated leader.

With today's data-driven tools for decision-making you can get lured into keeping your eyes down on the data and not raising them to see and tackle more sophisticated tasks. In a recent ad, CEOs were encouraged to watch dashboards instead of spreadsheets to help them lead more effectively. We thought that was encouraging, as we often suggest that to perform at the next level, leaders should raise their eyes by employing qualitative dashboards measuring critical high-level factors like executive team health, outside stakeholder attitudes, and coaching successes.

But we realized that the ad wasn't advocating dashboards of the kind we had in mind. It advocated dashboards that simply made spreadsheet data easier and faster to absorb. Clearly, the maker of the ads did not understand that leaders should be raising their eyes above the data. If this data-driven dashboard is the kind that serves you, you may have hit an inflection point and can't see how to drive beyond it. You're stalled.

This is not to say that you should ignore key data or not know the crucial facts about your organization. But you must assess whether you're raising your eyes to focus on what's most valuable, most decisive, because not many other people in your organization may be able to see and make the difference that you can. Do you have to see all those reports? Attend all those meetings? Review all those line items? Ask yourself: Should I even be in this meeting? Am I adding value? Is my presence decisive?

Assess examples of work from your current role: Should you personally be seeing all your customers for their quarterly business reviews?

When there's a problem in in the organization, should it be brought up to you? Should you be writing the first draft of the next board presentation? If there's an initiative to address an operational issue, should you be chairing that task force?

Your assessment needs to tell you whether you've acquired "Napoleon's Glance." You look across a welter and maelstrom of activity in your enterprise. In a snap, with your coup d'oeil, you decide what few but critical things you need to keep your eyes on; which activities require your leadership; and most of all, which require your presence.[85] Are you essential to the discussion or decision making? When you're not, giving others your precious leadership time is an indulgence you can't afford.

Do, Manage, or Lead?

The most helpful way to start your inquiry is to examine how you divide your time between acting as a doer, a manager, and a leader. When do you get in the trenches to do the work? When do you manage, or coach, others in executing the work? And when do you inspire and lead others into action? Is your time explicitly split into those three parts? Ask what proportion you devote to each. What allocation will deliver maximum results for your organization?

If you ask yourself these questions, you'll see better whether the problem in managing your time and energy is you yourself. We recently worked with a company president who wanted to get better at focusing. We asked him what percentages of his time he thought he was spending on "doing" versus "managing" versus "leading." As a doer he was focusing on strategic thinking, project management, information systems security, database administration, and financial and operational issues. As a manager he was focusing on setting goals, holding people accountable to them, and deploying resources to help people get things done. As a leader he was focusing on higher-order "why" questions such as organizational purpose, as well as the "where," "what," and "by whom" questions that fill out any organization's story.

This president responded that he felt he was allocating about 40 percent for doing, 20 percent for managing, and 40 percent for leading. Among his top three priorities: first, ensuring the organization was thinking big about the future while people worked together to advance key projects; second, helping shape strategy with his top 300 people; and third, "being the face and voice of change" to a more profitable, promising business.

Then we asked: Do you think you have the right breakdown for focusing your time and energy?

Only in part, he responded. He recognized that he needed to focus less on doing and more on managing and leading. He made a commitment to allocate more time to coaching his senior team members on objectives. He also realized he needed to devote more time to helping his people grow as leaders, in part by engaging in more one-on-one conversations as a coach and mentor. These conversations would aim at helping each of his people create plans to develop as leaders. Since he wanted to transform his organization, he concluded that his top priority—and something nobody else could bring about with the impact he could—was to put more personal effort into communication, role modeling, shepherding, rewarding others, and celebrating wins.

As a simple exercise, draw three columns on a tablet of paper, one each for "Do," "Manage," and "Lead." List all your activities and actions for this quarter, allocating each, in specific and measurable terms, to one of the columns. Estimate your time devoted to each, and calculate each column's relative percentage. Then ask yourself: Given my role and what I want to accomplish, am I investing my time and energy commensurate with the best returns?

If you hold yourself accountable for keeping a Do-Manage-Lead inventory, and check yourself against it regularly, you will see whether you're falling into the focus stall. There are some things that leaders *must* "do." We're not arguing that you give up "doing" altogether, whatever your seniority. But are you keeping your focus on higher-level work and not weed-whacking or overbooking yourself into a frenzy?

The Calendar Question

Another way to assess whether you've stalled is to have an honest look at your calendar and calculate where you actually spend your time. The only way to know if your estimates are right is to tally the hours. An executive will tell us, "Oh, I spend a good 20 percent of my time working on team alignment." But a look at the numbers often doesn't confirm that estimate, even if the belief reflects good intentions. The leader finds a lot of postponed and canceled team meetings and that the team hasn't invested in any of the efforts suggested in chapter 3 in more than a year.

Taryn Owen went through an exercise like this at PeopleScout. She examined her Outlook calendar for the previous year, capturing all of the data in a pie chart. The slices indicated time spent with clients, with stakeholders, on managing the organization, for "white space" strategic thinking, and so on. The results showed that, on the upside, she was spending time on the long-term development of her leaders, albeit only five percent. On the downside, she was spending more than a quarter of her time on unplanned operational problem-solving. Less of her time than she wanted and felt was required was spent on innovation and forward thinking. Meanwhile, she was averaging ten hours of scheduled meetings a day, including ones she had to cancel at the last minute.

Assessing your calendar in this way is a useful but humbling sanity check. Break questions about your time commitments into five parts:

1. Do you attend to *vision*: Where the organization is going, why, what success will look like, and who will care?

2. Do you attend to *goals*: What people specifically need to accomplish to realize that vision?

3. Do you attend to *alignment around strategy*: How exactly your organization will accomplish those goals, what might get in the way, and how you can overcome obstacles to success?

4. Do you attend to the *present*: Where your organization is today, as well as an honest assessment of what's working well, what's not, and what everyone needs to do about it?

5. Do you attend to *relationships*: Who on your stakeholder map most needs your time, and attention, from your team to the broader organization to your external stakeholders?

Once you've finished examining your calendar, you should see clearly where your time is really going. How much of your time and energy is being devoted to the work that really matters?

Urgent? Important? Both?

You are probably familiar with the concept of managing work that's "urgent versus important." Often attributed to President Dwight Eisenhower and popularized by business writers like Stephen Covey, the concept remains a useful guide to assessing how you manage your time and energy.

Draw a two-by-two matrix where the X-axis represents "importance" and the Y-axis represents "urgency." The upper right-hand quadrant will then stand for "most urgent and most important." The lower left-hand quadrant is "least urgent and least important." The upper left is "most urgent and least important," and the lower right is "least urgent and most important." See Figure 7.1.

If you consider all the things you do in a day or week, from meetings to project work to phone calls and emails, where does each of your tasks or investments of time belong? Assign each to one of the quadrants. Do you find the quadrant that gets most of your time and energy is the upper-right one that is designated "most urgent and most important"? This quadrant should include major deadline-driven projects and deliverables such as business reviews, key hiring interviews, a strategic company offsite, or the materials for second-quarter board meeting. It might also include crises, both business and personal: a client

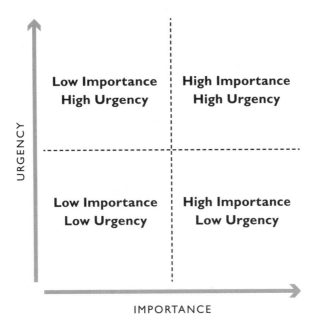

Figure 7.1 The Urgent/Important Matrix

emergency, family health troubles, or pressure from a maneuvering competitor or an angry board member. This urgent/important quadrant should typically feature the central things in your life—the ones that most demand focused attention.

How about the bottom-left quadrant, "least urgent and least important"? In the crudest terms, this is the quadrant for junk mail and any time-sucking, low-payoff activities. In other words, work you shouldn't be spending any time or energy on at all. If you're spending much time here, these activities should mostly be omitted.

And how about the upper-left quadrant, the "most urgent and least important" one? This quadrant is tricky and seductive. Attending to it offers immediate gratification, and when you're immersed in these activities you probably feel productive. You tell yourself, "I dealt with those three unexpected employee requests, answered sixty-three emails, and even managed to post an update on our new product on LinkedIn!

Now I'll go to lunch, and when I get back, I can start working on the really important stuff on my to-do list." Now ask yourself if you can deprioritize some of the things in this quadrant—or, better, delegate them to others.

That brings us to the lower-right quadrant, "least urgent and most important." This one is challenging. Work in this quadrant offers big payoffs but none of the tasks here vibrates with urgency. Here we find innovation ("Where do I want this organization to be in three years, and how can we get it there?"), strategy ("How can we better differentiate ourselves from our competitors?"), professional development ("How can I deepen my capabilities as well as those of the people I'm responsible for"), vocation and career management ("What's the right next step for me, and how can I develop and position myself to get there?"), and personal matters such as exercise, health, leisure, and family.

Check yourself to see if you fall into the tragedy of the lower-right quadrant. Do you leave many of the items there simmering on the back burner? Do you let promising windows of opportunity close while you delay action? Maybe you could have launched that project before your competitors did. Or maybe you could have gotten your team working together effectively, but now you're dealing with attrition. Or maybe you could have discussed that idea with a key board member, but because you didn't, that relationship soured. Or maybe you could have taken the family on that dream vacation, but now your eldest child is off on her career.

Have an honest conversation with yourself: Which quadrant do you live in most of the time? If it's not the upper right with mindful attention to the lower right—and deciding when you should shift things from the lower right to the upper right—you are risking a stall.

One parenthetical postscript for those who find the urgent/important matrix concept a bit too basic. An especially brilliant client of ours, a highly successful founder of several global companies, argues that you should actually seek to keep the upper-right quadrant *empty*. He refers to the high urgency/high importance quadrant as "*avoid.*" In other words, if you do a good job of clearing the unimportant half of the matrix, you can focus on the low urgency/high importance quadrant and keep the items there from moving into the upper right, and doing so will make you even more productive when it comes to the truly important matters.

Do You Reflect?

One of the simplest ways to assess whether you're in a focus stall is to track how much time you spend in undisturbed reflection or solo thought. Do you set aside real and meaningful time to let your brain slow down? To pull back and develop situational awareness? To see your goals and responsibilities from a more detached and strategic perspective? When asked, almost all executives admit that they have little time to themselves since their days are packed with back-to-back meetings. And that they have no time to stop, catch their breath, and ponder creatively. Surveys of CEOs routinely reveal that the number one thing on their wish list is "more time to reflect and think."

Despite the value of group brainstorming, research shows that genius often strikes people when they are alone. If you value your intellect and creativity as a leader—if you feel this is a strategic and differentiating asset—give your brain a runway of its own. Let it take off with your best ideas. If you do the calendar test and find you're booked twelve to fourteen hours a day, you may be focused on some of the right things at the expense of one of the most important ones: distilling your insights and experiences into new value and ways to have impact.

Recover: Raise Your Leadership Sight Picture

Management guru Peter Drucker used to say that no effective leader can remain effective in tackling more than two tasks at once.[86] His observation over many decades was that the best executives concentrated their time and energy on a critical few priorities—rather than many that are relatively important. Drucker's observation is a reminder that you should regularly rethink and remake the way you invest your time and energy. A sophisticated leader recognizes that the "critical few" may change as quickly as your organization.

As a general rule, each time you take on a new leadership role adjust your sight picture. "Back off and elevate" your sights, as we suggested in chapter 4, in terms of how to "see" which stakeholders to most closely manage. Now that you have more landscape to oversee, identify new risks and opportunities, near and far, big and small. Some are complex, some sophisticated. Make a discipline of fending off distractions and focusing on what really counts.

When we say you need to "back off," we mean several things: re-determining what you as a leader should be doing; retraining yourself to do so; realigning your team to pick up the slack; and developing your leaders so you can delegate more to them. When we say "elevate," we mean adopting a loftier target of attention: Take your eyes off the project team and put them on the division. Take your eyes off the division and put them on the company. Take your eyes off the company and put them on the marketplace. In successive coups, reorient your time and energy. Develop a new coup d'oeil.[87]

Prescribe "Do, Manage, Lead"

One of the best ways to learn to better develop your coup d'oeil is to pull out your Do-Manage-Lead list. Now that you've identified where you've been spending your time and energy, how should you re-focus tomorrow? What work should benefit from your periods of peak energy? If you're spending too much time *doing*, how will you shift your mindset to more *managing* and *leading*? You may want to make changes to systems or structure, and yes maybe you *should* hire a chief of staff. But more often you'll want to target more sophisticated behaviors.

The Do-Manage-Lead exercise challenges you to identify those behaviors, requiring above all that you change your notion of what and how to delegate. Many leaders have trouble with this one. What do you hold close to the vest and what do you hand off? Our general rule—intentionally a bold statement—is to *delegate everything someone else can do.*

We say this for two important reasons: First, as a leader, you must delegate all the activities that someone else can do because that frees you up for work *only you* can do. Second, only by delegating do you create opportunities to develop the leaders below you: Give them a chance to step up, learn new skills, and get the experience and visibility to turbocharge their careers. Delegation motivated by this logic is a hallmark of the sophisticated leader.

That said, we do believe that as a leader you should never delegate three responsibilities. The first is being the face of the organization—especially in bad times when everyone is watching. If you send lieutenants out to take the heat at times of a flare-up, the heat only intensifies, and your own authority will get singed. The second is acting as "Chief Strategy Officer." You should always be looking out from the bridge of the ship, even if you have strategy experts working for you. The third is taking charge of developing your leaders, the subject of the next chapter. Neglecting this last responsibility will hurt the organization most of all.

Not delegating everything she could caused Taryn Owen to recognize she might be facing a stall. She says she now routinely asks herself, "'Is this something that only I can do?' And if the answer is 'No,' then I must delegate it." For example, her calendar exercise told her that she had spent 25 percent of her time dealing with unplanned challenges and 16 percent on administration—almost two days a week on just those two items. She set a goal to zero out both.

As for her travel, she was logging nearly 90 percent of her time on the road. Her goal was 60 percent, and she has moved closer to that though she is not quite there yet, the realities of PeopleScout's business being what they are. That travel savings has given her more time and energy for strategic work like identifying the right kinds of acquisition targets, building new technologies, and developing her team to take on more client responsibilities.

An exercise in stakeholder mapping helped on that last point. She shed the responsibility for nurturing relationships with twenty formerly "must-see" stakeholders by introducing them to members of her team and making her direct reports responsible for those relationships, for the good of all parties. "I had capable leaders on my team whom I could trust to partner with our clients, and by empowering them to do so I created more time to focus on strategy myself," she says.

You should expect to go through an evolution when it comes to the Do-Manage-Lead mix, and you'll probably shift at key inflection points, such as a merger, acquisition, or promotion. But consider making this shift on your own when the challenges you are facing feel like they are demanding more sophistication. Keep asking yourself: Where should I be focusing as a leader of change?

On that subject, Jonathan Bush of athenahealth identifies three overarching phases of change in his growing organization. In the early years, the firm was an "execution company" where everyone worked on building products and services. Then it became an "administrative company" where, he says, only some people worked on building products and services while others worked on how to make the work more productive. Now he says it has entered a phase of "becoming an institution where some people work on stuff, others work on making the work go better, and then others work on helping people be successful."

"My job is much more 'meta' now," he reflects. "For a long time, I thought how absurd it would be to be one of those guys who had an assistant—why would I need one? Today I have a staff of three working hard to help me keep my time allocated in the right places."

Bush adds, "It has felt like a totally different job each year. And things that didn't even exist before have become the highest and best use of my time." He admits to still having a hard time resisting the allure of weed-whacking: "I like to get in and do stuff." But most of the time today he devotes his time and energy to building the institutions and capabilities of growth and management, externally as well as internally, rather than rolling up his sleeves and doing things himself. "We have an almost-religious set of icons and practices that make up life, work, and culture at athena. And most of my time is focused on those icons and practices."

As an example, he refers to athenahealth's "one pager," a list that varies from five to ten accomplishments that everyone in the company is responsible for working on, inventing whatever solutions are needed to advance the company. Recent items: complete the company's transformation to an agile organization, launch athenahealth in at least one new market, and deploy the current doctors-office systems into hospitals. As another example, he refers to the venerable athenahealth scorecard, a dozen or so metrics—employee turnover, employee engagement, bookings, operating-income growth, several measures of service to customers—aimed at helping the company grow and change. That way, he jokes, "I know when to celebrate or panic."

Bush's one-pager reflects the approach of a sophisticated leader. It is akin to the qualitative dashboard we recommended earlier for all leaders, one that reflects what you consider to be your decisive acts as a leader. At a glance, can you see where you need to personally direct energy? Developing that dashboard forces you to weigh the urgent versus the important. And it demands that you consciously separate the decisive versus the non-decisive actions that make the difference between winning and losing.

Find Your "Third Space"

A second way to cultivate the mindset and behaviors that discipline your focus is to set aside time for reflection. Make sure to provide blue sky for contemplative thinking and allow open space for fledgling ideas to mature. Also set time aside for your mind to surface and process the big issues that get flooded by the daily chaos. We are not encouraging executives to indulge in prolonged bouts of dreamy chin-stroking, hoping that lightning strikes. Rather, reflection should be a disciplined and pragmatic practice for leaders to ponder crucial issues that otherwise might go unattended. If nothing else, you need to discipline yourself to step back and elevate to ensure you're focusing on elements in work (and life!) that really matter, and not on the low-value, low-impact duties and chores.

We recommend adopting the notion of a "third space." In the 1980s, urban planner Ray Oldenburg coined the term "the third place" to describe those locations other than home or work that foster social interaction and creative dialogue: cafes, playgrounds, lobbies, malls, and parks.[88] Good and enlightened city planners make every effort to create lots of third places, the settings that allow people to step away from their workaday responsibilities and routines to recuperate and recharge.

In the same way, we recommend that you as a leader establish a third space where you're mentally transported away from work or home. We call it a "third space" because it doesn't need to be a physical place. But it *does* need to be a state where you can think differently about what you're doing and where you're focusing your time and energy.

Here's how it works. The first space is your personal life, and that should be the most important one. The second space is where you spend the majority of your conscious time: work, which usually happens in the office or in the field, but all too often these days can also be on an airplane, commuting, or (often preoccupied) while you're with family or friends. Most leaders spend nearly every waking hour engrossed in the first and second spaces. Some people even claim they have so well mastered their "work-life balance" that they toggle effortlessly back and forth between the first and second spaces. Others say they choose to make one space or the other a priority. But rather than just figuring out how to balance the two main spaces, how about carving out another space whose purpose is to make each of the first two more productive?

Create for yourself a third space—a place or even a mental mode you can enter to stop, catch your breath, take stock, think and reflect, see things more clearly, and find ways to be more successful in the rest of your life. How can you hope to do well in either the first or second space if you never make time to assess, plan, learn, and refresh? In the third space, you can be productive in ways you cannot in either your first or second spaces, so dedicate real time to it. Treat it like an important meeting—and don't let it be canceled for other commitments. If necessary, bundle the rare few fifteen-minute or half-hour free spaces on your calendar into a block of time to spend thinking alone. Capturing intervals of a calm and composed state of mind will help you recuperate, re-energize, and reset your focus—so you "do less, better" and feel more in control of getting results.

Taryn Owen offers a good example of these benefits. After losing a bid for a big contract, she asked the client's head of human resources to brief her on why PeopleScout lost, what the company could have done better, and above all, what her industry could do to support companies in accelerating the recruitment of talented employees. After the meeting, Owen spent several hours contemplating the feedback on her drive home. Those drive-time hours serendipitously became her third space.

And it came at just the right time. "Because I allowed myself to reflect on that conversation during that drive," she says, "a new product was born." She imagined creating a technology platform that would be embedded in PeopleScout's solutions. The product would connect clients with the best talent faster, in essence reproducing an experience for job candidates that would mimic the simplicity and usability of the best consumer websites. She also imagined a platform that would deploy best-in-breed technology and leverage artificial intelligence, recruitment marketing, machine learning, predictive analytics, and other emerging technologies.

From the clients' point of view, Owen foresaw a product that would deliver speed and scalability while streamlining the process for hiring managers and job candidates. Clients recruiting talent could still use their existing applicant-tracking and vendor-management systems, but

PeopleScout's platform would integrate all major systems in one place for easy implementation.

"That vision would not have occurred to me if I had used that drive to return calls and respond to crises the way I would have a year or two ago," she says. "I used that 'white space' to think strategically about how to leapfrog the market. The drive reaffirmed the importance of scheduling planned time for me time to think strategically."

Owen pitched her parent company on investing to develop the new technology, and TrueBlue embraced the business case right away. Owen's idea was to change completely how companies engage great candidates, starting from the moment a hiring manager opens a requisition for a job. With the help of artificial intelligence and machine learning, the technology platform would source active and passive candidates within seconds and leverage digital and social recruitment marketing to reach candidates wherever they were with a mobile-first experience.

In a competitive talent market in which candidates expect everything to be one touch away on their smartphones, PeopleScout's investment to streamline the sourcing process and create a consumer-like candidate experience would provide the company's clients an edge in the people business. "Having those four hours driving without phone reception," Owen says, "with time to reflect, this vision was born." The company brought that vision to life when it launched its Affinix system eight months later in November of 2017. Such is the power of third space to help a leader reap the benefits of focused time and energy.

Make the Pledge

Carving out a third space is one part of another means to recover from a stall in focus: reworking the allocation of time on your calendar. You need to make decisions: Which activities and roles will you drop? Which will you adopt? Take responsibility for answering these questions, because making explicit calendar decisions couldn't be more important. Don't remain a servant in thrall to the Outlook invitation. A good assistant, if you delegate the responsibility to him or her, can help you to commit to rethinking how you allocate your time. Your calendar application can then become a forcing device for establishing new habits, gaining a focused mindset, and changing your default behaviors to invest your time and energy where they will really make a difference.

Take a look at your Do-Manage-Lead list. That's what Owen did, and with the help of an assistant as an enforcer she now schedules according to priorities and not merely requests. She has decided how much time she wants to spend with customers, direct reports and team, her boss and parent company executives, and how much to spend focusing on innovation and new technology, assessing acquisition opportunities, and thinking about strategic direction. Her assistant keeps a watchful eye on all appointments, declining or rerouting ones that don't fit Owen's commitments, and even suggests items to delegate. "I've seen a massive difference," Owen says.

We like the Sherlock Holmes quote about filling any empty space (like a calendar) with what matters. When Watson inquires in *A Study in Scarlet* why Holmes isn't curious about knowing everything, Holmes replies: "I consider that a man's brain originally is like a little empty attic, and you have to stock it with such furniture as you choose. A fool takes in all the lumber of every sort that he comes across, so that the knowledge which might be useful to him gets crowded out, or at best is jumbled up with a lot of other things, so that he has a difficulty in laying his hands upon it."[89]

As with attics, so with calendars. Make sure you put in the right furniture. Don't let urgent and unimportant lumber crowd out everything else. To switch the metaphor, when it comes to your calendar, events are like gases: by nature they expand to occupy any space you give them. Think instead about what space *you* want to create for the work that is urgent and important, for time leading and managing (not just doing), and for your own valuable third space.

Every leader will make his or her choices, but in our experience the leaders who own fewer responsibilities grow better with their organizations than those leaders who take on too much. What three ideas or strategies are your signature initiatives? In which meetings do you drive the agenda and decision making? In which meetings do you just share your opinions while letting others drive the agenda?

If you're seeking to recreate yourself to lead at a more sophisticated level, strip from your time and energy expenditure all but the essentials, focusing on the issues where you are decisive. Doing less in the middle of the maelstrom of change and growth feels unnatural to most leaders—especially the "hard-chargers" or "alphas." But if you want to avoid a focus stall, you may need to learn to go against your natural grain.

When asked, we give leaders some broad guidelines on how to make calendar tradeoffs: Our experience is that you should bias tradeoffs, first, toward the future and away from the present; second, toward the important and not the urgent; third, toward managing up the chain of command rather than down; fourth, toward spending more time on action and not analysis; and fifth; toward close compliance with the organization's mission, vision, and values. If you follow these rules of thumb, you will send a powerful signal that you're not letting the small stuff crowd out the big.

Tap Your Energy

Yet another way to recover from a stall owing to a lack of focus is to come up with a plan for allocating your energy. What items on your Do-Manage-Lead list require peaks of brain power, attention, and zeal? You might have your own list, but we highlight four jobs that benefit from high energy: running meetings, fostering non-transactional conversations, asking questions (that is, inquiring instead of advocating), and making the most of your third space. None of these tasks should be abandoned to those times of the day when you tend to hit an energy trough.

You may think of meetings ordinarily as low-value time wasters. But our observation is that most of the waste in meetings stems from people thinking of them as a time to sit back and coast. If that attitude characterizes your meetings, you're not operating as a sophisticated leader. For a productive meeting, you should arrive with a storehouse of energy to follow an agenda based on meaningful objectives, facilitate dialogue and insights in a highly interactive way, and be sure to have specific and actionable next steps.

You can make simple policies to ensure your meetings are more productive. The rules should be the same for team meetings and one-on-ones. Taryn Owen tells us that she no longer accepts meetings without an agenda. "That's a hard line," she says. "People always have good intent. But I want to be sure that others get value out of the meeting as well." Meetings on her calendar are automatically canceled if she hasn't received an agenda a day in advance.

We talked in chapter 4 about the core skill of fostering dialogue with stakeholders, and especially non-transactional conversations. On the surface, such dialogue can sound like freeform gab sessions for the singular purpose of building rapport. But plan instead to animate a deep and open discussion, enough to surface sensitive issues and spark new ideas. Such conversations should result in interactions based on empathy, intimacy, and understanding, as opposed to persuasion, deliberation, and action.

Non-transactional conversations require you to be fully present and energetic. If you conduct them the right way, both you and the other person will find that you leave the conversation with clearer focus and a real commitment to doing something that will have meaningful impact. For example, think about your regular update meetings with your boss. If you're like most executives, these tend to be hurried, dominated by daily "firefighting," and often rescheduled because of something "more important." When they do happen, you stay transactional until a perfunctory check-in at the end: "Everything going okay otherwise?" "You bet."

Instead, try to frame one of these meetings every quarter as a breakfast or early morning coffee, and rather than jumping right into your tactical list of updates say, "I'd like to do a general update with you. I'm going to review at a high level the four or five things I think are going well for me and the business, as well as the two or three things I'm struggling with and could use your counsel on. I'd like it if you'd give me some feedback, and then also tell me what you think I need to be paying more attention to, or doing more or less of." This way you've set the scene for a productive and interactive give-and-take, a dialogue that will deepen intimacy, trust, and commitment.

Much of a leaders' work comes down to making a case persuasively. And you can't underestimate the energy that demands. But we suggest you reserve your highest-energy periods for questioning, or as we described in chapter 4, inquiry instead of advocacy. As with non-transactional conversations, it often takes more energy, and more creativity, to foster inquiry. If doing what's best for the organization is your objective—as opposed to what's easiest for you—save your moments of mental acuity for such sessions.

Finally, we recommend a high-energy period for your third space. This, again, is not just a time to grab a table at a café to relax or to throw back a drink and listen to a podcast after work, even though doing those things has benefits. Rather, find a way to energize your third space. Research has shown that exercise, for example, increases your mental prowess.[90] Whatever you do, practice matching hot topics with periods of high energy and engage in energy-producing habits. Stop treating every minute of the day the same. Some moments offer returns in gold, others in tin.

Find Your Zone

Above all, dedicate your best time and energy to fulfilling your organization's purpose, as we detailed in chapter 2. Purpose, if you recall, underpins long-term performance, resilience, commitment, employee engagement, and other critical success factors. Your people, in ways both big and small, want to become heroes in the story of their own lives, in effect making a mark on their own personal histories. How can you focus your time to make that happen? See our breakout summary at the end of this chapter for some ideas.

It's easy to think that only leaders of NGOs or nonprofits are driven by missions to do greater good. But caring about greater purpose is important for all leaders. In their own ways, the admired (and valuable) companies of our age are led by leaders who express a desire to make history—the leaders of Amazon, Facebook, Alphabet/Google, and Tesla. The same is true of the leaders of all the organizations featured in this book.

Look at Jonathan Bush's work at athenahealth. That organization has for almost two decades been committed to creating a private, nationwide network for physicians, hospitals, and patients—one which will enable doctors to operate in an internet-enabled ecosystem of services, in the same way as consumers operate in the ecosystems run by Facebook or Apple. athenanet can simplify, speed up, and deliver many services, and substantively improve healthcare.

As athena draws hospitals into this network, the company does indeed have a shot at history: new ways to deliver health care not yet even invented, including the longtime aspiration of health-care experts to establish a nationwide electronic medical record for each patient. athenahealth is well down the road to making this happen, all without government help.

But Bush couldn't have given athena this chance if he had not religiously practiced focus rather than giving into the temptation to whack weeds. His practice of focus began right from the start. In the early days, he says, "we always had the idea that we were 'playing house,' pretending we would make it to the institutional phase." He admits he was never fully confident things would work out.

However, he says, "We had a meeting in my yard every Friday called the 'one-one-one'—one week, one month, one year. Everyone stood up and said, 'Here's what I want to get done in the next week . . . in the next month . . . and in the next year. Every week, we updated the one-one-one waterfall."

The one-one-one and its focusing effect endured for years. It evolved into a list of company priorities and the company-wide scorecard. Today, Bush admits that his weed-whacking impulse still crops up. But he long ago recognized the sophistication of his challenge, which is not just mastering the complexity of serving 85,000 physician practices, but mastering himself in how he most effectively manages his time and energy.

Bush looks at the most important part of his job as a leader every day in just that way. Using a sports metaphor, he observes, "In the beginning, in the start-up days, it was a lot of man-to-man defense. Then it became zone defense. And that's a huge percentage of my life today, managing which zone to put my time into." The upshot of this practice: The company has been growing in double digits annually for a decade.

If you are part of growing an organization like athenahealth, take your cue from Bush and ask yourself, "What's my zone?" Can you reinvent yourself so that you allocate your time and energy to their highest and best use? So that you gain a refined coup d'oeil? So that, as a sophisticated leader, you don't have toxic impulses to focus on unimportant things? If you can do this, you will have positioned yourself not only to avoid a stall, but to have a shot at history. What will it be: the weeds or the tall timber?

~Reinventing Your Leadership~
A Stall In Focus?

Invest Your Time and Energy Wisely.

Beware of Danger

- You feel exhausted and overwhelmed, less energetic and passionate about what you're doing and its impact.
- You aren't comfortable delegating and/or your people complain you're not delegating enough.
- Your meetings are time-wasters, often without clear objectives.
- Urgent demands whipsaw you from crisis to crisis. You don't have control of your schedule.
- Your work/life balance is so out of whack that you can't seem to please anyone: peers, employees, or family.
- As the organization grows and changes, you are taking on more responsibilities rather than fewer, more important ones.

Assess & Troubleshoot

- Ask yourself "Where are my eyes?" On which key issues, opportunities, challenges, and metrics am I focused?
- Ask "Am I decisive to this action or decision? Or not?"
- Divide your work into "do," "manage," and "lead" activities. Are the weights of each appropriate for your role?
- Add up your calendar hours. Are you devoting most of your time leading and managing valuable work?
- Create an "urgent" versus "important" grid. Are you devoted to the most urgent, most important items?
- Keep track of which work you do when you have the highest energy. Are you using peak energy to fuel peak leadership?
- Do you set aside dedicated time for reflection? When was the last time you had a chance for a "Eureka!" moment?

Reinvent & Recover

- Commit to a new set of "do," "manage," and "lead" tasks, and decide which "do" tasks to delegate or drop.

- Enforce, with the help of an accountability partner (including your administrative assistant), rational percentages of time on your calendar to the leadership work that matters most.

- Set aside a "third space" for reflection, and use it regularly to re-weight your priorities and activities.

- Match your highest energy moments with your most important work. Defend time for it on your calendar.

- Regularly review your personal priorities and your organization's strategic priorities.

- Revamp your meeting to highlight agendas, objectives, goals, and the people responsible for them.

- Allocate your time as if you're going to "make history."

- Develop a "coup d'oeil" dashboard.

CHAPTER 8

COACH OF THE B TEAM

Stalling When You Can't Keep Your Leaders from Failing

"A teacher affects eternity; he can never tell where his influence stops."
—HENRY ADAMS, *The Education of Henry Adams*

"The greatest leader is not necessarily the one who does the greatest things. He is the one that gets the people to do the greatest things."
—RONALD REAGAN, interview with Mike Wallace,
60 Minutes, December 14, 1975

If Hector Batista had known, he would have had a different game plan in mind when he accepted the job as CEO of Big Brothers Big Sisters of New York City (BBBS) in 2010. A former professional musician with a knack for playing piano and drums, he found himself confronting a team of struggling leaders who tested him like never before. "When I came here, I realized the orchestra was playing all different music, rock and jazz." But he then came to realize that his leaders weren't just playing different music. "People were playing the wrong notes. And I had some players who didn't even know how to play the instruments."[91]

This weakness in developing leaders was not Batista's, if you recall from chapters 1 and 2. The precarious situation of the senior team stemmed from a different set of priorities pursued by the previous CEO, who had stalled in the ability to develop the next tier of staff—leaving the organization with a painful lack of leadership capability. When he arrived, says Batista, "There was a huge opportunity to make changes for the better."

For example, just three months after Batista started he became aware of a significant BBBS program that he had not heard of previously—and he became aware of it in an embarrassing way. When he met with a major foundation to provide an update, the funders asked him about this program. He was nonplussed: "What program?" he asked. Only later did he learn that a longtime staff leader had stepped away, and only a single board member had any visibility into the program. The abdication of leadership by his staff stunned Batista.

In another instance, he noted that a wealthy entrepreneur had been donating $2,500 to BBBS every year. Batista called him to thank him for his gift. The entrepreneur expressed surprise, because he had never gotten a call before. Batista, just as surprised, promptly made a personal visit, and the man upped his gift to $50,000 a year along with a $50,000 gift for a new "Going the Extra Mile" initiative. And then he put BBBS in his will for $1 million. Batista still marvels: "There was no cultivation of donors going on."

Faced with these realities, Batista realized he had some grooming to do to avoid further dysfunction. "I've never had to change every single person in senior leadership," says Batista, a veteran leader at the American Cancer Society, New York's Housing Commission, and Way to Work, a force in youth workforce development. "With BBBS, I had to learn everyone's jobs and learn about the people each leader would supervise." He had to remake his senior team to start, replacing some leaders and promoting "diamonds in the rough." He also had to align the team around a strategy and reverse behaviors in which leaders at the top formerly did little to help the leaders below them grow and thrive.

Batista's story helps us raise the question we would ask of any leader: "Are you going to leave a legacy of leadership behind?" If you're not building a bench of capable leaders, you're lapsing into one of the most tragic stalls of all: putting at risk your organization's near-term performance and longer-term success.

Many leaders get failing grades in developing the people below them, but they often have little self-awareness of it. And this is not a

C-suite-only problem. It dogs leaders at all levels. Whether you are a twentysomething overseeing two or three peers as a first-time boss or the seasoned leader of a large organization full of other accomplished leaders, the dynamic is often the same. When we visit companies, we often hear executives exclaim, as if they're talking about someone else's problem, "My leaders can't handle what I've delegated to them!" Whose fault is that? If you're the boss, it's yours. You may have worked through other stall points in your leadership, but you have come to a full stop on this one.

We are reminded of an inner-city charter school headmaster we once coached. He took it upon himself to manage every detail of running the school, even taking out the trash and doing the shopping. He was adored by parents for the way he sacrificed to pull his students out of their underprivileged surroundings, teach them in innovative ways, and guide many of them on to college. His board urged him again and again to develop a strong set of institutional leaders, including a successor. Although he accepted the logic, he never took the responsibility or action. The result? When he had to step down due to serious illness, there was no leader waiting to step up to take his place, not even on an interim basis.

Not just at BBBS, but in organizations public and private, the job neglected by too many leaders is that of developing other leaders. And that's ironic, because creating other leaders is probably *the* most important job of any leader. We attribute this neglect to the cause underlying every other stall: the difficulty of rising to the challenges of sophistication, which often require more substantive change of self than it seems.

As a leader, you can't simply hope people below you will raise themselves up by their bootstraps, inspired by you as a role model. Your followers need help, coaching, and investment to make themselves better leaders. And *you* have to help them. If you are focused only on your own leadership and results, not dedicating time and effort to your people and successors, the leaders you should be grooming almost certainly won't be able to hoist themselves higher.

So misunderstood is this stall that even when leaders recognize it, they rarely address it with the sophistication it deserves. Our experience is that they persist in not seeing that their behavior and role is the heart of the problem. Executives phone us or other consultants and say, "We need to create a leadership program!" Since we've seen this movie before, we start by explaining that leaders don't create other leaders just by financing a program. They also have to fix *themselves*. When they want to know, "What happens now?" we tell them they must recognize that their own leadership effectiveness depends on their willingness to personally and passionately own the leadership development of others.

Some leaders in this bind might sensibly delegate the job to experts in the human resources or talent development department. But that move, as in other stalls, is an organizational maneuver that dodges taking personal responsibility for the stall. Traditional management and leadership programs are necessary but not sufficient. They can tempt you into ignoring the harder role of reinventing yourself to become a sophisticated leader of leaders.

Programs can create a basic understanding of required leadership skills and competencies, but they rarely spur the mindset and behavioral change people need to make it on their own. If you ground your leadership development efforts only in basic programs run by the leadership development function or outside providers, you risk building a training edifice but never entering it to take charge of the transformation of the people within.

You might think, cleverly: "Why not let the HR team create the next generation of leaders? That's their expertise, and by delegating that duty I can redeploy my time and energy!" A strong HR or development team can indeed pull together a strategy, programs, and courseware. They are experts at classroom work, leadership retreats, brown-bag lunches, mentorship programs, and partnerships with business schools. Their work can indeed help to frame a philosophy of leadership for the organization, but they can't breathe essential life into it.

Or you might want to outsource the task, sending executives to external programs to develop themselves. Doing so lets you convince yourself that you are "investing in your people and your talent." But again, this action is a fix for an organizational challenge—a complex one—and while perhaps helpful it encourages you to avoid the real challenge. You are not developing the sophisticated capabilities that will make you a great leader known as a developer of other leaders.

Only you can judge if your leadership development programs are producing leaders consistent with your organization's values and culture. Are your people equipped for the strategic and operational ambitions of your enterprise? Do they possess the interpersonal skills you want to see in your team? Only you can coach your most important leaders in the capabilities for playing at the next level. You should not wait until you are leading a full organization to master this task. Make it part of your syllabus on leadership growth the first time in your career you assume a supervisory role.

As we said in the last chapter about where you focus your time and energy, this is a job you cannot delegate at any stage in your career, lest the leadership demands of the organization quickly outrun you. We like to ask: "If you wouldn't imagine delegating strategic oversight of your company's or project's or team's finances entirely to the finance function, why would you delegate the job of developing people entirely to HR? Aren't your people—especially your leaders—your most valuable resource?"

Few executives are natural leaders of leaders. Fewer still feel inclined or equipped to coach or teach leaders. But you should aspire to and develop yourself in this role, even as you overcome all the other stalls. If not, this stall will put your organization at real risk, and you will find yourself grinding your teeth when you eventually face a leadership talent shortage. Your team, meanwhile, will be grinding their teeth as they vent about you. Why, they will ask, won't the boss invest in developing us as leaders? Why won't he make time for coaching?

If you're a front-line leader, you may think you don't need to be personally involved in leadership development. That is a huge a mistake. People at every level need to grow, and in today's fast-moving world of ad-hoc and virtual teams, those with titles are not the only ones who need the capability to lead. Every one of your employees must lead at some point. If you don't make a concerted effort to develop others' capabilities, whether you're a factory-floor supervisor or the head of a unit, you're not going to be a leader of a high-performing team. At best, you're going to lead the B-team.

In some ways, the ultimate question for every leader is this: How should you think, behave, and act to create a culture of leadership and a cohort of great leaders? Where do you need to focus your time and effort to achieve this outcome? When you figure out the answer and adjust your behaviors accordingly, you'll have a good chance of leading an A-team. And if you fail, you won't be the only one who will stall. The leaders who look up to you will stall also—and possibly stall in every one of the sophisticated challenges discussed in this book. The consequences are dire.

Beware: That Second-Rate Feeling

How often have you wished you could just give people a manual for leadership and ignore personally helping them improve? You would have far more hours in a day as a leader. But if you were to do so, you would be sending the wrong message. If you want to have an A-team, you need to be a strong coach. In fact, when you reach the higher rungs of leadership, no matter your industry or sector, your priorities for running a successful enterprise change. You are mainly in the business of creating other leaders—often one leader at a time. You need to be like Trevor Boyce, the Microbac Laboratories CEO from chapter 1, spending as much as 50 percent of your time developing your followers.

B Team Blues

So what are the warning signs that you haven't properly attended to developing the leaders around you? The first sign, obviously enough, is that you don't feel the energy and satisfaction generated when you lead a strong team of strong players. Instead you feel unsure people are behind you, and that ill feeling usually comes along with some other uncomfortable thoughts. One is that you haven't gotten to the point where you implicitly trust your people to perform. Another is that you're uneasy delegating tasks that your leaders should be able to do.

You may be like Hector Batista, not actually sure people are up to driving the right results. What's more, you may not be sure that they'll get things done in the right ways. Maybe you're not confident your people are aligned with you. Says Batista, "I inherited a lot of directors and VPs here, and I didn't know what they did." That dearth of leadership clarity explains why the BBBS board chose not to promote a new chief executive from the inside. They had to go outside to find a leader with the right strengths.

Batista is a bit unusual in having to build a new senior team from scratch. If you join a new organization, you may expect to inherit people with skills and potential. As for Batista, he eventually and painfully came to realize that he had to reboot his entire team, and not just with new capabilities but by rekindling the sense of commitment that had waned: "I sometimes tell people, 'You're either on the train or not. It's going to be a great ride. We're going to do great things. But you're going to be on that train or you're not going to stay on this team.'" Batista keeps a model train on his office windowsill to remind people of this metaphor.

Even if you're facing a milder stall of your own making, if you lack trust in your direct reports you're surely in trouble. The same is true if you're unsure you've put the people below you into the right roles, which in turn suggests that you don't have a disciplined approach to assessing and managing your talent. When it comes time to assess people, you may be one of those leaders who simply fills out the HR performance appraisal template with little thought. You don't see managing talent as core to your job as a leader, and that is dangerous.

As for Batista: "When I arrived, I asked to look at the personnel files to see how people were evaluated, but the files were not up to par." He worked with the organization to develop a new performance appraisal process. Even today, he says the rebuilding process has not gotten to the point where he has an inside leader ready to take over the organization.

Like Batista, you should be wary if you don't have a boss-in-the-making (or, better, more than one) on the bench. Some hidden reasons can explain this failure. One is that you may be reluctant, even subconsciously, to hire people who are smarter and more talented than you. You may also unwittingly contribute to high turnover among your up-and-coming leaders, the people who say in exit interviews that they hit a dead end in their career path so they had to leave. You may even make a habit of always looking outside your organization for new hires. All of these practices send a bad message to your followers, but, more important, they should send a big message to you—you're stalled.

Of course, sometimes you should and must hire people from the outside. But that alternative should not be your default, your reflex, as if that's the only way you're going to succeed long-term. After all, few talented people want to join an organization without other A-level players. Talent attracts talent. You want to cultivate a crop of leaders with A-team DNA. If you haven't shown a commitment to developing your talent, your hunger for the brilliance of an A-team will never be satisfied.

"Not My Job!"

Another sign that you may be slipping into the stall of failing to develop leaders is that you don't think about leadership development as a core part of your job. You think of yourself mostly as a player, not a player-coach. We often run into leaders who are most motivated by "getting results." After all, that's how they rose so fast through the management ranks. They are uninterested in developing people with and through whom they could get even better results. Their personal achievements, not institutional ones, take priority.

Maybe you think that a sign of leadership is exhibiting superhuman results to inspire your team. Harvard psychologist David McClelland looked deeply into this subject years ago. Since then, research on tens of thousands of leaders has showed that, over the long term, leaders who model only relentless, heroic, results-driven behavior demoralize their teams. Although that behavior can spur short-term results, it is eventually likely to exhaust or disempower employees.[92]

Among the signs of being an overly heroic leader are several we often highlight: You prefer to accomplish great things instead of mobilizing others to achieve greater things; you prefer overcoming obstacles to teaching others to find opportunity in adversity; you prefer measuring personal success to measuring the success of followers; you prefer achieving the impossible instead of reimagining what is possible and empowering others to pursue it; and you prefer reveling in adulation for yourself to reveling in the adulation given to your followers.

Of course, leaders who themselves are high-performing, heroic leaders and personally drive results are not a bad thing—what organization doesn't need players who are great at scoring points? But if you're a leader who takes *all* the shots yourself, maybe you're better off not being a leader and remaining an individual contributor. You're not going to be happy or effective as a player-coach, let alone a general manager or team owner.

Odds are, if you can't get your mind off your own personal performance, you probably consider leadership development a burden and distraction. Maybe you're not even completely aware of it. We suggest you double-check your calendar—and not what you schedule but what you actually do. Do you keep appointments and commitments to help other leaders grow? We can't tell you how many leaders say they spend meaningful time developing others, but after checking, sheepishly admit that just about every other urgent matter has taken priority. Developmental conversations get bumped.

Recall Taryn Owen, president of PeopleScout, in the last chapter. When Owen hit a stall in managing her time and energy, she discovered that one misallocation was in the time spent developing leaders: She gauged it as just 5 percent of her time. While there are no firm rules, and a lot depends on your organization and role, our experience suggests the percentage should be much higher, 30 to 40 percent for front-line leaders and 10 to 20 percent for C-suite executives. Owen immediately raised her target, realizing she needed to be more focused on developing her people as PeopleScout underwent significant organizational change.

Nobody's Thinking Succession

Another obvious sign that you've stalled in developing leaders is hardly surprising: You have no succession plan for yourself, never mind for anyone else. A subtler sign is that you don't have succession planning baked into all your systems, including reports, regular meetings, one-on-ones, and performance metrics. If you bring up the subject only at succession planning events, you show it's just another program on par with other, often forgettable ones—a bureaucratic reflex. You're not approaching the task in a sophisticated way.[93]

Succession planning is only "baked in" when you make it a discrete subject of regular conversations with your leaders. You need to show you've expressly allocated your energy to thinking about developing the leaders of the future. Kim Pendergast, CEO of Magnuson Superchargers, calls work her number one priority, and leadership development number one at work. A veteran of five startups of her own, she bemoans the tragedy of what she calls "fifty-five and out." That's when hotshot leaders rocket upward fueled by natural skills, only to flame out in their fifties because they exhausted their natural fuel before anyone engaged them in discussions about their weaknesses and career paths.[94]

"I've lived through a lot of fifty-five-and-out people, because they did not develop the skills they needed and were left behind and therefore let go at that point where they should have been adding real value," she says. Pendergast pans the formal annual performance appraisal because she feels it fails as a tool to help her move people up the leadership ladder. "Every time someone comes into my office, it's a coaching moment," she says. "I don't really believe in annual reviews; I think they're useless. I think people only remember the one bad thing you said."

She notes that people's limitations are mostly interpersonal in nature—another nod to the importance of sophisticated leadership competencies. "They have their own demons that keep them from developing," she says. "So the question is, in their twenties and thirties, can I catch it and do anything about it?"

"Take the guy who's brilliant at strategy, but he's a bully," Pendergast suggests. "Or the one who grasps the vision, understands costing, but has an ego that gets out of control. Or the one at a meeting—when research shows the best teams have people speaking equally—and he can't stop talking."

Echoing the theme of our book, she adds, "What happens is that they have a tool in their toolbox that has made them highly successful, and every time they get in a stressful situation, they pull out that same tool, and it rewards them. But somewhere along the way, they don't develop—and it's not because they don't have vision or understanding of structure or technology. It's because they didn't develop all the other elements to become the next-level person, the manager, the leader." And they probably also didn't have a leader over them who helped them to develop and avoid their own stalls.[95]

"My own journey as a leader has been how to get the most out of these individuals," she says. She does so by making development an issue "every time you touch a person." "I'm always asking people and making people feel safe to talk about what their issues are and how they develop." In our experience working in many organizations, if you're not similarly making a habit of thinking about each of your leaders' future roles in the organization, you're headed for a stall. Too many leaders focus on performance but not succession. All they get in return is the sound of one leadership hand clapping.

Give It to the Scientists

Failing to focus on development brings us to a point we raised at the start of the chapter: an overreliance on your HR department to run leadership development programs. If you let others run the programs, disconnected from business strategy and your own priorities, you're probably seeing symptoms of a stall. Don't think it's enough to send your leaders to a generic program at a top university or leadership training center. Those programs, no matter how good the content, are conducted in a vacuum without the essential oxygen provided by your involvement.

Are your leaders getting better at sophisticated capabilities such as interpersonal style, translating your organization's strategy, role modeling its purpose, communicating in an inspiring way, fostering innovation, building relationships, or acquiring executive presence? We all have flat spots, but creating well-rounded leaders requires that people benefit from the guidance of other leaders. If you outsource this process, count yourself as a candidate for a stall.

A danger sign, even if you run all your leaders through your organization's leadership development program, is when you yourself don't make the personal investment. You need to be on hand to ensure the program reflects the culture, strategy, and competitive advantages of your organization. How active a role have you played in the design, shaping, and championing of the program? What kind of leaders, specifically, do you want and need? Do you teach and facilitate key modules? Or are you like the parent who pays the college tuition, and after four hands-off years wonders why the experience didn't result in both an honors student and a sophisticated adult?

Perhaps you see your HR programs as more of a cost center than a profit center. That's yet another bad sign: You haven't cultivated trusted partners in the HR department. Maybe you're working with off-the-shelf programs and generic outside providers. You don't feel HR offers programs customized and tailored to your objectives. If this is the case, you may be inadvertently creating the conditions for a future drought in leadership.

You might also be intimidated by the "science" involved in leadership development. What was once considered an art has become professionalized, technical, and research-based. This shift sometimes encourages leadership development professionals to warn you off having a hand in the process. But giving in to the training experts, instead of devoting your personal and expert counsel and coaching to your leaders, should cause you to feel wary.

When John Hillen was leading a 1,500-person unit at American Management Systems, the award-winning head of HR from the company headquarters suggested that the team of talent-management professionals choose Hillen's vice presidents. The HR head's confidence was admirable: his people had already earmarked a dozen new VPs to serve on Hillen's team. But Hillen didn't want leaders chosen via generic testing and developed in programs served up by others. He was charting a huge new growth direction for the enterprise and wanted to match leaders to the traits he needed to enable the new strategy. He opted to make final decisions himself.

If you do otherwise, check yourself. The two approaches aren't mutually exclusive, of course. But if you even think about hiring and training leaders based solely on their expertise, without judging their fit with the context only you as the leader understand, you'll end up with students of leadership, not leaders of people. The fault for misdirected leadership is then all yours.

WARNING: YOU'VE HIT A LEADERSHIP-DEVELOPMENT STALL

You get an uneasy feeling about your leaders' ability to lead. They don't seem to be in the right roles, you don't trust them to perform, and you tend to hire from the outside. You consider leadership development and coaching as the job of the HR department.

Assess: Spending Quality Time?

If you're seeing warning signs such as these, it's time to assess whether you yourself might be the problem. When it comes to developing leaders, you may come around to the position of Dev Ittycheria, whom we met in chapter 2. Ittycheria founded software startup Applica in the 1990s, sold it for a pittance in the dot-com crash, founded BladeLogic in 2001, sold it for $900 million, and took over as CEO of MongoDB in 2014.

Stung by struggles from early inexperience, Ittycheria says that in starting BladeLogic, "I didn't want to be one of those internet bozos who thought they were a lot better than they were." He decided to seek strong mentors, and he built a management platform that included a central plank on developing people. About his approach today, he says, "My philosophy is all about people. I view my job as a glorified HR job. If I see problems, I'm like a dog on a bone."

When describing his time leading BladeLogic, he says the software company's success quickly outran the skills and sophistication of his leaders. "We weren't successful and systematic in how we developed the next tier of management, such as figuring out who to recruit, how to develop them and their people, and getting them to produce results consistently quarter over quarter."[96] That's when, he says, "I realized the existing leadership had tapped out." So after a year, he hired a new CFO, sales chief, and head of engineering.

Trying to keep his focus on not making the mistakes of the past, he redoubled his efforts to assess early how to avoid making those mistakes again. "We had been pretty reactive about developing people. It's more art than science: people don't know how to delegate, and if they do delegate, they don't know how to empower their teams or educate their teams and involve them to produce results." That meant the "glorified HR chief" had to step in.

"People ask, 'what's your strategy?'" he says, because they think that strategy is what has made the difference in his success. "Yes, strategy, and making sure we're clear on goals, is important. But that's something you don't do every day. The day-to-day stuff is keeping the machine running, and that's all about people. That's why I spend a lot of time on leaders. The capacity of any organization to perform is directly correlated to the quality and size of its leadership team."

Do You Outsource?

One way to assess your involvement in a stall in developing leaders is to examine how decisions are made about leadership. How many of the decisions related to developing people do you make, and how many do you hand over to a consultant or your HR head? How often do you balk because you don't think of yourself as an expert in how to develop people or believe that's the domain of a specialist, not you as the boss?

Another way to assess your stall is to look carefully at your own 360-degree feedback. Check for comments on how you're doing as a coach, at giving feedback and guidance, or at being a boss that people say they learn from. Do your leaders feel they are growing and advancing in their careers under your guidance?

Tally the number of outside hires on your leadership team, and on the teams of your direct reports. How does that number compare to the number of homegrown leaders? What are the proportions? If you're buying too much talent rather than growing your own, your leaders may not be developing as you need them to. Does the proportion of outside hires suggest you are being reactive? Are you developing the number of people in-house that you think you should? Are you forced to hire because you are losing frustrated high-potential people?

Ittycheria notes that he considers it a trap to think you always have to go outside to get good people. He believes in promoting his insiders. That means finding candidates who can step up to the next level and therefore retaining and strengthening your culture through promotions. Doing so also lessens the risk of expensive external hires failing to fit in. If your tally shows you're inclined to internal hiring, this also signals to the organization that you run a meritocracy committed to its members. People can trust that if they do good work and develop themselves, they will advance. This practice can also help with retaining people, since managers who are promoted are less inclined to seek greener pastures. "You still have to set people up for success," Ittycheria says. "I don't abdicate that role."

Where Does the Time Go?

Another way to test whether you're risking a stall is to review your calendar, much as we urged in the last chapter. How much time do you spend on deliberately developing your people and helping them with career planning? How much time do you spend giving feedback to your followers and coaching them? The feedback time should be separate from management tasks such as reviewing progress and tracking progress against milestones and deliverables. During a business review, you're holding your people accountable for results; during a feedback session, you're holding yourself accountable for other people's development.

Ittycheria at MongoDB offers a great illustration of how a leader can and should make the time to develop other leaders. He stays plugged into each leader's development during both the performance-review cycle as well as what he calls "skill/will" assessments. The skill/will technique, adopted from longtime Intel CEO Andy Grove,[97] serves as Ittycheria's favored personal assessment and development tool. Leaders at every level rate each of their people on a 2x2 grid, high/low skill on one axis, high/low will (or motivation) on the other. "If someone fails," says Ittycheria, "they fail because of one of two reasons. They don't have the skills to do their job or they lack the will and desire."

Ittycheria prefers the skill/will matrix to ranking people against others, since it better explains why people are performing as they are. It offers a framework to probe why someone is performing poorly and then how to develop him or her accordingly. It also allows room for understanding how peoples' personal challenges—family strains, marital issues—can affect motivation. "Each leader who reports to me has to give the skill/will of their team members. And those managers have to rate the skill/will of the people below them. It all cascades."

"This process really forces people to assess," Ittycheria adds. "The day-to-day job of a leader is three things: recruiting, development, and getting people to execute. A lot of leaders focus on recruiting. And a lot focus on execution. But very few leaders focus on developing their teams." So, tally up your own time: How much do you invest in coaching and giving feedback versus reviewing numbers and addressing tactical problems? Let your self-assessment suggest whether you're on the road to a stall in developing leaders.

See Your Fingerprints?

A third way to determine whether you are facing a leadership development stall is to examine your company's leadership programs and activities for evidence of your fingerprints. Which of the formal programs reflects your input into objectives, design, and delivery? Which ones do you and other senior leaders participate in leading and facilitating? Look at talent assessment, training, and performance-management systems. It's a real warning sign if the fingerprints of the top leaders of a company or business unit aren't all over these, too.

Trace back the elements of your leadership development initiatives to specific ways they support your business and people-development objectives. In particular, how does each development initiative contribute to creating the leadership skills, behaviors, and mindsets that will reinforce your strategy, objectives, and culture? If the senior leaders of the company aren't engaged, your programs probably won't have the impact you need. And if you rationalize by essentially saying, "Smart people will figure out how to be effective," count yourself at serious risk, because you're abdicating one of the most important parts of your job. If your leaders fail to reach their potential, the problem is not with them. It's with you.

Are your leadership training programs true to your organization, tailored so people will both see the path and feel the inspiration to commit to their own development? Do they see you as personally sending that strong message? Does each program help your leaders answer questions to avoid their own stalls? Among key questions all your leaders should ask: How can I understand my core strengths and what I need to improve or do differently? How can I come across as strategic, forward-looking, organization-focused, and committed to my people's success? Am I personally modeling my organization's values and culture? What do other people in the organization need from me? How can I get feedback on how I'm doing as a leader?

Recover: Getting Personal With Leaders

We can't reiterate enough that the essential factor in recovering from a stall in leadership development is to commit to getting personally involved. Spread your philosophy and influence across all formal and informal efforts and programs to develop your people. Your investment sends a powerful message that will align and engage your followers. Doing so will also help each of them get better as developers of leaders themselves. Strive to reinvent yourself so that you're known and recognized as a leader who is intent on and committed to creating other leaders.

Over the course of our decades of work with executives and organizations, we have come to see three elements that matter most in developing leaders: helping leaders clarify and prioritize goals, deepening their understanding of the others whom they must engage and influence to achieve results, and developing a keener knowledge and awareness of themselves. When you are working to develop other leaders, help them keep their focus on all three: goals, others, and self. We call this model the Leadership Triangle.

Use the Leadership Triangle as one way to convey the mindset that self-knowledge and self-awareness are a means to an end, not an end in and of themselves. Bringing your best self to the fore as a leader is how you will engage others to achieve the organization's goals.

Also underscore that self-awareness must be balanced and informed by understanding the views of stakeholders. What do they want and need from me as a leader, and how can I best provide that to them? How do I come across to others when I'm under pressure, and how can I better self-manage? Helping your leaders answer these questions is the ultimate move of a sophisticated leader. As you rise to the challenge of doing so, you yourself will attain a higher level of maturity and effectiveness.

You have to balance a great many things to avoid, or to recover from, the leadership development stall. When you want to know, "what happens now?" we propose six ways to evolve to become a true leader of leaders. Each of them, in the following sections, involves heavy doses of your time and energy. Remember that your actions, not merely your words, are what enable you to grow and change as a sophisticated leader as you help others to do the same.

1. Grow Your Own Leaders

Despite the limitations of generic leadership programs, the most pragmatic way to begin your change in mindset and behavior is to spearhead the creation of a structured program for leadership development at any level in the organization. Although you may work with your HR team or talent department to develop the strategy and approach, position yourself as the champion of the effort rather than a passive sponsor. Integrate the company's strategic and business challenges, what you believe the organization needs from its leaders to excel, how each individual can get better, and how people will be held accountable for changing. Whatever your level or role as a leader, get involved in helping to create the best possible formal programs to develop other leaders, and let the Leadership Triangle be your guide.

Just as Hector Batista and Dev Ittycheria played lead roles in their organizations' leadership development programs, so did Jonathan Bush, whom we met in the last chapter. Bush's work began a decade ago when he concluded that leadership development was one of those "highest and best uses" of his time. This was in a period of growth, he says, when, "I went from doing work, to helping my leaders do the work, to actively avoiding doing the work and purely handling obstacles to the work."[98]

"That's a very different person," he says. "I changed from a guy who gravitated toward good helpers to gravitating toward people who are good challengers, standing up to me. They don't want me in the room until they're stuck." That was all part of his creating the culture and management initiatives on which he now visibly spends much of his time and energy. "I am surrounded by a lot more alphas than I was in the beginning," he adds.

In keeping with his own growth and aspirations as an enterprise leader, in 2010 he asked Mark Nevins to help design and launch a "transformational leadership program" custom-designed for the top level of executives in the company, those right below the senior team. The intention was to create strong business leaders who could drive the strategy, foster the culture, and effectively coach and mentor others. The aim was to spark a personal transformation of leaders in the face of a tide of change in the healthcare industry, ideally *before* they might stall.

Bush played a meaningful role in the design and delivery of this program, one that eventually all his vice presidents and directors—the top three hundred or so leaders across the organization—took part in. He kicked off the program with a challenging, highly interactive session on athenahealth's vision and strategy. This was not the typical talking-head brief that starts many corporate leadership programs. Rather, it was an intensive dialogue to wrestle with the fundamental questions to which Bush himself didn't know all the answers. Given the upheaval in the competitive landscape, he was challenging himself as much as his leaders. And these often spirited dialogues not only anchored the program in athenahealth's strategy, but allowed Bush to play an active role in leadership development.

With nary a presentation slide in sight, this kickoff day sparked insights that led directly to product and technology decisions for athena.

It informed everything else the participants did over the remaining days of the group session as they worked individually and in peer teams to identify specific ways to be better leaders. It gave Bush a chance to model the behaviors he expected of all the company's leaders. And the program ended with each leader crafting a detailed individual development plan.

In keeping with Bush's philosophy of making leadership development the top leaders' foremost job, in 2017 athenahealth added a program designed for all leaders moving into new roles. Not only has Bush served as a "faculty member" for most of these programs, but so do most members of his senior team, including the COO, CFO, head of strategy, head of product, head of people, business-unit heads, and even some board members. This engagement by senior leaders fuels an intense culture of leadership development. It also ensures that veteran leaders are constantly aligning themselves with the leadership capabilities needed for effective execution—and not waiting for the organization to outrun their skills.

2. Assess Your Talent

A second way to pull through a stall in leadership development is to challenge yourself to put in place a disciplined approach to assessing the talent in your organization. Once again, if you've long focused mostly on delivering results, you may not have adequately figured out how to help your leaders deliver results or help them figure out how to help those below them.

Assessing talent shouldn't be a complex or bureaucratic process. As a tool, consider making use of the classic 9-box framework popularized years ago by GE and adopted by many organizations since. Figure 8.1 shows this simple 3x3 grid indicating where to place each member of your team on a map to rate them on two dimensions: performance ("how well are they delivering today?") and potential ("do they have the capability to take on even more responsibility tomorrow?").

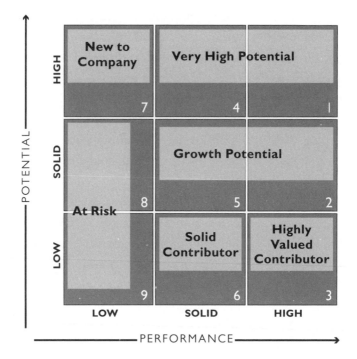

Figure 8.1 The 9-Box Team Assessment Tool

This is not a tool for performance reviews or compensation decisions, and it's not intended to pigeonhole people. Rather, its purpose is to help you as a leader decide where and how you should invest your time and energy to bring your followers and your organization to the next level of excellence. The 9-box is a snapshot that most of all can provide clarity on how better to develop the leaders who report to you.

Plot your employees onto the grid, and see what insights that mapping generates. Following are a few recommendations, depending on where you place your people in the 9-box:

New to company: For people who fall in box 7, we recommend ensuring a robust on-boarding plan (30-, 60-, 90-day, six months, and one year). This plan needs clear milestones and objectives, and you should provide your leaders with formal coaching.

Very high potential: If your people end up in boxes 4 or 1, think about their next likely position, and prepare to promote them. Get successors lined up. Double down on developing these people, to be sure you retain them and are getting the absolute most out of them.

Growth potential: For people who land in boxes 5 or 2, plan to coach, reward, and engage them. Consider expanding the scope of their roles, moving them laterally, giving them stretch assignments, assigning them a cross-functional project, or promoting them.

Highly valued contributor: Assign high-visibility projects to those people in box 3. Engage and reward them and tell them how much you value them. Continue to develop them as valuable functional experts.

Solid contributor: Engage people in box 6 in development dialogues and coach them to maximize performance. Be sure to celebrate their successes to keep them motivated.

At risk: If people are landing in boxes 8 or 9, seek to understand the root cause of their performance issues. Perhaps they are a poor fit for their jobs. Perhaps their bosses aren't investing enough time and effort in training them. Commit to formal performance-improvement plans for them, but if they persist in lagging, you must move them over or out.

The major benefit of using the 9-box team assessment tool is that the exercise should cue you to do *something* to support, develop, or address each of the people you're responsible for. The 9-box tool puts you in a people-development frame of mind: What can I do to make each of my people more successful? How can I ensure I am building the right leaders for today and tomorrow?

Once you have your team mapped, you can decide on what to do for each of them. Everyone on your team, depending on where each falls on the grid, will have his or her own development needs. It's up to you, personally, to decide how to help them get there. The grid helps you tackle perhaps your most sophisticated challenge as a leader.[99]

3. Give Better Feedback

Another powerful way to move yourself through a leadership development stall is to make a commitment to delivering feedback to your leaders. Time and again we find that leaders may intend to give feedback to their followers but don't. For one reason or another they never get around to it—or else they give a lot less feedback than they think they do. "Provide me with more feedback and coaching" is usually the most common request from followers to bosses on performance or 360-degree appraisals.

Be sure to distinguish between feedback and criticism. Feedback is an exchange of information that helps people understand how others perceive them. Feedback allows people to enhance their self-awareness and adapt their behavior to achieve better results. At its best, feedback is specific, descriptive, tough on issues, and future-oriented. You direct feedback toward pragmatic solutions and productive behavioral change. Criticism on the other hand, generally comes across as telling people how they *should* be. It is critical, generalized, judgmental, tough on the person, mostly about the past, and appears to place blame on them.

Feedback is not all about giving. It is as much about receiving and about dialogue. In other words, giving feedback is not about filling out elaborate multi-page appraisal forms. It's about employing the personal touch. Your leaders need to hear from you, and you from them. And that interchange should happen frequently, and be disassociated from any formal performance management process that affects their compensation or career path.

As an example, one of our investment banking clients, a hot-shot performer who was named a managing director, couldn't convince his bosses to promote him to a higher level because he hadn't developed a strong successor. As he committed to getting better at developing those below him as managers—not just as "deal guys"—he developed a simple feedback tool: a coaching card for each of his leaders.

On the front of an index card he wrote three or four things each leader did well and that he wanted them to do more of. On the back side of the card he wrote three or four other things each leader didn't do well, needed to get better at, or should just stop doing. He kept this stack of cards in his leather iPad case. Whenever he met one-on-one with one of his directs, he would pull out the card, review key points, ask the person how he or she thought they were doing, and provide his own feedback, suggestions, and reminders of improvement. Since the day he adopted the coaching cards, he has ascended two levels in the bank. What's more, he is known not only as one of the smartest guys in the company, but also the leader who has developed some of the best leaders in the firm.

You can devise your own approach, but the point is to create a process or system so you give more feedback—and keep it simple so that you can do it easily. And then exercise discipline to do it. For another example, when you start a new year, consider scheduling regular "pulse conversations" at specific intervals—one hundred days after the start of the year, at the midpoint, and at the end to recap how the year went. These don't have to be formal, but as in other coaching sessions, ask people to have a big-picture conversation on how things are going. Ask to hear their thoughts, tell you what's going well and not, and what they can do about it. And then ask what they need from you to be more effective.

When conducting one-on-ones like these, ask your direct report to go first, and remind yourself to listen and take notes. Inquire to see if your follower's self-assessment aligns with yours. Respond with your perspectives and suggestions. Ask what kinds of feedback they are getting from others, and whether they are soliciting it. Ask what they are worried about. Share pragmatic ideas on behavioral changes that could improve their leadership right away. Discuss blind spots. Agree on specific changes and ask them to create an action plan—as simple as books to read, specific changes to make, a top-three list of improvements—and share that with you. You're likely to spark a marked turnaround in their performance *and* their potential. Meanwhile, you will have demonstrated that you really are committed to their development.

4. Discover Your Inner Coach

Giving feedback is all a part of a larger change in mindset that you must undergo to break out of a leadership development stall. If you are to become a genuine leader of leaders, you will jumpstart yourself if you make a distinction: Sometimes you are a manager, the boss; other times you're a coach or mentor.

As a manager, you set goals, monitor and measure, hold people accountable and reward them. You tend to focus on transactional questions: How are we allocating resources? What's getting in the way? What do you need me to know or to help you figure out? What should you be escalating? How can I tell you if you're not doing a good enough job? The manager role is a critical one for execution, but it cannot be your sole role if you aim to develop your leaders.

The other role you need to play is coach, and that's when you focus on *how* people lead rather than on *what* they should seek to accomplish. When you focus on the "how" you engage more in non-transactional questions. Your purpose is to help people learn and grow via dialogue to bring out their best, to allow them to understand that your job is also to make them better, and to show you care about them as people and about their careers. Think of these conversations as conducted side by side, not head to head. They are "porch swing" conversations. They don't happen over spreadsheets.[100]

You'll be less successful if you flip-flop between these two modes in the same meeting: the carrot-and-stick of the boss alternating with the ear and empathy of the coach. The fact is, the honest boss role, which is more urgent and tactical, will usually dominate most meetings. So be deliberate about when to engage in "manager meetings" versus "coach meetings"— and don't let "urgent matters" drive coach meetings off your calendar.

Here's an illustration: We once had a client who had two coffee mugs. One said BOSS on it, the other COACH. When he met one-on-one with a subordinate he would choose the mug that best fit the meeting's purpose and slide it onto the desk as a centerpiece. That was a reminder to his leader (and to himself!) about what kind of meeting it was. And he made sure that the COACH mug appeared no less than every six weeks.

"Boss" meetings are fine to have in your office, where you have access to background materials, spreadsheets, and reports. But "coach" meetings are better held in a place more conducive to open dialogue—not in your office, with its trappings of power, but in a comfortable conference room, huddle room, local coffee shop, or outdoors during a walk. This kind of dialogue needs to feel different, as you adapt your behaviors to catalyze the development of your leader.

Trevor Boyce, whose story kicked off this book, says that when he identifies a talented employee he follows up by "finding out what makes them tick, what their future motivators are." He spends time with his people not just in teams but individually. For leaders who appreciate the outdoors, he favors spending time on his fishing boat in Rhode Island, where they can catch fish together, and Boyce can ask about the leader's joys and frustrations with the company all while building intimacy and engagement.

Don't hold coach meetings only once in a blue moon—or, worse, when you feel you have to give tough feedback. Have them minimally every two months, and when possible in a place where your subordinate wants to meet: over breakfast, at the end of the day, or adjacent to a meeting or offsite. Recall Hector Batista's habit, in chapter 1, of having a monthly meeting he refers to as his leaders' meeting, as distinct from the monthly meeting he calls "his" meeting. Or Kim Pendergast's ideal of coaching at every touch point. More frequent meetings give time for people to think, act, and reflect—and then come back for debriefing and more coaching. Greater frequency leads to more open and authentic conversation, trust, and transparency.[101]

5. Planning for Development

When we coach leaders, and coach them to coach others, we require them to create a formal leadership plan. The specific template for this plan is less important than the thoughtful investment in creating it. Still, most executives like to respond to a framework rather than start from a blank sheet of paper, so we created what we call a Leadership Growth Plan. See Figure 8.2.

If you sit down and thoughtfully work through this template, reflecting on your own leadership role, you'll find you have much better clarity on where you need to invest your time and effort to be a more effective leader. You can then take each of your direct reports through the same exercise. Box by box, you can employ this simple tool to compel yourself to answer fundamental questions for success. The template then also gives you a great dashboard with which to coach your direct reports. The leadership growth plan helps you hold yourself accountable for coaching and hold your people accountable for adapting their mindsets and behaviors to become better leaders.

As an example, we once worked with a leader who presented to his boss a plan that pinpointed three distinct weaknesses: poor collaboration during crises; trouble asking for feedback; and difficulty developing meaningful client relationships. He suggested to his boss three behaviors for practice: creating and then consulting with a dedicated team during crises, polling a team of peers for feedback regularly, and working with his boss to identify key clients with whom to communicate better and more regularly.

This plan gave his boss, who was until then not the best coach, an easy way to ease into the coaching process. Here again, the power of the leadership growth plan came from using it to facilitate interaction and aid in overcoming a hesitancy or inability to coach. Ask your people to fill out a plan like this one and then take you through it. As in any good feedback session, take pains to listen, ask questions, and make suggestions. If it helps, invite a third person to join these discussions: A facilitator or referee can help you be sure to behave as if your COACH mug is on the table.

Your Organization/ Function	Your Role	Your Team	Your Leadership
		How strong is your team, and how can it improve? (Collaboration, communication, execution, decision-making, and conflict resolution.)	
How would you describe the core purpose of your function?	What are your core responsibilities?		What core strengths should you most rely on?
What are your critical goals for this year? And longer-term, over the next 18 months?	What early wins can you secure?	How do you assess each member of the team? (Core strengths, key development areas, performance, potential, and career trajectory.)	What things can you do differently or get better at?
Who are your customers/clients, both internal and external? How will you best understand their needs and requirements?	How will you and your boss measure your success? (Key metrics, financial targets, etc.)	What is your talent strategy? (Hiring, succession planning, training, advancing, redeploying, coaching.)	Where should you focus your time and energy as a leader, including to make your organization transition successful?
What changes need to be made? (Execution, process, structure, etc.) What are your enablers for success? What are the barriers?	How will you manage your relationship with your direct boss?	How will you lead this team? (Meeting cadence, communication, delegation, and execution of goals.)	What will you personally do to reinforce and model the culture of your organization?

Leading the Enterprise

Who are your key stakeholders? How will you ensure collaboration and communication on important issues?	What do other parts of the organization need from you? What do you need from them?	How will you get feedback on your organization and leadership effectiveness from key people across the organization?	How will you help the broader organization drive meaningful change initiatives?

Figure 8.2 The Leadership Growth Plan

Source: Nevins Consulting, Inc.

6. Commit to Developmental Dialogues

If you are to recover from a stall in leadership development, you can see that underlying a lot of actions we suggest (which we capture in our final breakout summary below) is one fundamental act of all great leadership: fostering dialogue. We stressed this capability in chapter 5, but we want to underscore it again here. No matter which stall you are working on, you must always come back to this most important executive capability. You can see as much in the stories of Hector Batista, Dev Ittycheria, Kim Pendergast, Jonathan Bush, and the host of other leaders whose experiences we chronicle throughout this book. *You must foster dialogue* to pull yourself through each of the leadership stalls we have identified, and foster dialogue as well to develop the leaders below you to help them avoid their own stalls.

As we've written elsewhere,[102] when you don't use dialogue, along with the other techniques we've described in the book for development, you risk creating what we call "your most dangerous employees." These are the high-performance stars who may stall and bring others down with them. Such a designation could describe any leader who is "missing" something sophisticated—and it could also describe you!

For managers at any level of an organization, growth and change as a leader require increasing complexity to keep the plane flying—indeed to keep an air force of planes flying. As we've stressed, you can respond to complexity partly with the tools of an organizational mechanic. Keeping your force of high-altitude jets in flight is to a large degree about having the right machines and the organizational structure to keep them aloft.

But growth and change also demand more sophistication as a leader—much more, disproportionately more, as you rise in the organization and hit one inflection point after another. You can only handle these kinds of sophisticated challenges with dialogue. Dialogue is the preeminent tool for any organizational leader, at any level, who wants a team of leaders who can take the organization to new heights and not get outrun in the process.

As Chuck Yeager once said, "There's no such thing as a natural-born pilot."[103] Don't succumb to the tragic flaw of so many leaders, those who fail to develop new capabilities to master the layers of sophistication required for transcendent leadership. If you commit to reinventing yourself as a sophisticated leader, you will find you can travel far beyond what you ever thought you could do naturally.

Yes, you will have to work hard to create the A-Team. From storytelling to stakeholder management to time mastery to building authority to developing sophisticated leaders as your legacy—you need to apply steady effort to leadership development for yourself and for your people. That's how, like Trevor Boyce, you will avoid hitting all the predictable stalls. You will help your people avoid them, too. And you'll get on a wave, rough or not, and keep riding it.

~Reinventing Your Leadership~
A Stall in Leadership Development

Aspire to Be a Leader of Leaders.

Beware of Danger

- You don't consider your leadership team an "A-Team."
- You're not sure your leaders are in the right roles, and you can't always trust them to perform.
- You tend to look outside the organization for talent.
- Coaching your followers to be better leaders feels like a distraction from "real work."
- You don't have leadership succession plans, and you don't integrate succession planning into all systems and conversations.
- You have little to do with your company's leadership development programs and initiatives.
- You don't tailor leadership development to your company's goals and culture.
- You feel you don't have the technical expertise to put a personal stamp on leadership development.

Assess & Troubleshoot

- Count the decisions being made about leadership development—How many are yours? How many are coming from your HR team or consultants?
- Review your 360-degree appraisals. How many of your people call you a great mentor or coach?
- Look at the percentage of new hires on your team. Are you buying or growing your own talent?
- Tally how much time you actually spend on one-on-one coaching or leadership development.
- Do you regularly map and assess your talent?
- Have you made efforts to develop customized, high-impact, in-house leadership programs?

Recover & Reinvent

- Take command of shaping your organization's leadership-development programs and playing a meaningful role in leading them.

- Systematically assess your talent, using a tool such as the 9-box to identify development actions.

- Give feedback, and practice giving it more frequently and effectively. Find your own authentic way to have coaching dialogues: don't rely on checklists or forms.

- Commit to becoming a coach as well as a boss, and dedicate discrete time for both.

- Hold regular "pulse-check" conversations with your leaders, at least two or three times a year.

- Ask your leaders to create their own leadership growth plans—and coach them on focal areas and action items.

- Make a habit of conducting "developmental dialogues."

CHAPTER 9

From Stall to Success

Some Final Thoughts

"Wise men ne'er sit and wail their loss, but cheerily seek how to redress their harms."—WILLIAM SHAKESPEARE, *Henry VI*

"How wonderful it is that nobody need wait a single moment before starting to improve the world."

—ANNE FRANK, *The Diary of a Young Girl*

Wallace Stegner once wrote, "There is a sense in which we are all each other's consequences."[104] As a leader, as the head of a human community, however big or small, what will your consequences be? How will you perform at higher levels of effectiveness, again and again, so you can send ever bigger ripples of positive and beneficial consequences to the world around you?

Or to come back to the way this book started, how will you become not just a better leader, but your "best leader ever"? How would you want people to draw or depict your leadership qualities? What mix of skills, traits, and behaviors do you aspire to as the hallmarks of your own leadership?

Throughout this book, we proposed a natural progression for leaders in all fields and walks of life, a shift over time such that, if you're one of those leaders, your effectiveness will increasingly be based less on your technical and tactical mastery and more on your strategic and interpersonal skills. To some extent, this progression is a shift from depending solely on "hard" skills to also on "soft" ones. That shift is consistent with the generally accepted theory that the best leaders enhance their intelligence and technical knowledge (IQ), with emotional intelligence ("EQ"). Both are necessary.

But in our work over the decades, we have come to believe that describing the progression as merely a shift to combine soft with hard doesn't properly characterize the growth we see in the best leaders. Neither the hard, nor the soft, nor even both together, will fully enable leaders to move to their next level of effectiveness. The best leaders, out of the hundreds if not thousands we have worked with over the years, take a different route. They master the sophisticated challenges of leadership with an almost counterintuitive blend of capabilities and mindset.[105]

Whether you are a leader in a business, a nonprofit, a civic group, or government agency, you will become a more sophisticated leader not by abandoning the managerial mastery, analytical skill, business smarts, or work ethic that have served you so well for so many years. Those are the things that brought you to the top of your game as you grew your organizations and grappled with increasing levels of complexity. You will instead add to and evolve your leadership repertoire with a new set of executive capabilities, mindsets, and behaviors.

This new repertoire of leadership competencies is what's required to overcome new challenges of sophistication. In essence, best leaders reinvent themselves: their role, their approach, their sources of authority, how they focus their time and energy, the way they interact with people, and, most fundamentally, how they come across to others as leaders.

In our experience, those leaders who have triumphed over the toughest challenges of growth and change do not fit a model. These "masters of sophistication" range across every possible personality and type. Still, all tend to have a number of characteristics in common, however differently expressed in their own styles.

If you are to become a sophisticated leader, you will be one who tends to be more empathetic and skilled in dialogue than leaders bent primarily on tackling increased complexity. You will seek to start conversations rather than issuing orders. You will ask questions rather than giving answers, at times even frustrating those around you who are looking for quick decisions or new analytics to deliver a solution. In short, you will be more dialogic.

At the same time, the dialogue and searching you engage in with stakeholders will not betray uncertainty or a wishy-washy approach. You will be more determined and resolute when it comes to organizational purpose, ethical decisions, or cultural values because you know meaning and values drive long-term success. You will have an inner compass, and that compass will help you guide your organization's direction, identity, and values, which you will reinforce through dialogue and more inclusive decision-making.

You will find yourself a changed person when you perform at the highest level. That's when you are a better listener than ever before, and yet at the same time you are forceful and determined in the way you elaborate ideas, take action, and communicate needed change. You are ever more aware of competing value systems among your stakeholders, and you take extraordinary steps to understand discord and accommodate people with different ideas. And yet you are firm, confident, and compassionate in making the "right versus right" judgment calls on questions for which there are no pat, formulaic answers.

As a master of sophistication, you will sometimes face confusing and elaborate challenges brought about by growth or change. That's when you may actually depend on less data to make decisions, not more. You will simplify issues without dumbing them down or turning a blind eye to tangled matters. You will be ruthless about the investment of your own time and energy, devoting yourself to the important things only you can do and that you can or should not delegate. In other words, you will be the active captain of your own team.

It will sometimes come as a surprise to your followers, but as you master sophistication you may at times appear to be more detached or less interested in the details. In the past, you may have relished as the highest compliment, "She really rolls up her sleeves and gets her hands dirty," or "He's a real take-charge guy." But if you're among the best leaders, your purposeful resolve will be matched by flexibility, your resoluteness by openness, and your calm decisiveness by a willingness to engage. You will exemplify the seemingly counterintuitive concept proposed by researchers Robert Goffee and Gareth Jones: "tough empathy."[106]

Leaders who successfully keep pace with their growing or changing organizations can acquire new capabilities and reinvent themselves to conquer sophisticated challenges.

As we've shown in previous chapters, overcoming a stall in purpose requires you to become more strategic, incisive, and attentive to the need for a narrative that captures purpose and values.

Getting through a team stall requires you to be more inclusive, dialogic, and focused on alignment and accountability.

Preventing the stakeholder stall demands that you acquire political astuteness, a strategic perspective, and the ability to persuade and influence rather than control.

Triumphing over a stall in leading change calls on you to combine empathetic understanding with discernment, creativity, and determination.

Being able to avoid a stall in your authority necessitates a commitment to acquiring range and being trustworthy, reflective, and judicious.

Avoiding a stall in focus, where you're working harder but not getting commensurate results, requires new discipline, decisiveness, a honing of intuition about what matters most, and a commitment to delegating.

And finally, avoiding a stall in leadership development calls on you to become an expert at achieving through others by devoting more time than ever to being a coach, a teacher, and a creator of other leaders.

This may all sound daunting, especially when you add it all up in just a few paragraphs. But don't despair. Reinventing yourself as a leader can start with something as simple as taking on the exercises in the previous chapters one-by-one. Each exercise is an aid to helping you change your mindset and behavior. We could have offered any number of other aids, and many business books do, but these are the ones that we and our clients have found most useful and powerful.

In our work with many leaders, we sometimes kick off our programs with one additional exercise where we ask people to identify leadership in others—in this case, others portrayed in film. In particular, we ask the leaders to watch the 1982 movie *Gandhi* and then choose clips they feel illustrate the leadership behaviors and capabilities that matter most in their organization. Which scenes, we ask, show Gandhi practicing the sophisticated elements of leadership that matter most to you?

If you know the life story of Mohandas Gandhi, you know he was not just a role model for nonviolent civil disobedience. He was also a paragon of highly engaged leadership. Gandhi was a marvel at creating a purpose-driven narrative (to bring about India's home rule), managing stakeholders (of all backgrounds, classes, and faiths), developing other leaders, and tirelessly focusing his time and energy in just the right places to pursue a goal that must have seemed almost inconceivable.

What Gandhi accomplished dwarfs what any of us might aspire to as leaders. But the film clip exercise hits home in our leadership sessions because it enables people to think in new ways about how they can try to be the best leaders ever in their organizations. What's more, the exercise allows leaders to see how different their answers are from those they would naturally come up with in another exercise—for example, drawing up a conventional job description.

Formal executive job specs for hiring tend to stress functional knowledge, relevant experience, role-specific competencies, and professional certifications. These descriptions prescribe someone who is highly committed, works hard, sets goals, executes actions accordingly, and identifies and appoints strong managers. Although conventional job descriptions give a customary nod to interpersonal skills or "cultural fit," they essentially describe a leader who can master the challenges of complexity.

Inspired by Gandhi, many leaders in these sessions start to appreciate even more what we have been calling the sophisticated dimensions of leadership: vision, teamwork, caring, dialogue, coaching, self-awareness, stakeholder engagement, and systemic thinking. They choose and discuss scenes that characterize the kind of leader who has mastered the sophisticated capabilities we stress for overcoming the seven stalls of leadership.

One organization inspired by the Gandhi exercise is Schlumberger, the world's largest oilfield services company. Few companies on Earth present the level of complexity of Schlumberger, which has 100,000 employees in nearly 100 countries. In recent years, the company's leadership team has set an ambitious goal: to become the best-run company in the world. Their thinking is that only companies running with the highest levels of excellence will remain competitive among global leaders.[107]

To achieve that goal, Schlumberger kicked off the formal deployment of what it has called its "transformation" one August day in 2015, as the company's sixty most senior executives gathered for a meeting in London. The question they debated at the start: What matters most in leading transformation? "What really makes the difference?" asked Dominique Malard, one of the executives chosen to spearhead the effort. "Not all of us are natural leaders, and some are better than others."

Schlumberger needed to crack this question of leadership if the executives hoped to lead a change that would sweep across the ranks of their 13,000 senior managers around the world, the people who would bring the transformation to all 100,000 employees in creating the sought-after "step change" in efficiency, reliability, and integration. And the company's senior leaders committed to this ambitious effort at an unimaginably challenging time, as the price of a barrel of oil fell from over $100 to $30, in turn creating profound operating and financial challenges.

As leaders in a company made up almost entirely of bright engineers, Malard and his colleagues naturally broke the leadership question down into its component parts. First, they decided the differentiating factor could not be intellect, at least not at Schlumberger. The company had a structured recruiting process for hiring engineers. It hired only people with degrees from the best universities in the world. On average, its engineers have a consistent IQ level in the 120–135 range.

Second, the difference could not be education and training. Every engineer, already a top student, graduates from Schlumberger's fixed-step training program. "So the second type of intelligence, acquiring technical and functional knowledge, is pretty consistent," says Malard. In other words, it was not education that set great Schlumberger leaders apart.

And what did that leave? "The message was, as a leader, if you have high IQ and the same level of education, and if you want to be successful in deploying changes, what sets you apart is your level of emotional intelligence," says Malard. And that's what he conveyed to his peers: To succeed with the transformation, Schlumberger's 13,000 leaders around the world would need a new level of leadership sophistication.

And thus, Schlumberger, in its quest to become preeminent, was kicking off the deployment of its transformation not just by focusing on technology, and not just by means of management systems and tools, but by focusing on those capabilities that require a different approach to leadership. Different skills, mindsets, and capabilities.

As a part of this process, the company's leaders screened thirty minutes' worth of specifically chosen clips from *Gandhi* to stimulate conversation about sophisticated leadership skills. The exercise was part of a larger effort wherein Mark Nevins helped create a two-week "academy" to equip Schlumberger's change leaders to evangelize change across the organization.

In a session around the whiteboard, Malard and his team used colored markers to describe different dimensions of the transformation deployment. In red, they listed technical changes: improvements as simple as using more bar codes and GPS location technology. In blue, they itemized project management or systems components, including how to define, measure, and monitor progress in implementing those red changes. In green, they listed different approaches required in leadership skills, mindsets, and capabilities.

Everyone quickly came to realize that "the green stuff"—the sophisticated capacity to "align, engage, and empower" the workforce—was what would enable the transformation to take hold across the world. "We have an army dedicated to realizing the red stuff, and we do the project management with the blue stuff," Malard explains. "But unless we get engagement and buy-in, it's going to be 'push' and not 'pull.' We know that the more you push, the more people resist, so to overcome resistance we went into an extensive campaign of green stuff."

Although the company's leaders were intent on getting red stuff accomplished—the mechanical changes of a complex enterprise—they knew the muscle-building to do so would require more green for instilling greater self-awareness in leaders. For understanding and managing large and diverse groups of stakeholders, often in remote locations. For fostering dialogue and getting better at "difficult conversations." For understanding how people respond to change, and how to coax and coach them through resistance to engage them as evangelists. For communicating in ways that link execution to purpose.

The point was not that red, blue, or green was more important; it was that mastering *all three* was necessary for success. For a company built on and proud of its engineering capabilities, this was a novel—indeed foreign—idea. Malard, a top executive who started as a field engineer and rose to president of one of the business units, says "this role completely transformed my thought."

"Funnily enough," he adds, "I became quite passionate about 'the green.' It really transformed me professionally and personally in how I approach situations and how I deal with people." He says that in the past he was a "very directive" leader. Now he likes to cite a quotation attributed to Gandhi: "I suppose leadership at one time meant muscles; but today it means getting along with people."

Schlumberger's story helps us raise one more question: How should you act as a leader today if you expect yourself to succeed in your career by mastering "the green stuff"? What will make you the person who confronts and overcomes the subtle, sophisticated, and deeply embedded challenges of the seven stalls? How will you appear in the mirror with the judgment, character, presence, and savoir faire of a leader of leaders? You're not likely to be Gandhi—but how will you change?

Above all, you will always be thinking about remaking yourself, always striving to grow and adapt. You will be a leader who can't stand still. That's the message underlying this entire book. If there is any overarching warning sign of a stall, it's that if you haven't been pushing to grow your leadership capabilities, you're in trouble. If you haven't been eager, throughout your career, to figure out *how* to get to the next level as a leader, your stall is probably just ahead.

In the preceding chapters, we've outlined an approach for changing your mindset to become just that kind of constantly growing leader, an approach that spurs you to reinvent yourself constantly as your organization grows and changes, to wake up every morning and ask, "How can I be the best leader ever?"

And what are the consequences if you don't? We are reminded of an anecdote by one of our colleagues, a CEO who suggested to one of the leaders below him that he should consider working with an executive coach. The response: "I don't need a coach. I'm good at what I do." The CEO's comment: "That attitude is the kiss of death."

Don't let that attitude take hold of you. Commit to improving yourself on an ongoing basis as one of the most important and fundamental parts of your job. Pay attention to the warning signs of stalls, and remember that stalls are common and maybe even inevitable, even for the best leaders. Make a habit of asking yourself regularly, when you sense a stall coming and before you even hit it: "What happens now?"

In this book, we urge you to approach the answer to that question in three steps.

1. Become More Aware

First of all, scale up your situational awareness. What's changing in your organization? What do you need to change in yourself to tackle the emerging challenges?

You probably recognize new challenges of complexity, because they are concrete, systems-based, structural, and managerial. And because they are usually urgent and give way to quick resolution through known steps. But are you just as quickly recognizing new challenges of sophistication? These are subtle, resist resolution through fixed steps, are entangled in interrelated challenges—and are less urgent and can't be resolved with traditional solutions.

Ask yourself honestly: How perceptive am I as I look both within and outside myself to see the challenges of sophistication? Do I, dangerously, tend to conclude that problems are those of the organization rather than my own? How good am I at taking multiple viewpoints and looking at myself and my organization from a perspective removed from both?

Take stock of impending warning signs: When your people are behaving contrary to your values and culture. When your team members are acting like freelancers. When your universe of stakeholders seems indifferent. When your people react only when you command them to. When you feel like you're not even close to leading an "A-team." Awareness is the prerequisite for understanding.

2. Assess and Troubleshoot

Second, assess and understand yourself. Can you become a balanced critic of your own strengths and weaknesses? Can you struggle to see that, when faced with new challenges of sophistication, perhaps *you're* the problem? Are you a ready-fire-aim leader who misinterprets growing sophistication for growing complexity?

Test yourself for what you don't know—but perhaps should. Seek to better understand yourself, your enterprise, and your interactions with others and how they perceive you. Relish self-discovery, not self-importance. Be a student of the human condition. Be on the lookout for traditional practices or behaviors that may not work tomorrow.

And don't dwell only in introspection. Use the index-card test to see if your leaders are aligned, draw a map of stakeholders to pinpoint which need more attention, query people to see whether they can recite the mission and purpose, re-examine your sources of authority, ask if you're initiating enough developmental dialogues.

You have to be honest with yourself: What do the tests reveal? Am I picking up only the accolades and compliments? Or am I also in tune with my undeveloped capabilities, particularly as others see them and as the changing organization reveals them? Understanding is then the prerequisite for recovery.

3. Recover and Reinvent

Third, act deliberately to recover from—or avoid—those seven deadly stalls. Develop capabilities that change your behaviors and thinking. Ask, "What can I become?" Will I accept and do something with the feedback I'm getting, from others and from my own honest self-assessment? Or would it make sense to engage a coach, whether a professional one or one of my peers who can give me feedback and help me hold myself accountable? Can I make better use of my mentors? Am I focusing my time and energy in the right places? If I'm a star performer, how can I evolve into an engaging leader of others and a creator of other leaders?

Choose solutions to respond to complexity, but don't fall for the tragic flaw of ignoring what you need to do to meet the challenges of sophistication. Hold a story-creation session with people across your organization. Take your team off-site and ask: Where are we? Where are we going? How will we get there? "Lift and shift" your eyes to engage different stakeholders. Communicate in the style your people like to receive. Role model gravitas with the "seven wells": well read, well traveled, well spoken, well dressed, well balanced, well experienced, well reflected. To achieve that last "well," set aside a "third space" for active reflection.

And most important of all, don't let yourself become your own "most dangerous employee." When you get a whiff of your own stalling, trace the cause—and refocus on how to grow yourself into a more seasoned, holistic leader. You have to plant one foot in each of two parallel worlds, the worlds of complexity and sophistication, because every growing and changing organization challenges leaders in both areas.

If you've had a long run as a successful leader, it may not be easy to find this new path. Why, after a run of success, would you doubt yourself, check for flaws, and initiate changes to enhance your personal leadership? Doing so is not natural. It may make you feel uncomfortable. But check your leadership pulse regularly. Is it telegraphing that you have an opportunity for personal development to become a sophisticated leader?

With this three-part approach, you're on your way to growing as a sophisticated leader as fast as your organization will challenge you to do so. You'll focus on the important, not just the urgent. You'll have the vision to clarify and make tough decisions based on a compelling story about the future. You'll help others challenge the status quo and get better, as individuals and as teams. By distinguishing your roles as doer, manager, and leader, you'll focus your time and energy where you can have most impact. At the service of your followers and institution, you'll make your enterprise greater than the sum of the people within it.

And that's how you will gauge your success—not just on whether you deliver results but on the positive consequences you've created for your stakeholders and the broader enterprise.

At Schlumberger, some people were uncomfortable when company leaders asked them to think so differently about their roles as leaders. At one point, every change leader learned about the "change curve," a concept developed by Cynthia Scott and Dennis Jaffe[108] that mirrors Elisabeth Kübler-Ross's famous model of the stages of grief.[109] Every person experiencing change must work through predictable emotional and behavioral stages: denial, resistance, exploration, and commitment.

As the champion of a companywide leadership development program, Dominique Malard ensured that all 3,000 of the top leaders in Schlumberger learned how to situate themselves and their followers along that curve. "We had a lot of people either in denial or in passive resistance," says Malard. "We had deployed all this energy communicating the red stuff. People were not actively resisting, but they were saying, 'Yes,' and not taking action. People would think, 'We're different.' Or 'You can do that somewhere else, but not here.'"

"What was really a big aha," Malard says, "was how the change curve allowed people to identify themselves as to which box they were in: denial, resistance, exploration, or commitment. The breakthrough came when people started calling each other out: 'You are in denial" or 'Good, now you're exploring.'" And then they worked to teach and coach each other. The exercise was a good reminder for any leader that you can't possibly lead others through change until you first lead yourself.

The Schlumberger case is a special one. The company's top management recognized that, in undergoing a transformation, many leaders would hit stalls. Malard's effort, in which he armed a companywide force of change agents with tools ranging from stakeholder mapping to working through conflict to communicating more effectively without positional power, catapulted many of these change agents over leadership stalls before they even hit them.

Looking at your own leadership challenges, how can you do the same? Use this book as your guide: Open your eyes to the warning signs, assess your capabilities, and reignite your success with recovery actions before it's too late.

Malard says that Schlumberger leaders developed a new sensitivity to "the green stuff." Asked which capabilities have most benefitted Schlumberger leaders, he points to managing stakeholders and learning to communicate change, both highlighted in the Gandhi exercise. "We're a very transactional organization," he says, and points to the nature of the company's engineering culture. "People barely say hello to someone else. When you need something, you just call people on the phone, get what you need, and that's the end of it."

"The green stuff has added a non-transactional aspect to relationships," Malard says. "That doesn't put the transactional part in jeopardy. It just adds to it. The 'how' is completely different, and in the end, the results are much better."

Indeed, when it comes to tackling any of the sophisticated challenges you will face as a leader, the "how" is everything—*how* you tell the story, *how* you build networks, *how* you align teams, *how* you change your style, *how* you project character, *how* you make judgments, *how* you conduct a dialogue, *how* you inspire others, *how* you coach. In short, *how* you change and reinvent yourself.

No matter your level, don't assume you will grow as a leader without hitting a few bumps along the way. You can't avoid stalls entirely. But if you make the commitment, over your career as a leader, you will learn to sense impending stalls. And you will continue to grow without undue slowdowns. That's when you will become your own version of your "best leader ever." And that's when you will spread positive consequences beyond your job. You will create a lasting legacy for yourself, for others, for your organization, and for the world around you.

Notes

1 The story of Microbac Laboratories comes from author interviews with Trevor Boyce, 10 January 2017 and 15 June 2017.

2 Although we argue that leaders stall from not recognizing their weaknesses, we acknowledge that leaders can also overcome hurdles by better leveraging their strengths. For example, see Laura Morgan Roberts, Gretchen Spreitzer, Jane Dutton, Robert Quinn, Emily Heaphy, and Brianna Barker, "How to Play to Your Strengths," *Harvard Business Review* (January 2005).

3 Larry E. Greiner, "Evolution and Revolution as Organizations Grow," *Harvard Business Review* (May-June 1998).

4 See also Neil Churchill and Virginia Lewis, "The Five Stages of Small Business Growth," *Harvard Business Review* (May-June 1983).

5 The distinction we make between complexity and sophistication has parallels in the work of John Kotter, who has written "Management is about coping with complexity. Leadership, by contrast, is about coping with change." See John Kotter, "What Leaders Really Do," *Harvard Business Review* (December 2001).

6 This story is told, among other places, in Nathan Hodge, *Armed Humanitarians: The Rise of the Nation Builders* (New York: Bloomsbury Press, 2011), 155–161.

7 Author interview with Frank Lavin, 13 April 2017.

8 Daniel Goleman, "What Makes a Leader," *Harvard Business Review* (January 2004). See also Daniel Goleman and Richard E. Boyatzis, "Emotional Intelligence Has 12 Elements. Which Do You Need to Work on?" *Harvard Business Review (online)*, 6 February 2017.

9 See also Daniel Goleman, "Leadership That Gets Results," *Harvard Business Review* (March-April 2000); and Daniel Goleman, Richard Boyatzis, and Annie McKee, *Primal Leadership* (Boston: Harvard Business Review Press, 2004).

10 See also Michael D. Watkins, "How Managers Become Leaders," *Harvard Business Review* (June 2012).

11 Author interview with Sid Fuchs, CEO, MacAulay-Brown, Inc., 26 January 2017.

12 Warren G. Bennis and James O'Toole, "How Business Schools Lost Their Way," *Harvard Business Review* (May 2005): 100.

13   For a related view, see Deborah Ancona, Thomas W. Malone, Wanda J. Orli-
     kowski, and Peter M. Senge, "In Praise of the Incomplete Leader," *Harvard
     Business Review* (February 2007).

14   The story of Big Brothers Big Sisters of New York City comes from author
     interviews with Hector Batista, 6 January 2017 and 15 June 2017.

15   The Lululemon story is documented in many articles. For example, see Anon-
     ymous, "Lululemon's Chip Wilson," *BC Business,* 2 February 2006, https://
     www.bcbusiness.ca/lululemons-chip-wilson; Jim Edwards, "The Long,
     Strange History of Lululemon: North America's Weirdest Clothing Brand,"
     Business Insider, 4 September 2015 http://www.businessinsider.com/history
     -of-lululemon-2015-9; Laura Bogomolny, "Toned and Ready: Lululemon
     Transitions," *Canadian Business,* 24 April 2006 http://www.canadianbusi-
     ness.com/business-strategy/toned-and-ready-lululemon-transitions/; Marga-
     ret Brennan, "Lululemon CEO—Old And New—"Stress" High End Product
     Success," CNBC, 3 April 2008, http://www.cnbc.com/id/23939595; Anon-
     ymous, "Well Positioned," *The Economist,* 13 December 2007, http://www.
     economist.com/node/10286974; Marina Strauss, "Lululemon's Christine Day:
     In Sweaty Iursuit of innovation," *The Globe and Mail,* 8 March 2013, https://
     www.theglobeandmail.com/report-on-business/careers/careers-leadership/
     lululemons-christine-day-in-sweaty-pursuit-of-innovation/article9559457/.

16   "Dent in the universe" is attributed to former Apple, Inc., CEO Steve Jobs in a
     variety of places.

17   Author interviews with Michael Barnett, CEO, InGo, 5 January 2017 and 16
     June 2017.

18   For example, see most recently, Simon Sinek, *Start with Why: How Great Leaders
     Inspire Everyone to Take Action* (New York: Portfolio, 2009).

19   The story of Big Brothers Big Sisters of New York City comes from author
     interviews with Hector Batista, CEO, 6 January 2017 and 15 June 2017.

20   The story of Gymboree comes from author interview with Gary White, for-
     mer CEO, 8 March 2017.

21   Peter Drucker, "What Makes an Effective Executive," in *Harvard Business
     Review* (June 2004).

22   For more on personal stories, see Herminia Ibarra and Kent Lineback, "What's
     Your Story?" *Harvard Business Review* (January 2005).

23   James Collins and Jerry Porras, "Building Your Company's Vision," *Harvard
     Business Review* (September-October 1996).

24   For more on the role of strategy in a corporate story, see David J. Collis and
     Michael G. Rukstad, "Can You Say What Your Strategy Is?" *Harvard Business
     Review* (April 2008).

25   The story of MongoDB comes from author interviews with Dev Ittycheria,
     CEO, 27 January 2017 and 23 June 2017.

26 For more on the critical importance of values in effectively leading change, see James O'Toole, *Leading Change* (New York: Ballantine, 1996).

27 For a related view on culture, see Dan Stravinski, "Driving Results Through Culture," *HR Magazine* (January 2014).

28 The quotes attributed to Rebecca's team have been altered in form, but not content, to protect confidentiality.

29 See for example Linda A. Hill, "Becoming the Boss," *Harvard Business Review* (June 2007) and John Gabarro, "When a New Manager Takes Charge," *Harvard Business Review* (January 1985/2007).

30 For example, see W. W. Burke and G. H. Litwin, "A Causal Model of Organizational Performance and Change," *Journal of Management,* 8(3), (1992): 523–546.

31 Patrick Lencioni, *The Five Dysfunctions of a Team* (New York: Jossey-Bass, 2002).

32 Jon R. Katzenbach and Douglas K. Smith, "The Discipline of Teams," *Harvard Business Review* (July-August 2005): 6 [in reprint]

33 For those with interest, Wikipedia nicely summarizes the ancient roots of the "Blind Men and an Elephant" story. See https://en.wikipedia.org/wiki/Blind_men_and_an_elephant

34 On the meaning of authenticity, see Herminia Ibarra, "The Authenticity Paradox," *Harvard Business Review* (January-February 2015).

35 http://adst.org/oral-history/fascinating-figures/george-shultz-country-united-states/

36 Author interviews with Hervé Sedky, President, Reed Exhibitions Americas, RELX Group, 25 January 2017 and 9 June 2017.

37 http://foxtrotalpha.jalopnik.com/here-is-what-all-those-colored-shirts-on-an-aircraft-ca-1757896999

38 Author interviews with John Rogers, CEO, Ariel Investments, 6 April 2017 and 13 July 2017.

39 For readability purposes, we relate the personal story of coauthors in the third person.

40 When working with executives in helping them map and understand the need for and nature of different networks, we often cite the article by Herminia Ibarra and Mark Hunter, "How Leaders Create and Use Networks," *Harvard Business Review* (January 2007). See also Brian Uzzi and Shannon Dunlap, "How to Build Your Network," *Harvard Business Review* (December 2005); Jay A. Conger and N. Anand, "Capabilities of the Consummate Networker," *Organizational Dynamics* 36 (2007); and Rob Cross and Laurence Prusak, "The People Who Make Organizations Go—Or Stop," *Harvard Business Review* (June 2002).

41 Sidney E. Fuchs, *Get Off The Bench: Unleashing The Power of Strategic Networking Through Relationships* (Charleston, South Carolina: Advantage Media Group, 2012).

42 Author interview with Dawn Halfaker, CEO, Halfaker and Associates, 14 July 2017.

43 Ken Aultetta, "The Raid," *The New Yorker,* 20 March 2006.

44 For examples of different kinds of networking diagrams or stakeholder maps, we sometimes give clients the work of Brian Uzzi and Shannon Dunlap, "How to Build Your Network," *Harvard Business Review* (December 2005), or Rob Cross and Laurence Prusak, "The People Who Make Organizations Go—or Stop," *Harvard Business Review* (June 2002).

45 Rob Cross and Andrew Parker, "The Hidden Power of Social Networks," (Boston: Harvard Business School Press, 2004).

46 Author interviews with John Rogers, CEO, Ariel Investments, 6 April 2017 and 13 July 2017.

47 For more on advocacy and inquiry, see Peter Senge, Art Kleiner, Charlotte Roberts, Richard Ross, and Bryan Smith, *The Fifth Discipline Fieldbook* (New York: Crown Business, 1994). Many experts, most notably Chris Argyris and Donald Schon, have also written well about these concepts in business literature.

48 Author interview with Ron Jones, formerly Chief Strategy Officer and Executive Vice President, Corporate Development, for Veridian, Grey Hawk, GTEC/Sotera, and Vistronix, 30 December 2016.

49 For more on managing the emotions of change, see Ellen R. Auster and Trish Ruebottom, "Navigating the Politics and Emotions of Change," *Sloan Management Review* (Summer 2013).

50 https://www.youtube.com/watch?v=2I91DJZKRxs

51 For more on inspirational communication, see Jay A. Conger, "Inspiring Others: The Language of Leadership," *Academy of Management Executive* 5:1 (January 1991).

52 Author interviews with John Hassoun, CEO, Vistronix, 19 January 2017 and 15 August 2017.

53 Russell Eisenstat and Michael Beer, "How to Have an Honest Conversation About Your Business Strategy," *Harvard Business Review* (February 2004).

54 Author interview with Gary White, President, GW Retail Consulting, 8 March 2017.

55 For a complementary view of what to communicate, see John Hamm, "The Five Messages Leaders Must Manage," *Harvard Business Review* (May 2006).

56 David Garvin and Michael Roberto, "Change Through Persuasion," *Harvard Business Review* (February 2005).

57 John Kotter, "Leading Change: Why Transformation Efforts Fail," *Harvard Business Review* (May–June, 1995).

58 Author interview with Gary White, President, GW Retail Consulting, 8 March 2017.

59 Author interviews with Michael Barnett, CEO, InGo, 5 January 2017 and 16 June 2017.

60 For more on how to manage conflict and foster "the conversations that need to happen," see Douglas Stone, Bruce Patton, Sheila Heen, *Difficult Conversations* (New York: Penguin, 2000).

61 Author interview with Chris Howard, President, Robert Morris University, 7 July 2017.

62 See also Robert Goffee and Gareth Jones, "Why Should Anyone Be Led by You?" *Harvard Business Review* (September-October 2000).

63 For more on the subject of paradoxical decisions, see Wendy K. Smith, Marianne W. Lewis, and Michael L. Tushman, "'Both/And' Leadership," *Harvard Business Review* (May 2016).

64 Warren Bennis wrote, "The most dangerous leadership myth is that leaders are born—that there is a genetic factor to leadership. This myth asserts that people simply either have certain charismatic qualities or not. That's nonsense; in fact, the opposite is true. Leaders are made rather than born. And the way we become leaders is by learning about leadership through life and job experiences, not with university degrees." See Warren Bennis *Managing People Is Like Herding Cats* (Executive Excellence Publications: 1997), 163.

65 Author interview with David Kriegman, former COO, SRA, and president Z2B, LLC, 26 July 2017.

66 John Nicas, "Google Cancels Meeting on Diversity, Citing Safety Concerns for Employees," *The Wall Street Journal*, 10 August 2017.

67 James Damore, "Why I Was Fired by Google," *The Wall Street Journal*, 11 August 2017.

68 John Hamm, "Why Entrepreneurs Don't Scale," *Harvard Business Review* (December 2002).

69 For a deeper understanding of the factors in trust, see David H. Maister, Charles H. Green, and Robert M. Galford, *The Trusted Advisor* (New York: Touchstone, 2001).

70 https://www.youtube.com/watch?v=WqitLNTTUzc

71 Author interview with Dawn Halfaker, CEO, Halfaker and Associates, 14 July 2017.

72 For communicating during a crisis, see Maurice E. Schweitzer, Alison Wood Brookes, and Adam D. Galinsky, "The Organizational Apology," *Harvard Business Review* (September 2015).

73 See for example, Warren Bennis and Robert J. Thomas, "Crucibles of Leadership," *Harvard Business Review* (September 2002); and Max De Pree, *Leadership*

is an Art (New York: Doubleday 1989); Warren Bennis, *On Becoming a Leader* (New York: Basic Books, reprint edition 2009); James O'Toole, *Leading Change* (New York: Ballantine, 1996); and Daniel Goleman, Richard Boyatzis, and Annie McKee, *Primal Leadership* (Boston: Harvard Business Review Press, 2004).

74 For more on defining moments, see Joseph L. Badaracco, Jr., "The Discipline of Building Character," *Harvard Business Review* (March-April 1998).

75 For a view on courage needed in decision making of this kind, see Kathleen K. Reardon, "Courage as a Skill," *Harvard Business Review* (January 2007). For tools on ethical decision making, see Constance E. Bagley, "The Ethical Leader's Decision Tree," *Harvard Business Review* (February 2003).

76 James O'Toole, *The Executive's Compass* (Oxford: Oxford University Press, 1995).

77 For related thinking on this concept, see William W. George, Peter Sims, Andrew N. McLean, David Mayer, and Diana Mayer, "Discovering Your Authentic Leadership," *Harvard Business Review* (February 2007).

78 https://www.morehouse.edu/pdf/Five-Wells.pdf_"The Soul of Morehouse and the Future of the Mystique: President's Town Hall Meeting" (Robert M. Franklin, 2009).

79 Marcus Aurelius's, *The Meditations,* translated offers tremendous wisdom on how to be an effective and fulfilled person and leader. See, for example, the translation by Gregory Hays (New York: Modern Library/Random House, 2002).

80 David Rooke & William Torbert, "Seven Transformations of Leadership," *Harvard Business Review* (April 2005).

81 https://en.wikipedia.org/wiki/I_know_that_I_know_nothing

82 Author interview with Jonathan Bush, CEO, athenahealth, 13 January 2017.

83 Author interview with Taryn Owen, president, PeopleScout, 11 August 2017.

84 For more on the subtleties of political skills, see Pamela L. Perrewé, Gerald R. Ferris, Dwight D. Frink, and William P. Anthony, "Political Skill: An Antidote for Workplace Stressors," *Academy of Management Executive* 14:3 (2000).

85 Ronald Heifetz and Donald Laurie call this "getting on the balcony." See Ronald A. Heiftez and Donald L. Laurie, "The Work of Leadership," *Harvard Business Review* (January-February 1997).

86 Peter Drucker, *The Effective Executive* (New York: Harper Collins Publishers, 1967).

87 For a complementary view of how to focus, see Daniel Goleman, "The Focused Leader," *Harvard Business Review* (December 2013).

88 Ray Oldenburg, *The Great Good Place* (New York: Paragon House, 1989).

89 Sir Arthur Conan Doyle, *A Study in Scarlet,* 1887.

90 https://www.scientificamerican.com/article/why-do-you-think-better-after-walk-exercise/

91 Author interviews with Hector Batista, CEO, Big Brothers Big Sisters of New York City, 6 January 2017 and 16 June 2017.

92 Scott W. Spreier, Mary H. Fontaine, and Ruth L. Malloy, "Leadership Run Amok: The Destructive Potential of Overachievers," *Harvard Business Review* (June 2006): 72-82.

93 For another view on succession, see Joseph L. Bower, "Solve the Succession Crisis by Growing Inside-Outside Leaders," *Harvard Business Review* (November 2007).

94 Author interview with Kim Pendergast, CEO, Magnuson Superchargers, and founder of Pendergast Partners LLC, 2 August 2017.

95 For more on the career stalls of star performers, see Barbara E. Kovach, "The Derailment of Fast-Track Managers," *Organizational Dynamics* 15:2 (Autumn 1986); and Manfred F. R. Kets de Vries, "Leaders Who Self-Destruct: The Causes and Cures," *Organizational Dynamics* 17:4 (Spring 1989).

96 Author interviews with Dev Ittycheria, CEO, MongoDB, 27 January 2017 and 23 June 2017.

97 Andrew S. Grove, *High Output Management* (New York: Random House, 1983).

98 Author interview with Jonathan Bush, CEO, athenahealth, 13 January 2017.

99 For more on the unique needs of leaders transitioning at different levels, see Ram Charan and Stephen Drotter, *Managing Transitions* (San Francisco: Jossey-Bass, 2001). For a standard text on helping managers through the first few months on the job, see Michael Watkins, *The First 90 Days* (Boston: Harvard Business Review Press, expanded edition 2013).

100 For additional insights on how to ask questions that open up dialogue, see Tony Stoltzfuz, *Coaching Questions: A Coach's Guide to Powerful Asking Skills* (Virginia Beach: Coach22 Bookstore, 2008).

101 For a good general guide on coaching as a manager, see David Dotlich and Peter Cairo, *Action Coaching* (San Francisco: Jossey-Bass, 1999). For a more philosophical approach, see James Flaherty, *Coaching: Evoking Excellence in Others* (New York: Routledge, third edition, 2010).

102 John Hillen, "Do you know who your most dangerous employee is?" *Washington Technology,* 13 July 2016. https://washingtontechnology.com/articles/2016/07/13/insights-hillen-most-dangerous-employee.aspx

103 Cal Fussman, "Chuck Yeager: What I've Learned," *Esquire,* 25 December 2008.

104 Wallace Stegner, *All the Little Live Things* (New York: Penguin, 1991), 8.

105 As an excellent complement to our thinking, see also Marshall Goldsmith, *What Got You Here Won't Get You There* (New York: Hachette, revised 2007).

106 See also Robert Goffee and Gareth Jones, "Why Should Anyone Be Led by You?" *Harvard Business Review* (September-October, 2000).

107 Author interviews with Dominique Malard, President, Schlumberger, 21 September 2017.

108 Cynthia D Scott and Dennis T. Jaffe, "Survive and Thrive in Times of Change," *Training and Development Journal* 42 (April 1998).

109 Elisabeth Kübler Ross, *On Death and Dying* (New York: Scribner, reprint edition, 2014).

Index

About the Authors

Mark Nevins *(left)* and John Hillen

John F. Hillen, DPhil, is a leadership and strategy professor in the School of Business at George Mason University, a consultant, and a director for many companies. His views on leadership draw from his experiences as a CEO of public and private companies, a board chair and director, a US Assistant Secretary of State under President George W. Bush, and a former US Army officer and decorated combat leader. He holds degrees from Duke and King's College London, received his MBA at Cornell and his doctorate from Oxford. A *Washington Technology* columnist, he writes regularly on leadership and strategy, both of which he teaches in George Mason's MBA program. Recently recognized as one of the one hundred most influential business leaders in the Washington DC area, Hillen is the winner of a number of prestigious leadership awards in the military and business and the author or editor of several books on international security.

Mark D. Nevins, PhD, is a consultant and advisor to top executives, teams, and organizations. Earlier in his career he was responsible for learning and development globally for Booz Allen Hamilton, and for organization development and human resources globally for Korn/Ferry International. He has coached and advised a broad range of executives from the C-suite to high-potential vice presidents at large corporations such as American Express, Citibank, NBCUniversal, and Time Warner, as well as at smaller companies, high-growth startups, and top-tier professional and financial services firms. A Harvard PhD (alma mater College of the Holy Cross) and former literature professor, his views on leadership and business are informed by universal themes of the human condition as well as extensive pragmatic work with hundreds of executives and senior managers across almost all industries as well as the higher education, not-for-profit, and military sectors. Nevins has worked, taught, and travelled in more than sixty countries. An author and business writer, his previous work includes *The Advice Business*, a book on management consulting.

The insights Hillen and Nevins share in this book build on their thought leadership in some of world's most prestigious venues. Over more than twenty years, they have led, helped direct, or consulted with hundreds of companies and executives in many different types of businesses. They originally met at the Aspen Institute, where they served as executive seminar co-moderators, leading intensive week-long seminars for leaders from around the world. They are united in their passion for helping all leaders—even the most skeptical of executives—to discover the root causes of stalls and to develop their mastery of sophisticated leadership.